EAT A PEACH

EAT A
PEACH

A Memoir

DAVID CHANG

WITH GABE ULLA

CLARKSON POTTER/PUBLISHERS
NEW YORK

CLARKSON POTTER is a trademark and POTTER with colophon is a
registered trademark of Penguin Random House LLC.

Library of Congress Cataloging-in-Publication Data

Names: Chang, David, 1977– author. | Ulla, Gabe, author.
Title: Eat a peach: a memoir / David Chang with Gabe Ulla.
Description: First edition. | New York: Clarkson Potter/Publishers, 2020.
Identifiers: LCCN 2019052985 (print) | LCCN 2019052986 (ebook) | ISBN
9781524759216 (hardcover) | ISBN 9781524759223 (ebook)
Subjects: LCSH: Cooking.
Classification: LCC TX714 .C463 2020 (print) | LCC TX714 (ebook) | DDC
641.5—dc23
LC record available at https://lccn.loc.gov/2019052985
LC ebook record available at https://lccn.loc.gov/2019052986

ISBN 978-1-5247-5921-6
Ebook ISBN 978-1-5247-5922-3

Printed in the United States

Book and jacket design by Ian Dingman

10 9 8 7 6 5 4 3 2 1

First Edition

For Grace and Hugo, with love.

In memory of Joe Chang.

And to all the underdogs.

PROLOGUE

I CAN CONVINCE MYSELF OF ALMOST ANYTHING.

Four years ago I signed a deal to write this book. I swear I told the publisher that it would be a self-help manual about leadership or entrepreneurial strategy or advice for young chefs. Unfortunately for me, they beg to differ. It wasn't until many months after my original deadline that my agent finally put her foot down: "Tell yourself whatever you want, Dave. It's a fucking memoir."

For the record, I'm still thinking of this as a textbook on what not to do when starting a business. It's my brain defending itself from considering the monumental weirdness of being asked to write a book about my life, as well as the worrying amount of ego it took for me to say yes.

And frankly, I just don't understand my appeal.

How can it be that, after fifteen years of hearing me wax on about food and restaurants and many other subjects I'm far less qualified to talk about, people still want more? Why is my word more valuable than anyone else's? What makes anyone think I know better than they do?

I'm not asking hypothetically. I asked my publisher the same questions.

Should I include recipes?

No, that's not what this book is about.

You're sure? Can't I lean on some culinary content to pad this thing out?

We're sure.

Much later, when it came time to design the book, there was some debate over what the cover image should be. The publisher proposed a photo of me, as is the custom for memoirs. But I couldn't summon the courage necessary to imagine my face on a bookstore shelf.

Eventually we settled on using an illustration. The publisher mocked up a cover with a portrait of Idris Elba to give me a sense of the style they were looking for. I liked it so much that I pushed to use Elba's image instead of mine, but I lost that argument. We came up with several alternatives: a couple of gentle landscapes and watercolors of peaches like you might find in a dentist's office; a couple that riffed on the myth of Sisyphus, which I've always viewed as an inspirational tale; and a couple of portraits of me painted by my friend David Choe, including a version without any facial features (I'm still unclear on the symbolic significance of that one).

I liked the Choe portrait that did include a face and thought it was a fine compromise. It was still a picture of me but impressionistic enough that I could live with it as a book cover. Of course, now the publisher was pushing for one of the Sisyphus covers as the more consumer-friendly route. I worried that it would seem too self-important to draw a comparison between my journey and that of a mythological character. (Although, if you look closely, it's not technically me pushing the peach up the hill; it's Oddjob, the arche-typal cinematic Asian bad guy.) We went back and forth for a while, but I'm not easily swayed by unsubstantiated opinions or general wis-dom. I'm a devout believer in data, so we commissioned a survey.

Of the hundreds of people we polled, most had never heard of me, and about 7 percent knew "a fair amount" or "a lot" about me. Altogether they overwhelmingly favored the cover you're holding, which was fine by me. I'm not too proud to change my mind. Strong opinions loosely held and all that.

I appreciated how thorough the survey was. For example, each of the respondents was asked to highlight the parts they disliked about their least favorite covers. Their preferences were displayed on charts highlighting the most frequently selected—that is, most disliked—areas. Here, I'll just show you:

We also asked respondents to select what they liked least about their favorite covers. Those who preferred the cover with the blank-face portrait chose my name as the part that bugged them.

*Frequently
selected*

*Frequently
selected*

Okay, so my face and my name were the problem. I have to admit that was a little confusing for someone who (1) has historically been sensitive about the particulars of my appearance and the general Asianness of my face and name, and (2) was already struggling to understand why people would want to read this book. But again, I respect data. We deemphasized the name and removed the face. If it helps you enjoy the book, I have no problem with your imagining it was written by a white author named David Chance.

The one aspect of this book I cannot change is its perspective. For better or worse, that's mine.

I won't pretend that I can recount everything exactly as it happened. I'm not a security camera. I apologize to anyone whose role I've exaggerated or downplayed in my memory. Throughout the book I've erred on the side of caution and changed a lot of names to protect colleagues and friends from being irritated by how I remember events. The details have likely fallen out of order here and there, too. Without a doubt, the chronology in the second half of the book is all screwy. I'm sure I've also contradicted statements I've made in the past, whether it's because I've changed my mind or I was play-ing fast and loose with the facts before or I'm misremembering them now. Just know that this is as honest and true a story as I can offer.

In case you can't tell, I'm doing all this throat-clearing as a stall tactic. I'm delaying you from getting into the book, because honestly, I'm extremely nervous about you reading it.

It doesn't make sense that this memoir exists. I've been wrong about so many things.

My friends say I should stop with the false modesty, that I should be able to own who I am by now.

But I'm not supposed to be here.

PART ONE

UP THE HILL

A more or less linear account of events I've had many years to reflect on with my psychiatrist: a vengeful God; other kids; a little golf; an ultimatum; the underground and the overground; opening a few restaurants; paranoia; early signs of a tendency to flee.

THE TEA LEAVES

WE USED TO GET A LOT MORE SNOW IN NORTHERN VIRGINIA. WHEN IT was especially heavy, my older brothers and Thomas, their Finnish friend from up the street, would build a makeshift luge course and ride a sled from the top of the hill down past our house. Whenever someone asks me about my childhood, that's the first thing I remember.

On dry days, Thomas and my brothers would race a go-kart down the same incline. I say *go-kart,* but it really wasn't much more than a wooden crate on wheels, built for one passenger. And on the rare occasion that the older kids invited me to ride with them, I leapt at the chance. Thomas, who had about ten years and eighty pounds on me, would launch us with a running start before jumping into the cart from the back. I was always tucked tightly in front.

Once, when I was seven or eight years old, I tried lifting my legs in the air during one of these runs, like you might throw your hands up on a roller coaster. I somehow managed to get my left leg jammed under the front wheels, dragging me out of my seat and under the cart. Thomas ran over me and continued down the hill.

The next thing I remember is being sprawled out on the big yellow couch in the living room with my mom, sister, and grandmother hovering around me. Their prescribed course of treatment went as follows: every half hour they'd slather my knee with a mysterious yellow-red paste, stand me up like a marionette, and see if I could walk a few paces. No chance. Every stumble hurt worse than the last. I wouldn't stop crying.*

My dad came home from work and looked at me as though he'd never seen a person with an injury before. He demanded that I get off the couch and walk. I cried some more.

After failing to heal me with the power of his commands, Dad reluctantly packed me into the car and took me to a Korean acupuncturist, who poked me head to toe with pins. I did what I did best and kept on crying. Dad grew more frustrated. He was convinced that the pain was in my mind and the only remedy was to suck it up.

"Walk."

After a few days, he moved on to other matters. My mom, ever the good cop, had waited through all the crying, fruitlessly slathering me with that paste. She drove me to a pediatrician in McLean who took X-rays of my leg. There was a lightning-bolt-shaped crack that stopped just short of passing through my whole femur.

The doctor set my leg and we went home, where life went on without another mention of the accident.

Back then, Dad was the archetype of a certain Korean man who

---

*I was a notorious crier. Whenever they wanted a laugh, my brothers' friends would come over and make me weep. They'd whisper something to me about my mom leaving forever, and instantly the waterworks would start. Assholes.

remains completely foreign to non-Asian America. Yes, they scold and punish us for poor grades and the slightest misbehavior, but it's not just tough love. It is love that feels distinctly conditional. The downside to the term *tiger parenting* entering the mainstream vocabulary is that it gives a cute name to what is actually a painful and demoralizing existence. It also feeds into the perception that all Asian kids are book smart because their parents make it so. Well, guess what. It's not true. Not all our parents are tiger parents, tiger parenting doesn't always work, and not all Asian kids are good at school. In fact, not all Asian kids are any one thing. To be young and Asian in America often means fighting a multifront war against sameness.

A year or so before the go-kart incident, Dad told me that I could no longer be ambidextrous—one of the few natural skills I possessed and took pride in—and said I'd be using my right hand from then on. He was worried that any potential golf career would be derailed by my being a lefty. Just like that, the matter was settled. The cost of questioning his authority was always higher than sucking it up and dealing with it.

Our family dynamic was far from perfect, but it had its bright sides, too. My parents were always working, so my grandparents on my mom's side practically raised me. They were gentle and doting to an almost comical degree. My grandmother would carry me on her back while she cooked, feeding me little pieces of dried fish snipped with scissors or bites of sweet potato cooked in the fireplace. My grandfather came from a well-to-do family that lost everything during the Japanese occupation of Korea. He was one of many men who were essentially brainwashed to think of themselves as Japanese.* He would take me on the bus to get sushi in a nearby town.

While we're talking formative food experiences, my parents' favorite story from my childhood revolves around a dinner at our

---

*Read *Pachinko* by Min Jin Lee if you want a better understanding of what I'm talking about.

special-occasion Chinese restaurant: Wu's Garden in Vienna, Virginia. This must have been right around the time I broke my leg. My older siblings weren't with us on this particular night, more than likely because they were at a church function. The meal was winding down and I asked the adults if we were bringing back food for them. My parents said they would be fine and fed wherever they were. That should have been the end of it, but I was dismayed that no one seemed concerned about my brothers and sister. How could they be sure the kids had eaten? I started going around the table, clumsily scraping leftovers from each person's plate onto mine, so I could bring them home. The adults had a good laugh.

That's the extent of cute stories I have about eating as a kid. Mom is a great cook—much better than I gave her credit for at the time. As a kid, I was embarrassed by the smell of our kitchen and the look of our Korean food, so when Sherri Chang wasn't around, I mostly sustained myself with mozzarella sticks, chicken fingers, Hungry-Man dinners, microwave burritos, quesadillas, and Ichiran ramen and Shin ramyun. Latchkey kid fare, which was all right by me.

I got by fine. I did tae kwon do and played basketball with my two older brothers. Family get-togethers were consistent and nice. I had a solid mix of friends. I was completely, certifiably average. My school participated in a program to find "gifted and talented" students. If you tested high enough, you'd be placed into Thomas Jefferson, one of the most prestigious high schools in the country. My whole group of friends made the cut, except for me. The only other Asian kid at our school who didn't get selected was Brian Zhu, and Brian Zhu, I never tire of pointing out, was a dummy.

By all metrics, I was a terrible student. I never broke 1000 on my SATs. I would get so nervous during test taking that I'd spend more time fretting over the consequences of a low grade than actually doing the work. I graduated from Trinity College—the farthest school from home that I could get into—near the very bottom of my class with a 2.78 GPA.

Like I said, my dad would get upset, but it didn't make a difference. I wanted so badly to please him and my mom. I was simply incapable. What happens when you live with a tiger that you can't please is that you're always afraid. Every hour of every day, you're uncomfortable around your own parent.

I'm only telling you all of this because it's what a memoir calls for: tea leaves. Selected stories that foretell the person I would become. But I'm reluctant to put too much stock in these anecdotes. People have survived much worse suffering and much tougher parents. If you grew up as a first-generation Asian American, there's a good chance you're saying to yourself, "Whatever. Big baby."

• • •

Korean immigrants tend to fall into one of two very different and mostly incompatible camps. They're either doctors and lawyers, or they run laundromats and convenience stores. But no matter what they do for a living, they go hard at church.

My extended family all sold Bibles or worked in Bible-adjacent businesses, carpentry and the like. I have cousins whom I've never met because they travel full-time to far-flung places trying to spread the word of Christ. Before immigrating to the States, my dad's mom was one of the earliest Christian converts in Korea. In my mind, she couldn't have been taller than four-foot-seven, but I can't be sure of her true height because she always wore floor-length hanbok dresses that obscured her feet. Despite her stature, she was a terrifying presence. Etched into her face were the pain and sorrow and stoicism of someone who had seen far too much shit. I took up Christianity out of fear of displeasing her.

We were Presbyterian. Our church was connected to a working farm where you could buy fruit and old-fashioned candy. It has since evolved into one of the largest Korean congregations in America, but back then, we'd have to wait until the afternoon to attend services. It was understood that the white people used the place to worship in the morning.

Between my grandmother, my parents, and my sister, my family waterboarded me with religion. I never tried to rock the boat, but I recall looking at my parents and their fellow devotees and thinking, *If they really mean this—if the only thing that matters is the afterlife—then why aren't we out in the field every day trying to bring more people into the fold? What are we doing just sitting around planning barbecues?*

That's not to say that we weren't a militantly religious family. As it is for many Korean immigrants, church was the center of my parents' daily life. It was a physical hub for the community and, more important, the spiritual anchor that gave them security in a new country. Mom and Dad would host Bible study at our house. They'd pray all night. My sister would have her youth group over to the house every weekend. We spent all Sunday at church: Korean service with our parents, then the English service with our youth group, then Bible study. I'd watch family members go from being blind drunk Saturday night to God-fearing disciples the next morning. Any time there was a family gathering, whether it was Thanksgiving or New Year's or a birthday, we'd have two hours of Bible study. At least the food was always good.

On long car rides in our faux wood–paneled Chrysler minivan, we listened to tapes about Revelation that, in retrospect, were essentially radicalizing materials. The end was always near. There was religion all around me, all the time—and for a stretch, I counted myself a believer. I took all the eschatology stuff very seriously, even if other people's lack of conviction made me dubious. I would always sneak peeks during family prayer to see who was phoning it in.

Gradually I got more comfortable asking, "But why?" I suppose that's important to the person I would become, but doesn't every kid do that? There was one Sunday school session, when they brought out a felt backboard with little cutout figures to illustrate how everyone in heaven is able to look down at the nonbelievers in hell. For the first time, I felt bothered by the idea that someone would burn eternally for not accepting Jesus Christ as their lord and savior.

So, you're telling me that I'm going to be fine as long as I believe? How do you know if I really believe? All I have to do is say the words? How does Jesus know that I mean it? What if you live in seclusion and have no idea J.C. is an option? You go to hell?

It was all so crazy to me.*

In time my skepticism grew into a full-blown rage. My sister, Esther, took the brunt of it, by her own choice. She was eight years older than me and had abandoned any hope of getting my two older brothers to be as devout as she was, so she focused her energies on me. After college, Esther went to seminary school and led the church youth group—the whole deal. She even served as a missionary in Mongolia. The more she tried to lure me out, the more I retreated. On Friday nights, I'd literally hide in the sales racks of my dad's golf store to avoid going to youth group service. I couldn't stand her for it, and as I approached my teenage years, I gave her relentless shit.

I attended a Jesuit boarding school, Georgetown Prep,** where I learned that Presbyterianism had descended from Catholicism. I was like a flat-Earther seeing the planet from space for the first time. I

---

*I was strangely delighted when, in 2018, the American missionary John Allen Chau managed to reach North Sentinel Island—home to an isolated, uncontacted people who have made clear over hundreds of years that they wish to remain isolated and uncontacted. He went in knowing that he might die for his proselytizing, and that's exactly what happened. The Sentinelese killed him for his intrusion. This guy had asked the same questions, and it bothered him to the extent that he could not let anyone burn in hell simply because they hadn't heard about Christ. If all the believers around me as a kid had held their convictions as tightly as Chau, I honestly might still be one of them. His plan was incredibly stupid, but I admired his commitment.

**The same school—about a decade later—as PJ, Tobin, Squee, and Justice Brett Kavanaugh.

had no idea that one church could come from another. They were all human-made constructs, products of politics, not divinity.

I felt alienated from the outset. On the first day of classes, I noticed another student waiting at the door of the classroom trying to get in. I tried pointing him out to our teacher, who responded by shouting, "JUG!"

"What's JUG?"

"Double JUG!"

"Judgment Under God" was a demerit. Interrupting the class to draw attention to my stranded classmate was a JUG-worthy offense. Getting JUG meant I would be late for freshman football, which meant running laps at the beginning and end of practice, which earned me another JUG for being late to dinner. That translated to nighttime resident JUG and yet another punishment—writing an essay about God or holding a Bible for some absurd amount of time or picking up trash around campus. Every day at that school was another spin on the same self-perpetuating cycle.

I know everyone takes some emotional damage in high school, but that place left an impression that I'm still trying to shake. I'd excelled at golf as a kid, which opened the door to a number of top-tier options for me. When Georgetown Prep came calling, my dad committed me to them. Though it was close to home, the school was worlds away from where I'd come from. The students were touted as the best of the best, which was another major reason I chose to attend, but I never found my place. One of my second cousins, another prep school kid, once beat the shit out of me because I wouldn't join the Korean clique. I wasn't Asian enough to hang with the other Asians, and I wasn't book smart or talented enough to keep up with anyone else. I internalized the atmosphere of superiority and processed it into an overwhelming awareness of my own inferiority. Everything was a struggle for me there, with the exception of my religious studies. By that time, I'd read the Bible enough to teach the classes myself.

Later, at Trinity College, I had designs on studying comparative economics, Asian studies, or philosophy, but I realized early on that I couldn't follow any of those tracks unless I actually showed up for the classes. I changed my major every semester before settling on religion because that stuff was still a breeze for me and I liked reading about non-Christian faiths—Taoism, Hinduism's *Vedas* and *Bhagavad Gita,* ancient Judaism, and Mahayana Buddhism's idea that you should be so sympathetic to the suffering of the world that you would choose not to attain nirvana but rather return as another spirit to aid the living. That made sense to me. The religious study led me to philosophical texts—Plato, Kant, Nietzsche, and all your usual college-class suspects. I took every course offered by Ellison Banks Findly and Howard DeLong.

I made it a point to learn as much as I possibly could about religion, partly so I could defeat Esther during our arguments. In my sophomore year, while studying abroad in Europe, I met up with her in Switzerland. I hadn't seen her for a while. I should have told her about being moved by Buddhism, or explained how I had finally discovered that the right faith for me was secular humanism. But the security Esther had in her own beliefs made me angry. She wasn't exactly smug about it, but she was so damn *sure.* In my anger toward her, I felt righteous.

I came prepared to unload all the worldly wisdom I had picked up in two years of college. I told her that if her omnipotent God had allowed for all the famine and tragedy in the world, for Stalin and Pol Pot and genocide, I would rather reign in hell than serve in heaven. I topped it off by saying that if I had been alive two thousand years ago, I'd probably be crucifying Christians, too.

I don't think she had ever viewed us as combatants. The battle was completely in my head.

• • •

When I was nine or ten, we moved from McLean to Vienna, Virginia, a transition that was as close to traumatic as my childhood ever got. Our new home was only twenty minutes west, but at the time it was a mostly rural area with more cows than people. I had to give up what had been a solid setup: school buddies Monday to Friday, Korean kids and neighborhood friends on the weekends. My social agenda had been pretty stacked, and now it wasn't.

If you're so inclined, you could stretch and say that running through the woods of Wolf Trap Park in the years after the move is how I learned to use my imagination. Being alone and unmonitored by my working parents meant a lot of solo play: forts and guns and video games and Transformers. I never really got bored.

We'd moved because my dad wanted to be closer to his golf store in Tysons Corner. In the early eighties, he had moved on from a career working in restaurants and tossed his lot in with a handful of other industrious Korean businessmen who had decided to band together to monopolize golf-supply sales in the D.C. area.

Yes, my father worked in the restaurant business. It's not that important. Like I said, I hate giving these early-life details too much credit. Cooking and serving food are what people do in America when their options are limited. Like so many immigrant parents, Dad toiled at blue-collar jobs in the hope that his kids wouldn't have to. Unlike his friends in the local Korean community, Joe Chang did not come from a prestigious background or study medicine or business. The family lore is that he got into college in some small Kentucky mining town by breaking into the registrar's office and altering his grades. Dad came from a long line of hustlers. His mom was essentially a loan shark in Korea, and he grew up hungry there in the postwar years. He opened a deli and eventually expanded to a sit-down restaurant in the Press Club in Washington, D.C. What *is* interesting—or at least ironic—is that my father explicitly banned his children from following in his footsteps. He never felt able to support his family until he got out of the restaurant business.

How's that for a tea leaf?

Back to the men and their golf plan: they determined that they'd each focus on a different section of the D.C. region. Being the least educated and least wealthy of the bunch, Joe Chang got Tysons Corner. The more well-to-do guys like Eddie Pak scooped up neighborhoods like Potomac, Bethesda, and Silver Spring.

Tysons Golf Center started out as something like a Price Club for golf. It was hidden in the back of a massive and unwelcoming steel hangar that was all but impossible to find unless you had been there before. Inside was all crappy green carpet and cardboard boxes full of golf gear, the idea being that whatever my dad saved on decor, he'd pass on to the customer.* Mom started working at the store, all while raising four young kids. I spent a lot of time in the shop doing different jobs as well, from stacking boxes to working the register.

What came next is further proof that the facts of life are fickle. No one would have predicted that Tysons Corner would turn into *the* modern shopping destination in the D.C. area, but within a few years, that's what happened. Eddie Pak came to envy my dad's location. It helped that Joe Chang was tireless, a man who believed he could bend reality to his will if he tried hard enough, but he was also very lucky. Good fortune beats any plan.

I was lucky, too. My dad introduced me to golf when I was five, and as I briefly mentioned, I was pretty damn good at it for a stretch. A bona fide prodigy, in fact. In the beginning, I never had to study any strategy or work on specific parts of my game. One day, my dad told me that I was going to play golf, and I was better than all the other kids. My stroke was naturally awesome. I sound like an asshole saying this, but it's impossible to talk about being good at golf without sounding like an asshole.

---

*Dad eliminated the extraneous whenever possible. He was the kind of guy who'd call in his order before arriving at a restaurant, then ask for the check halfway through the meal.

This was before Tiger and Vijay and Michelle Wie and K. J. Choi hit the stage. Golf was very much a white sport and something of a weird niche for a Korean kid. On the other hand, traveling around the South to play in tournaments showed me a side of American culture that I couldn't see in suburban Washington, D.C. I learned to eat and love Brunswick stew, country fried steaks, and redeye gravy. I got to know the other kids on the golf circuit, and I really enjoyed being around them. We were bound together by this incredibly uncool sport that we were all somehow good at.

At the height of my powers, a Korean television station sent a crew to Virginia to follow me around for a week while I played in local tournaments. I must have looked like such a cocky motherfucker. Golf was my first talent, the first thing anyone praised me for, and I ate it up. I loved beating everybody.

I won back-to-back Virginia state championships when I was nine. I beat everyone in my age group and everyone in the next age bracket up, too. One summer at golf camp, I beat all the high school kids and carried our whole team to the win, with a crowd of people cheering me on. All I did was golf. These days, if you go to a youth golf tournament, you'll see all these Asian parents yelling at their kids from the sidelines. Dad was a pioneer in the field. He preached the gospel of Ben Hogan, who almost died in a car accident, then won the U.S. Open the following year.* On probably 360 days of the year, I was playing or practicing with my dad, my brothers, or one of my two coaches. During the winter, I would spend my days inside, hitting into a net with a camera recording my swing. I would practice until blisters formed, then popped, then bled.

Given that I'm not a professional golfer, it's probably no surprise to hear that the whole thing fell apart. As high school neared, I got

---

*Personally, I was fascinated with Bruce Lietzke, who never seemed to practice and always played in the least possible number of tournaments. He always made the cut but never won a major.

into my own head and stayed there. Kids I used to destroy began to catch up and then surpass me. I was like a field goal kicker who's flawless in practice but shanks it when it counts.

From the time I was eight or nine, Dad would sit me down after every poor showing at a tournament to analyze each mistake I'd made on the course, identify the shots I should have taken, and emphasize that I could have done better. As my game began to unravel, he was adamant that I just needed to focus. I heard him telling people, "Dave just can't handle that other people outdrive him now." Richie Yu loomed large in those days. My dad would constantly compare me to Richie, a nationally known phenom at the top of the amateur level. He qualified for a PGA tour event when he was sixteen, and was essentially everything I couldn't be. *Be more like Richie Yu* was a constant refrain in our house. When I coincidentally met Richie Yu a couple of decades later, I told him that he had ruined my whole childhood. I was joking, mostly.

But this pursuit that had given me value and identity was slipping away. By the time I got to Georgetown Prep, I couldn't even make the team I had been recruited to join. I was such a basket case. I came to hate golf.

"Golf is ten percent physical and ninety percent mental," Dad would always say. The takeaway for me was far simpler: I wasn't good enough.

That embarrassment defined me for a long time. However, as with most other aspects of my childhood, I tend not to fixate on my failed golf career very much anymore. Not because it hurts, it's just that you're not supposed to dwell on something that didn't work out.

Right?

2

A RATIONAL CHOICE

FOR A SHORT WHILE AFTER COLLEGE, I WORKED AT A CORPORATE JOB. It was an entry-level post that you might describe as a stepping-stone to a career in finance, but that's probably too generous of a characterization. I was a glorified gofer. A friend of a friend hooked me up with the position after every other private wealth-management firm, brokerage house, and investment bank in New York and San Francisco had already rejected me.*

I can't recall every one of my specific duties, but they were all menial—sometimes it was cold-calling prospective clients, sometimes it was prepping a meeting room for the CEO, and mostly it

---

*No joke, the other day a woman stopped me on the street in Tribeca to say, "Hey! I interviewed you for a job twenty years ago."

was data entry. The job proved to be so soul-sucking that I ended up drunkenly telling everyone at the company holiday party exactly how little I thought of the job and the company and them. I hadn't even been at the company for very long, but I couldn't stand it anymore. I'd looked around my cubicle at all these smart, college-educated people being swallowed alive by this place, and I could imagine five, ten, twenty years slipping away from me before I could put a stop to it.

And you want to know what I got for my insubordination? A raise.

I swear to God it was exactly like *Office Space*. A consultant sat me down for an assessment, and I told him how little effort I was exerting and how much I loathed my job. He told me he appreciated my honesty and implored me to stay. He offered me more money. But I was done. I didn't have it in me to be any better at what I was doing. I told him I was going to culinary school.

Every one of my friends and family tried to dissuade me. They'd already warned me off of studying religion in college and now I wanted to be a *cook*? Come on, Dave. I couldn't argue with them, but anything was better than hurtling toward mediocrity at a desk job.

The restaurant industry had appealed to me even before I'd ever seen the inside of corporate America. During college, I worked as a barback at the local watering hole and then as a busboy at a steakhouse near home. I wanted to work in the kitchen, but that didn't exactly thrill Joe Chang. Before my interview with the chef, Dad spoke to the owner. I showed up, and they left me to wait in front of the salamander broiler for what felt like an eternity. When the chef finally appeared, I was red-faced and sweating through my clothes.

"The kitchen's no place for a boy like you," the chef said through his thick mustache. "We need bussers, though."

To Dad's dismay, I was undeterred and applied to Le Cordon Bleu in Paris during my sophomore year. *Everybody* gets into Cordon Bleu. I did not. After that, I put my culinary ambitions on the back burner for a few years until existential dread about what I was going to do for a living drove me there again.

The Culinary Institute of America was the preeminent culinary institution in the country, but I'd only recently finished undergrad and I didn't feel up for another years-long college experience. The French Culinary Institute, on the other hand, was located right in Manhattan, and I could be in and out within six months. I had no idea if it was the right fit for me, but I paid my first tuition installment and started immediately after leaving my job at the finance company.

From the first day of orientation, I began to notice a few different types of students. A good number of my new classmates had recently left jobs in tech and were looking for a change of pace. They had money and nothing better to do. Then there were a handful of working chefs in our class, too—people who were running small neighborhood restaurants but wanted more. They would always make a point of saying, "I don't even know why I'm here." Quite a few other students were older folks looking to fulfill a lifelong dream. And finally, there were some younger kids like me who were looking to the kitchen for salvation.*

Even compared to the other career changers in my class, I was a disaster. What a surprise—the classroom proved not to be my ideal environment. There always seemed to be vegetables flying out of my hands as I fumbled with one preparation or another. My classmates were unamused. At FCI, we were each paired with another student, and my partner already ran two of the hottest restaurants in town. She was attending cooking school so that she could take over the cooking responsibilities from her mom, who served as the restaurants' chef. As we approached the end of our first term, she requested a change. If she was stuck with me any longer, she told our teachers,

*Including Joshua Skenes, who would go on to become one of America's great iconoclastic chefs.

she'd rather quit. In the end, she decided that dropping out of school was better than collaborating with me.

I should have quit, too. The last couple of levels before graduation at FCI were basically unpaid jobs in the school's restaurant. In other words, I was paying them for the privilege of cooking food for customers. (Why anyone would want to go to a cooking school restaurant in the first place is beyond me.) But I was hooked. There was no romantic, come-to-Jesus moment about cooking, but I had at least found something I didn't hate doing. I became captivated by the industry, talking my classmates' ears off about restaurants—most of which I'd never visited. In New York, I loved Danny Meyer's and Tom Colicchio's Gramercy Tavern. It would be tragic if modern dining audiences only recognized Colicchio from *Top Chef.* He is an OG, who was embracing techniques like cooking over wood fire long before they were trendy. He helped define the modern American culinary sensibility, and my first preference was to work for him over any Eurocentric chef. I was all in on Americana.

As graduation neared, I developed a jam-packed schedule: a full slate of classes during the day, a full-time job at Jean-Georges Vongerichten's Mercer Kitchen at night, and weekend shifts answering phones at Craft, the much-anticipated restaurant Colicchio was opening up. Marc Salafia, my friend from Trinity, was going to be a captain at Craft and recommended me for the job.

My dream was obviously a proper cooking job at Craft, but they certainly didn't need—or want—my help, so I took a position as a reservationist. At age twenty-two, I felt so behind people who had been cooking since they were sixteen. I was scrambling to get experience under my belt as fast as humanly possible. I was stationed next to the prep kitchen, where I'd gawk at the products coming into the restaurant. Foie. Rabbits. All kinds of mushrooms—hen of the woods, bluefoot, St. George's, lobster, morels, chanterelles. I marveled as the cooks transformed raw product into mise en place.

When I finally weaseled my way into the kitchen, my real education began.

I showed up to my first shift and was greeted by a crew of heavy hitters: Akhtar Nawab, Karen Demasco, Dan Sauer, Brian Sernatinger, Mack Kern, James Tracey, Lauren Dawson, Arpana Satyu, Stacey Meyer, Ed Higgins, Liz Chapman, and Damon Wise, with Marco Canora and Jonathan Benno running the kitchen.* And then there was me, toting my tools from cooking school to my first day on the job.

"Nice knives, bro," someone snickered. Evidently the gear the school gave me was bullshit. I was like a kid showing up to the first day of school with his tighty-whities over his jeans. I had no idea what I was doing.

My first assignment, Benno told me, would be to prepare nine quarts of diced mirepoix—three each of onion, carrot, and celery. Perfect quarter-inch cubes, please. For a half-decent cook, it's maybe a forty-five-minute job. I spent all night. I knew exactly how to handle the task, but I froze up. Psyched myself out like I was taking the SATs again. By one a.m., I'd managed to demolish a couple cases of vegetables to produce one quart of each dice that I thought was usable.

When Benno saw what I'd done, his hand immediately went to his forehead.

"Yeah, we can't use any of this," he said, as he dumped it all into a pot of veal remouillage.

I don't know what prevented me from quitting on the spot. Pride, I suppose. I'd told everyone that I was going to be a cook. So I showed up for work the next day, and the day after that. In fact, I didn't take a

—

*If you know me, you've heard me recite these names over and over, as if they were the starting lineup of my favorite baseball team. Almost every single one of them—and I'm certainly forgetting a few people—went on to lead their own kitchens. That's an incredible anomaly in the restaurant business.

day off for a year. I worked for free until the magical day, six months in, when Marco sat me down and offered me a paid job.

I was always behind, but I relished the opportunity that the kitchen offered to take another swing with each new day. In a kitchen environment (as opposed to the golf course), I found a reserve of sheer, stubborn willpower to make up for what I lacked in talent. Here in front of my cutting board, I could see slow but definitive results. It gave me purpose. I would park myself on the couch at home after my shifts, watching recorded PBS cooking shows while practicing my technique. For hours I'd just sit and tournée potatoes, carrots, and turnips. I don't remember doing anything else for that whole period of my life other than cooking and studying cooking.

Some time during my first year at Craft, Marco asked why I hadn't come into the restaurant for a meal yet. Most cooks never dine at the restaurants where they work, because either it isn't encouraged or it simply feels too awkward to be served by one's superiors. Here Marco was urging me and I didn't have a good excuse, so I made a reservation for when my brother was in town. We ordered within our budget, but the kitchen crushed us with extra food. I mean *crushed*. More dishes than any VIP table ever got. When I opened the check at the end of the meal, I found a handwritten note from Marco: *Thank you for all of your hard work. This meal is on us.*

I wept like a baby.

I was still so bad at my job. Everyone knew it, yet they showed me patience. I recall crying another time at the restaurant after getting passed up for a position on the hot line—I'd be stuck on garde manger, the cold appetizer section. I was sobbing in the boiler room when Marco walked in to console me. I was good at this, he said, but I needed to get better. He told me I'd be fine. For some reason, I believed him. He left me to get myself together and then Benno came in.

"Garde manger is the place you want to work," he said. "Don't let anyone tell you otherwise."

Between the years he'd put in at Daniel, The French Laundry, and Gramercy Tavern, no one had spent more time at garde manger than Benno.* The result is that he'd become everything a cook should be. I had a lot left to learn. Benno took a special interest in my development. He pushed me out of my comfort zone at every opportunity. Looking back, I realize the huge debt I owe him. In the moment, I just thought he was trying to make my life hell.

I stayed at Craft for two and a half years, alternating as much as possible between morning prep shifts and dinner service. Morning prep gave me more hands-on experience with cooking in the purest sense of the word. I learned how to make everything in the mornings. I especially appreciated Saturday mornings, because it was just me and Ahktar Nawab working mise en place all day. I'd get in super early, turn on the island, grab all the stockpots and rondeaus. No one was there to fight for space on the stove or prep table. I think I learned more working on those Saturday mornings than any other time in my life. Vegetables, meats fabrication and butchery, vinaigrettes, charcuterie, sauces—all of it during my prep shifts. Dinner service, as anyone in the industry will tell you, is all about execution.** By dinnertime, everything is prepped and ready. Your job is simply to keep up with the constant influx of orders from the dining room.

I liked working both prep and service. I never became discour-

---

*Somehow, garde manger has been recast in the modern era as a lowly salad station, but in the history of the world's most esteemed restaurants—I'm talking about places like Kikunoi in Japan and La Maison Troisgros in France—garde manger was a position of strength and honor. It teaches you more about being a cook than any other job in the kitchen, because the variety of techniques and preparations there go far beyond, say, learning to grill a steak to medium rare sixty times a night.

**It used to be that there wasn't a divide between prep and service shifts. In old-school French kitchens, you worked both. And lunch, too. Labor laws changed all that. To no one's surprise in the restaurant industry, you'll still hear some chefs citing that fact as the reason why restaurants suck now.

aged by the long hours or the physical toll. It could all be overcome through willpower.

• • •

Willpower continued to keep me afloat when I started working at Café Boulud. I wanted to stay at Craft longer, but my family there encouraged me to work in the kind of French-style kitchen I had always found too intimidating. I was already in awe of one CB dish in particular: poularde en vessie. It's a preparation that has been around for a century, invented by Fernand Point at La Pyramide. A whole chicken is stuffed with truffles and foie gras, placed inside an inflated pig's bladder—an ingredient you couldn't even source in the States—and simmered in a bath of Madeira, Armagnac, and truffle juice. The bladder is sliced open tableside, sending a cloud of chicken-and-truffle-scented steam billowing out. I'd never seen anything like it, and deep down I knew I had to learn how it was made, so I joined the ranks of Andrew Carmellini's tough-as-nails kitchen.

It was 2003. I was sleeping on my college friend Tim's pullout couch across Central Park. This living arrangement was fine because I basically never left the restaurant. I'd spend the bus ride home after an eighteen-hour day debating whether I should take a five-minute shower or go right to bed. I get a headache just thinking about it.

New York City was just coming out of the 9/11 daze. People weren't going out to dinner. But ask anyone who was around and cared about such things and they will tell you that Carmellini was running the best restaurant in the United States. We all certainly thought it was true.

We were a small, spartan team. There were no prep cooks, no commis, no stagiaires, no help. That meant I was in charge of doing all my own mise en place. That might not sound like a big deal, but take the tuna carpaccio as an example. To this day, it remains the most illogically labor-intensive dish I've ever made: each morning I'd break down a side of bluefin tuna, making sure that the resulting product was completely devoid of sinew. I'd pound the fish into paper-thin circles that would fit perfectly onto the plate, then confit the scrap and sinew with a sachet of aromatics above the oven. (No matter how busy I was during service, I'd have to keep one eye on it, in case it started to get too warm.) Next, I'd wash the salt-packed capers and fillet a few pounds of anchovies, one by one, and cure them. Then wash the capers again. I'd have to make the bread tuiles: slice frozen bread, form it onto the back of a third pan, and bake the slices so they came out in a perfect U shape. I'd lose maybe half of the little fuckers to breakage. I'd then proceed to slice spring onions and chives into a decorative frizzle and make a "confetti" of brunoise shallots, red and yellow bell peppers, radishes, and Niçoise olives. Have you ever tried to make a perfect ⅛-inch dice of olives? Good luck with that. Oh, and let's not forget the maddeningly thin slices of baby yellow and green beans. At some point, I'd make a tonnato sauce out of the tuna scraps. And finally, I'd pick greens and make a lemon vinaigrette for a salad that sat in a perfect little nest on the plate. In kitchenspeak, the dish was a fourteen nine-pan pickup, meaning it called for fourteen individual containers of prepped components. It was made all the worse because tuna carpaccio is like catnip for Upper East Siders. I had to be prepped for dozens of orders a night.

There were also the terrines, which were not the rustic blocks of meat that you might get at a casual bistro. At Café Boulud, they were elegantly interlaced layers of smoked foie, potato, and apricot. A gorgeous presentation, as well as a significant pain in the ass. My station also included the oysters, the canapés, and a constantly changing amuse bouche for every guest, plus a separate amuse for VIPs. (Our only directive for the amuse bouche was that it had to be made from scraps, one bite, and incredibly delicious. There was no budget for it.) The hamachi dish. The seafood salad with cantaloupe purée. And those goddamned sugarcane shrimp skewers. Three times a week, I would be greeted by a towering forest of sugarcanes, two cleavers, and a wedge. My first task was to whittle down the sugarcanes to make the skewers.

Café Boulud gave a stodgy clientele the world when they probably would have been just as happy with messy terrines and frozen shrimp on toothpicks. The cook on the hot apps station would have to assemble small lasagnas, layer by layer, *to order*. It was way too much.

The reward, if you survived and showed a little verve in the process, was the privilege of working directly with Carmellini to come up with a special. You got to flex in front of your peers, but you'd need to conceive, prep, and have the special ready by the next service, while also taking care of your usual tasks. It's a common dynamic in high-end kitchens—the better you get at your job, the harder it gets—but it was especially pronounced at Café Boulud.

I once watched with a mixture of admiration and longing as a line cook—a Harvard grad, I should note—walked out in the middle of service. She left her sauces to burn on the flattop, took off her apron, and went out through the back door.

Chefs of an older generation will scoff, "This is nothing compared to what we had to endure in Europe." And, yes, I know how much of the chef-memoir library is full of descriptions of heinously complicated dishes. Regardless, I struggled every day I was there. Six months into my tenure at Café Boulud, my tenacity began to fall short. I'd always gone blindly and full speed into every situation, knowing I could hack it as long as I was ready to work and work and work some more. As long as I could embrace the numbing repetition of the kitchen, I could keep everything else in my life at bay. But doubt leaked into my psyche, and the lines between the kitchen and the real world began to collapse.

Mom was sick. During college, I'd taken the fall semester of junior year off to look after her after she developed breast cancer. Now it had returned. I'm convinced the relapse was a psychosomatic response to an ugly business dispute between my dad and my brother Jhoon. Everyone was acting like a jackass. It was a very shitty time

that broke the Changs apart and confirmed what I had always suspected: even your loved ones will let you down.

I tried my best to support my mom in my scant free time. At
work, with my defenses down, I began to get acquainted with some
thoughts that I had always batted away. *Why am I cooking this food? It
isn't what I want to eat, and it all feels so unnecessarily over the top. And even
if I stick with it, where will I end up?* There was one level left to unlock,
Thomas Keller's Per Se, which was set to open in a big, shiny sky-
scraper on Columbus Circle with a legendary kitchen team. Benno
was going to be the restaurant's chef de cuisine. He actually offered
me a position, which I declined.

I knew I wouldn't make it in a kitchen like Per Se. There was a
long line of better cooks ahead of me, and many of them would be
eaten up by the business before they made it. Meanwhile, my mom
was sick and my family members were calling on me to take sides in
the fight between Jhoon and my dad. Through the haze of doubt and
confusion, one thought began to surface repeatedly: I wanted to die.

• • •

With the benefit of many years of consultation with a professional
therapist, I can tell you that what I was experiencing toward the
end of my time at Café Boulud was my first full-blown experience
with the depressive phase of bipolar disorder. As simply as I can put
it, bipolar disorder is characterized by dramatic swings between high
(manic) and low (depressive) states.* This particular low lasted for sev-

---

*Let me emphasize that I'm not an expert. I can't even tell you if I have bipolar 1
or 2—I can't even remember. So, please don't infer anything about your or anyone
else's situation from reading about mine. Whenever I'm in a depressive state, my
therapist ends each session by saying, "If you feel that you need medical attention,
please call me immediately, or dial 911." That's just to give you a sense of how seriously doctors take this, and how important it is for you to seek professional help if
any of this resonates with you.

eral months and was the longest and most intense I've ever endured. But again, I can only tell you that in hindsight. At the time, all I knew was that everything felt shitty and I couldn't pinpoint a specific reason. I felt dislodged personally and professionally. Things I could always count on, like my palate, were failing me. It didn't seem normal to feel this way.

High school was where I first noticed that something was off. I'd spoken to the in-house therapist a few times, but I stopped because I didn't really feel comfortable spilling my guts to someone who had lunch with my teachers seven days a week. Instead I wrote about everything going on in my head. One day, my roommate dug through my computer and mocked me mercilessly for what he found. I saw another counselor in college. It took him two minutes to pull out the prescription pad and prescribe me Paxil. I never took it and I never saw him again.

I was embarrassed. I didn't feel justified in seeing a therapist or taking pills. For one thing, I didn't know any other Asian people who saw therapists. A lot of my friends had shrinks in college, but their situations were different. They were wealthy kids with actual bad shit going on at home in Westchester or whatever northeastern enclave had produced them. Rich kids are always the most fucked up. I didn't recognize my issues in anyone else.

At Trinity, I grew acutely aware of my otherness. The girls at school were mostly white and therefore off-limits. I'd seen how my parents reacted when my siblings had tried dating non-Koreans, and it wasn't pretty. Not that it would have mattered. The white girls at school were explicit in their pronouncements that they would never be seen with an Asian man. And so, aside from random drunken hookups, I never dated anyone in college. For years, any kind of meaningful relationship I had was one I found during the summer or while traveling abroad. I simply felt more comfortable somewhere else.

For a minute, I thought I'd attend divinity school after Trinity, but my grades weren't good enough to get me into a graduate program, much less one of the cushy jobs that my classmates were landing in New York. I didn't know what else to do with myself, so I showed up to a postgrad career fair and signed up to teach English in Japan, because the booth was closest to the door. I'd come to think that my problems were in America, and I wanted to live the life of an expat. Being away from home would be a fresh start, a chance for reinvention. I fled the States with the intention of being gone for good.

• • •

Cut to the cross-country track behind the high school in Izumi-Tottori and the largest Asian man within thirty miles running around and around and loving it: my first encounter with the highs of a manic episode, and the other side of bipolar disorder. I had boundless energy. I felt invincible. At night, I read dense Russian classics, plowing through the entire canon. I finished *War and Peace* in a couple of days.

I had originally requested an assignment in cold, northern Sapporo. The company sent me to this steamy town in Wakayama Prefecture instead. Imagine Jacksonville, only hotter. At night, I would hear wannabe yakuza riding their dirt bikes and motorcycles around the rice paddy that was my backyard. Most of my students were either the wives of organized criminals or kids prepping for college entrance exams. Once they realized that their English grammar was better than mine, they started using my class as an opportunity to nap. I lived in an apartment with my boss, next to a dorm for Jehovah's Witnesses, and I don't think I had a full night of sleep the entire time I was there.

I'd hoped to find something in Japan—a sense of belonging, maybe. No such luck. The women in Japan were no more inclined to date me than the women at Trinity. All the Japanese girls seemed to be paired up with a white guy. If not, they certainly weren't going to stoop to dating a Korean.

I did a little traveling while there, and saw that many of the Koreans living in Japan were downtrodden or wrapped up in gambling and shadier professions. Finding vandalism on the monuments to Koreans who died in Hiroshima was an early lesson in racism's ubiquity.

I'd always assumed Japan was a country of extraordinary punctuality, but the train would sometimes be late in Izumi-Tottori. I learned that the delays were caused by people jumping on the tracks, even though the government did everything it could to prevent it. They announced that they would fine the families of the deceased. They painted the station a calming pastel yellow. None of it seemed to have an effect.

Between Tolstoy and Dostoyevsky, I read Camus. I spent a lot of time mulling over his famous quote about finding an "invincible summer" within himself. I wondered about the car crash that ended his life, when he took a ride with a notoriously bad driver. When they examined his body, they found a train ticket in his pocket. Did he maybe *want* to get in that accident?

• • •

I don't know if all suicidal people fixate on suicide, but I did. I saw myself in Mel Gibson's character in *Lethal Weapon,* waking up every morning to a solitary game of Russian roulette. I'm aware of how stupid that sounds, but I'm saying it anyway. That's how it was for me.

It couldn't look like a gesture. As pointless as it is to worry over what people would think of me when I was dead, the last thing I wanted was to burden my parents with the dishonor of having a son who killed himself. There could be no drama, no note. I'd make it look like an accident, or just put myself in enough cars with shitty drivers.

When I returned to New York from Tokyo, I started my dead-end job at the financial services company. I would ride my Gary Fisher bike all over Manhattan, weaving in and out of traffic and blowing through stoplights as if I were the only person on the street. I once went skiing with friends who had to tell me to cool it because I was getting too close to the trees. I defied them and completely obliterated myself in the foliage. One day I stepped off the curb in Central Park as a bus was backing up; it hit me and it hurt a great deal.

There was a New Year's Eve party in 2000 that began with Valium, speed, pot, this, that, and the other, washed down with around twenty drinks, and ended with my falling through a giant glass table. Blood everywhere. Shards of glass embedded in my wrists. The ER doctors said I narrowly missed an artery. I wonder if my recklessness was a cry for help disguised as youthful indiscretion, or if maybe I was hoping that at the bottom of a bottle would be the courage to step in front of the train.

I didn't want to feel like this. I had no morbid curiosity about killing myself. I would rather have spent my time doing anything other than obsessing about death and trying to manifest it. Eventually I tried to approach the matter rationally. Step one was to ask myself if I really wanted to die. I'd decided the answer was yes, but could a professional talk me out of it? If they couldn't, step two was obvious.

The only reference points I had for therapists were *Frasier* and Robin Williams in *Good Will Hunting,* and some light reading I'd done on depression and mania. (Camus was my first source. Later, I came to love William Styron's *Darkness Visible* and eventually read everything by the psychologist Kay Redfield Jamison.) My main takeaway was that I didn't think Freudian psychoanalysis was for me. I didn't want some dude with elbow patches and a tweed jacket alerting me to the fact that I had a difficult dad. I certainly didn't want someone who would try to graft a "tested" approach to my case.

I scrounged together a stack of *New York* magazine issues to find the psychiatrists listed in the *Best Doctors* inserts. If you've lived in New York at some point over the past couple of decades, you probably know what I'm talking about. But I couldn't tell what distinguished one shrink from another. It was all so vague. I probably would have gleaned more information about each doctor's expertise and style if I hadn't hung up on every single one of their offices as soon as they got on the line.

As things were getting rougher at Café Boulud, I decided to call on a therapist on the Upper East Side. When I arrived at the appointment, I found a gentleman with silver hair and—you guessed it—elbow patches. A dead ringer for George Plimpton. Immediately after the first session, I was convinced he wasn't for me. I kept meeting with him for a few weeks anyway, trying to muster the energy to open up. I'd decided on a plan, and I needed to see it through.

• • •

"How is this supposed to work?"

I'd landed in the office of another doctor I found online. He'd attended a small liberal arts school for undergrad and a southwestern state university for med school—the kinds of colleges I wished I'd gone to. More stuff I liked: he had done a lot of work on children's suffering and PTSD, and he had just completed his residency, so I knew he was only a few years older than me.

I emailed him, he got back to me quickly, we hashed out the finances, we set up an appointment. Simple and efficient.

Our early sessions were uncomfortable. He barely spoke at all and I barely said anything of substance. I kept asking how the sessions were supposed to be structured as he stared at me blankly. No matter how hard I forced the issue, I'd get no response. I was smart enough to know that he was leaving these silences for me to fill in, but back then, articulating the most basic sentiment—I'm not even talking about feelings, I'm talking about stuff like ordering off a menu at a restaurant—took immense effort.*

But the few words Dr. Eliot did say at the end of our first session made me want to stick around.

"Hey, I'm really concerned about you. I think we should get into a rhythm here in my office and consider starting you on some medication."

It was a dry, almost mechanical expression of worry, but it felt entirely new. I had never really confided in family or friends before. It actually blew my mind to know that someone was willing to listen to me, and that he had detected the possibility that I could hurt myself.

What I wasn't ready to do was start medication. Partly, I was afraid that once I started taking meds the only way to be healthy would be to become an artificial version of myself. It's a common source of hesitation. But mostly I just thought meds were for pussies.

In any case, Dr. Eliot wanted a rhythm, and a rhythm is what I delivered. In those first three months, I unloaded on him. I talked very slowly—that didn't change—but I was able to tell him what he needed to know. It was in that room that I started to figure out how to articulate what I was experiencing, which was as morose and cheaply dramatic as it was deeply felt. I'm happy to give you a taste:

My depression morphs and adapts. There will be periods when I think it's gone, only to discover months down the line that it was actually pulling

---

*You can still find old video clips where interviewers ask me questions like "What's your desert-island dish?" and I visibly struggle to push the words out of my mouth. Watching footage of myself straining to talk about my favorite thing to do with leftovers, I'm genuinely surprised they didn't stop the camera and ask, "Are you okay?"

the strings with more intention than ever before. There are days or weeks that I look back on and realize I was manic and had no idea. Sometimes the depression will be obvious and oppressive, and other times it'll just simmer. It is a constant ache, a constant agony. The complete and utter suffocation of anything positive. Stimuli that should cause joy induce the opposite. Anything and everything in life is a reminder of the absurdity of existence. Depression plunders my confidence but somehow also boosts my ego, a very dangerous set of fluctuations that makes it feel as if everything around me is rotten and that everyone is aware of my plight and actively working to make it worse. My threshold for sadness is insane, because sadness is the only solace.

I spent a lot of time resisting Dr. Eliot's questions about my childhood, but it all came out eventually. There was the fear of abandonment, generated from being left alone so much as a kid. There was the toll of constant exposure to my dad's intensity and conflict with my mom. The God stuff came up a lot, especially how and why I took it so seriously. And there was the most consistent theme of not fitting in: not in my family, not among other Koreans, not in a WASP-y high school or college, not in the kitchen. I told him that I felt inadequate when I stood next to blue-blooded white Americans or in a French-style brigade.

I talked about 9/11 and my classmate who killed himself with his dad's pistol in third grade, and the three friends I'd lost right after college—one to suicide, one to an overdose, one to a freak accident. I felt surrounded by death.

I talked about always being a person to whom things were done. I told Dr. Eliot that at Georgetown Prep, I'd learned about the type of people who get what they want in life, and it wasn't anyone who looked like me. I couldn't stop thinking about how stupid and arbitrary life seemed. Even if I was outwardly a wallflower, I was angry at the entire world. I felt lied to or let down by everyone. I was insufficient, unnecessary, and I hated how much it all affected me.*

Dr. Eliot's office was the place I first actually said it out loud: the only thing that could possibly make the situation better is to turn it all off.

• • •

For me, depression manifests itself as an addiction to work. I work hard to control what I can. Thus, my conversations with Dr. Eliot weren't restricted to abstractions. We talked about restaurants—a lot. I floated opinions that had been bouncing around my head for a few years. I'd always been somewhat nervous about discussing them with anyone because I didn't want other cooks to laugh at me. Don't get me wrong, I thought the ideas were brilliant. I was an egomaniac with low self-confidence.

And so, I may have only whispered it at first, but I definitely said it: "I think the underground in food can become overground." It had happened before in music, art, fashion, in Europe and Asia. Why not food? Why not here? I couldn't relate to the people I was cooking for. At the time in New York, dining out was still the domain of the rich and privileged. That was definitely how my friends saw it: whenever I suggested going out for a nice dinner, they'd look at me as though I'd suggested we put our cash in a paper shredder. But in Asia? Man, it was the polar opposite. From the grocery stands and yakitori joints in Japan to the stalls along the hutongs of Beijing, enjoying food was

---

*I feel a compulsion to legitimize my depression even now, against the advice of my editor. I have never walked barefoot across the desert, lost an appendage, or fought a war. But these thoughts felt like a spike in my chest, my gut, the back of my eyes, every square inch of my brain. And if you're reading this book, hoping to glean some tidbits about the key to my success, know that you're looking right at it. Depression and the choice to resist it are the only reasons you're hearing from me now.

foundational. Dining out was attainable and affordable, a crucial part of daily life. Even in Virginia lower-middle-class Asian families would go out to dinner once a week at a Chinese restaurant. The idea that people with less money could not appreciate better food was a fallacy.

I told Dr. Eliot that I wanted to walk away from the traditional chef's path, but not because I was afraid of failing. I had already failed. There had to be another trajectory for me. I had nothing to gain from cooking in fine-dining restaurants and I had nothing besides cooking to live for. When I left Café Boulud, I wasn't trying to save myself. I was ready to die, and I had something I needed to get off my chest before I did.

I'd become a cook because it was the only job available to me. Somehow, my grades and disposition had landed me—a former golf prodigy with a liberal arts education—in the same place as the other misfits, ex-cons, alcoholics, and newly arrived immigrants that the kitchen tends to attract. At the same time, I'd also become a cook because it was real, honest work that I could understand and control. Like so many impressionable college students, I'd been captivated by Emerson and Thoreau, who helped plant the seeds for American Pragmatism. I interpreted their writing to mean that one's goal should be to live as an embodiment of philosophy, to test one's beliefs through one's actions rather than through study or discussion. Cooking was my way of making that happen. If I wasn't cooking food I believed in, then what was I even doing?

Our culinary memory is short and we live in a very different food world now. Chances are you won't remember the late nineties as a time when restaurants were basically inaccessible to most Americans, but it was. Our dining culture was, by and large, bifurcated. On one side, you had prohibitively expensive, mostly French-inspired restaurants with excellent service and comfortable dining rooms. On the other, there were far more affordable options serving the cuisines of Asia, Africa, and Latin America in humble settings—a genre that's been lumped together as "ethnic food" since the 1960s. But as delicious as those places could be, they were usually locked into the traditions and time periods from which their immigrant proprietors first came. There really wasn't a place where you could find something in between: innovative cuisine that was neither married to France nor fixed to the recipes of the motherland, made with high-quality ingredients, and available for, say, twenty bucks. I could tell that race played a major role in America's slow uptake on this concept, which only made it more personal for me.*

People often hear that I spent time in Japan and then came back to New York to start a noodle bar, and they fill in the blanks for themselves. I may have helped that narrative along in the *Momofuku* cookbook, implying that I was certain from day one about my desire to open a ramen shop and that I went to Japan specifically to study ramen. Yes, in that hellish town there was a ramen-ya, but I actually only managed to eat there once.

I passed by the shop every day, watching it longingly, carefully. People were eating well for cheap and they were having a good time. There was no pomp and circumstance, no smoke and mirrors. There were no barriers to entry, none of the artifices that make restaurants so difficult to run and so expensive to enjoy. The working stiff could sit next to a billionaire and neither of them would feel out of their element. The food would be carefully and thoughtfully prepared, while everything else—the decor, the plating, the service—was about fun and comfort.

I went back to Japan for a second time between my stints at Craft and Café Boulud. I wanted another crack at it—my first stretch there

---

*When I was a student at the French Culinary Institute, I once proposed a project using pork stock, which is common in Asian cooking. My instructor scoffed at me: "Pork stock is for savages." I walked away with my head down, wishing I had the courage to tell him he was wrong.

had ended too soon, I thought—so I scored a visa and my dad hooked me up with a Christian Korean missionary named Paul Hwang. Paul picked me up from the airport and brought me to a dingy old office building in Kudanshita, in Tokyo. The seventh floor held the ministry and church. Floors three to six were a blend of offices and living quarters for the homeless.* The first floor had been converted to an izakaya, which was run by a Japanese chef who was married to a Korean woman, a union that was still deeply frowned upon. The other head chef was schizophrenic. The whole building was a haven for broken people for whom there were very few resources in Japan. Their skill level was unbelievable, and the food they cooked was absolutely delicious.

For a hot second, I worked at the filthy ramen shop next door, but I quickly moved over to the izakaya. I slept in the back of Paul's office on a beanbag pillow and a single tatami mat. I enrolled in Japanese courses at the same university that my grandfather had attended during the Japanese occupation of Korea. I would get 2s, 3s, and 4s on my exams. *Out of 100.* Needless to say, my Japanese needs work.

I'd met a well-known physician in New York, and he took me under his family's wing in Tokyo. His nephew ran a soba shop. It was the only job I ever truly wanted and the only job I was ever fired from. Next, my old bosses at Craft helped me get a position at the New York Grill, the restaurant at the top of the Park Hyatt Hotel. We cooked American food with Japanese products, which provided me with a solid bit of evidence that labels are empty and that deliciousness is universal.

But amid all those gigs, the most eye-opening eating experiences took place in homes, on the street, and at McDonald's (which was cheap and consistently great). After paying rent at the ministry and

---

*Years later, I would return to Japan while filming our TV show *Ugly Delicious.* We searched everywhere for Paul's building but couldn't find it. I felt like I was being gaslit. Was it all a dream?

tuition at school, I was scrounging to make ends meet, but I could still eat like a king. That was the real epiphany. I could eat extraordinarily well in places that weren't punishingly expensive. I don't just mean "cheap eats." I'm talking about restaurants driven by technique and respect for ingredients and chefs who were just as devoted to their craft as those in the Western fine-dining kitchens that I had come to think represented the only legitimate path. Why didn't I see this in New York? Even Europeans had embraced Asian-influenced egalitarian dining at restaurant chains like Wagamama. Why hadn't the majority of people in America bought into this way of eating?

• • •

In general, Asian role models were hard for me to come by. I loved Bruce Lee, and in the sports world, I worshipped the golfer Jumbo Ozaki and the football player Eugene Chung, who was the first Asian American to be selected in the first round of the NFL draft.

With such limited and disparate options, I didn't know where to look for direction. At home, there were my brothers, but the only trait of theirs that I wanted to emulate was their size. I was obsessed with catching up to them. For five years I drank a gallon of whole milk every day and consumed meat like a starving bear.* Sophomore year of high school I sprouted four inches and gained a hundred pounds. (Part of the reason my golf game fell apart and I started playing football was that the growth spurt completely derailed my swing.)

As I imagine other big Asian boys can probably attest, there's a faint promise that separating yourself from the cliché of Asians

---

*We're not talking about grass-fed cows here. My family bought the cheap, chemically enhanced stuff. When people ask me about my disproportionate size, I tell them that I'm a product of bovine growth hormone.

as small, meek creatures will somehow make it easier to fit in with white America. But being big doesn't actually get you any closer to blending in. If anything, it further separated me from my own kin. My relatives began to look at me like a monster, while continuing to ply me with food, as is the Asian way. In the same breath they would tell me I was getting fat while imploring me to eat more of whatever homemade Korean dish they'd put in front of me.

Once I started cooking, I didn't recognize myself in the chefs I admired, either. Then I heard about a Chinese American man, Alex Lee, running the kitchen at Daniel Boulud's flagship restaurant. It was almost unfathomable to think that someone who looked like me could stand at the helm of one of the finest French kitchens in the world. Through word of mouth, I learned about what a serious and monomaniacal figure he was. He was the kind of chef who made it to the top the old-fashioned way: by sheer grit. One of my life goals was to work for him.

The day Lee quit Daniel and headed for the suburbs to run a country club kitchen was a monumental moment for me. He wasn't even forty yet, but he was done. Word on the street was that he wanted a better life balance, to take care of himself. By that time I was also coming to the end of my time at Café Boulud. I was never going to be Alex Lee. His story—a badass Asian chef who out-cooked everyone around him, regardless of skin color—was never going to be mine.

To be clear, there were other Asian chefs paving the way as well. By the time I opened Momofuku, Anita Lo was already doing something truly special and personal with Asian food at her restaurant Annisa. (She has never gotten enough credit for her accomplishments.) But she lived in the high end, as did Patricia Yeo, who earned three stars from the *Times* at her eclectic Asian restaurant AZ. To a miserable cook with dim prospects like me, there was an undeniable appeal in the idea of opening an American restaurant that didn't bother with fanciness.* By relaxing certain conventions of dining, we could bring more cooks and diners into the fold and make restaurant culture more like it was in Asia. Maybe this could be my contribution to the world. I was becoming ever more distrustful of and angry at mainstream America, and if I could somehow show that everything I had been told about American dining was wrong, perhaps I could disprove some larger cultural fallacies, as well.

I had a feeling, I told Dr. Eliot, that humans aren't all that different as you move around the world. What worked in Asia could work here, too. Someone just needed to give it a place to breathe.

Talking through these ideas with Dr. Eliot felt productive, but I hadn't had any overt aha moments about my depression. I didn't really feel any better. Going over the facts of my childhood didn't seem to be making a difference. My sole breakthrough was a private one: if nothing mattered—if I wasn't going to beat this depression and I wasn't going to make it in the fine-dining world—what did I have to lose? Why not at least try to create a world that worked for me?

Thoreau said, "I know of no more encouraging fact than the unquestionable ability of man to elevate his life by conscious endeavor." I took that very much to heart as I contemplated suicide. Elevation through conscious endeavor. Work toward something. Open a restaurant. If it doesn't pan out, there's always the other path.

---

*It should be said that I like fancy restaurants very much, but at that point in American dining, fanciness had become paramount. I recall a restaurant manager once telling the staff as we prepared to cook for the *New York Times* critic that, in order of priorities, the critic would be considering (1) service; (2) decor; and (3) the food. It was around that time when I first started thinking, *Fuck this. I don't want my work to be an accessory to the carpet and chairs.*

OUT OF MY DEPTH

Young chefs opening their first restaurant come to me for advice all the time.

The questions come in three flavors:

1. What does it take to be successful?
2. What kind of people should I go into business with?
3. What's a piece of wisdom that nobody shares with you at the outset but makes all the difference?

I don't always nail the message. If you're one of the many aspirants who have approached me for help, you know this. My answers to your concerns have likely made both of us dumber.

Usually I end up expounding on whatever subject has been consuming my thoughts at the time, vaguely connecting it to the topic at hand until I run out of time. There is too much to cover. It's hard to name a discipline or area of knowledge that isn't useful to the business of birthing and operating a restaurant. For starters, one needs to understand contracts, real estate, management, and publicity—not to mention the craft of cooking good food. This is what people call a "compound art."

Sometimes, if the conversation is private and I have more time, I'll ask pointedly, "Do you really want to open a restaurant?"

Then I give the following recipe:

1. Invite all the people who have agreed to give you their money to the home of one of the investors for a private and very special preview of your restaurant. Do not forget to mention that they will each need to bring a check in the amount of $5,000.
2. When they arrive, place a big bowl in the center of the table. Kindly instruct your guests to place their checks into it. Set the contents of the bowl on fire.

Your friends and family must be under no illusions: in all likelihood, their investment in your project will be gone forever. Perhaps there's a better way they can help you with their money. If so, you should take them up on it. Do not open a restaurant unless you must.

Does my advice ever work? Not really. I have a 99 percent failure rate. Practically everyone I have tried to dissuade from opening a restaurant has done so in spite of my warnings.

But who am I to warn people off this business? I knew nothing about what it takes to open a restaurant when I began, and I often cite that ignorance as the primary reason for my success.

• • •

I didn't have a space and I didn't have any money, but at least no one wanted to work with me.

That was the score in the spring of 2004. No funds and no location are a part of the process, but having no potential cooks is a tell. Most chefs who are opening a restaurant will alert like-minded colleagues well in advance about what they have in the works. Over beers at night or Chinese food on days off, they sniff out who might be ready for a change of scenery.

No one was biting on my concept. The cooks I admired from Craft and Café Boulud all said no. I tried to recruit my brother's golf buddy who ran a gourmet goods store in Pittsburgh. Nope. I even asked my friend Brendan, who wasn't a cook—he was a teacher.

I'd left Café Boulud six months earlier than expected. To this day, one of my great life regrets is not finishing my tenure there. According to kitchen custom, I should have left the business entirely or spent at least five more years training under great chefs before even *considering* running a restaurant of my own. Nobody wanted to work for a dude who had bailed on his job to chase a crackpot scheme.

I was spectacularly alone.

Lest we forget, my big idea for a restaurant was to make ramen. These days opening a noodle shop in America is a common enough dream, but it was a downright bizarre proposition in 2004. As far as deterrents go, it was a force field. I could have been Paul Bocuse and people still would have hesitated when they heard "ramen." A good number of folks assumed I was talking about the packets that you heat up in a microwave. I know this because I got questions about it all the time from guests visiting my restaurant in the beginning.

In retrospect, as foolish as I may have looked, this was actually the only time in my career that I would have a domain-expertise advantage over the rest of my industry. And it was pure chance. My travels to Japan had coincided with the exact moment that ramen was blowing up there. Artisanal shops were opening all over the country, and people were lining up for hours to get a taste. Here was this huge group of people with incredible food knowledge, and they were all going crazy for ramen. Was it specifically because they were Japanese? Given that I'm not Japanese and I also found ramen extremely delicious, I doubted it.

At the same time, there were small signs of budding interest in Japanese food in America. One day while I was still working at Craft, I was walking by a Korean bodega in Union Square that I'd passed a thousand times in the past. In their cold case, they sold all your typical convenience store fare: yogurt, fruit salad, orange juice, stale sandwiches. But then I saw it. In the far corner of the refrigerator, a plastic container of sushi. I told everyone I knew. *A bodega is selling sushi! This is it, man! This is it!*

None of my cook friends were into it, but in theory, I knew a noodle shop would work. I put staffing on ice to attend to other matters.

Finding a location was not that difficult. I briefly considered opening in Virginia, so I could be near my convalescing mother, but something—my ego—wouldn't let me quit New York City. I was going to either fail or thrive, and I was going to do it in full view of everyone I respected and resented.

I looked at a couple of spots in SoHo and the West Village but in the end gravitated toward the East Village. I already had an affinity for the neighborhood. Whenever I was passing through the area during the day, I'd grab a watery coffee at Veniero's, a hundred-year-old Italian bakery with very strong A/C. I'd go down there all the time to drink at Lucy's, Tile Bar, International Bar, or any of the other musty spots that used to let you smoke inside. If I didn't want to drink alone, I'd post up at Bar Veloce, where the mustachioed barkeep would keep me company. Veloce is still around, too.

Marco Canora, one of my mentors at Craft who has since become an older brother figure to me, had also recently opened his first restaurant, Hearth, with Paul Grieco on the corner of 12th Street and First Avenue. I figured that if the East Village was acceptable for them, it would be just fine for me. The rents were low and the area had character and was friendly enough to small Asian restaurants. More and more young people were heading there after being priced out of other neighborhoods, too. But I don't believe I'd have moved in without Hearth paving the way. I never gave Marco reason to think much of me while I worked in his kitchen, but once we opened, I'd go visit him and try to absorb knowledge from the sensei during his breaks. It was a comfort seeing his kitchen filled with line cooks and sous chefs I had worked with at Craft.

One East Village establishment that's no longer in business is Village Chicken at 163 First Avenue. Or was it called Village Barbecue? Either way, it was a fried chicken place—six hundred square feet for the kitchen plus dining room, and $6,000 a month. It was smaller and more expensive than most of the other locations I'd scouted. I zeroed in on it because of the foot traffic. I told the realtor straightaway I was going to put in an application.

The discovery of that narrow little shitbox made me happy. That same day I signed a lease on an apartment across the street.

Location was settled. Staffing not so much. And money was another story.

• • •

I had little reason to believe my dad would support me in this endeavor. I'd failed to land any kind of respectable postgrad job because my grades were too low, and now I wanted to chase a career in the one industry he said was unacceptable. I hyped myself up before approaching him, suppressing my dread by adopting a scorch-the-earth attitude: *I'll do this without you, Dad. This is a courtesy—your last chance to invest in me before I move on.*

The fact of the matter was I had nowhere else to turn.

Over the phone, I blurted out the forceful-sounding material I'd rehearsed without letting him get a word in. I outlined my case, to which he replied with one word.

"Okay."

"What do you mean, *okay*?"

"How much do you need?"

Dad agreed to help me out with a loan and an accountant refer-ral. In short order, he conferred with his inner circle of Virginia-area Korean movers and shakers and loaned me 100,000 bucks. Together with the twenty-seven grand I'd saved, it would get us open.

When I think about why Dad was so quick to agree, I wonder if he wasn't longing for a distraction from his ongoing struggles with my brother. Dad and I began a new routine—a schedule of check-ins about construction progress and nuts-and-bolts business stuff. There was no one else who could help me out with project management. This phase of our relationship turned out to be the closest thing to therapy I ever experienced with him: a reason to be in touch and on the same side, though I'm not sure that either of us was able to recog-nize it as good for us at the time.

One thing I knew for certain was that I would not take my father's contribution for granted. Sons don't have difficult relation-ships with their fathers because we *want* to disappoint them. When I think back on the bright moments of our relationship, this one stands out. There were no apologies or heartfelt conversations, only the money and the particulars of starting a business. He was vulnerable. I was vulnerable. We were leaning on one another, just as a family might.

Until I started writing this book, I'd forgotten that I named our business entity JCDC, LLC—Joe Chang and Dave Chang in the same company.

• • •

Lexapro made me feel nothing much at all.

At Dr. Eliot's suggestion, I'd finally decided to try medication, and some of my initial fears had come true.

I understood precisely what the doctor meant when he told me it would be a "mood governor." The drug has the effect of leaving you constantly wanting to sense more emotion. Everything was monotone and muted, including myself. I felt controlled, which, to be fair, was an improvement.

My new apartment was a dank and dreary dump that I made even more sad-sack by furnishing it like a sociopath's lair. I slept on the futon that had come with the place; I had a table, a lamp, and a TV, all procured from one of those corner shops that you walk by and wonder, *Who buys this shit?* I turned off the gas to the stove and unplugged the refrigerator because I had no intention of cooking at home. The floor was perpetually littered with half-full bottles of water I'd brought home from work. Every once in a while, I'd go to take a sip and find a cockroach waiting for me at the bottom. I stored paperwork in the fridge and kept the pantry completely unstocked save for a steady reserve of brown liquor: Bulleit, Elijah Craig, and Pappy Van Winkle, which was still relatively unknown and cheap back then. I'd drink half a bottle almost every night just to fall asleep. I couldn't figure out how to get the A/C unit to fit properly in my window, so I put books around the intake and duct-taped it to the sill. I've never seen the Unabomber's apartment, but I lived there for five years.

I chose that place solely for its proximity to the restaurant. When my dad saw that I was living within spitting distance of my business, he told me that that would be the key to my success. And so I immersed myself in the task before me. In between frantic visits to restaurant-supply stores along the Bowery and in Chinatown, trying to get the shopkeepers to print signs and build equipment, I tinkered with recipes. It would be generous to call what I was doing "R&D." My noodles were pitiful and they weren't getting any better. I had Japanese ramen cookbooks that I paid people on Craigslist to translate for me, but even with the necessary information, I couldn't produce what I needed. I isolated the problem as a lack of kansui, the alkaline solution that lends ramen noodles a sustained springiness, a slightly sulfurous aroma, and a distinctive mouthfeel.*

Today, a chef can ring up Sun Noodle in New Jersey and they'll happily make alkaline noodles to their specification. Fifteen years ago, I found myself harassing the brother-owners of a company called Canton Noodle Corporation on Mott Street, asking them about kansui and whether they could procure it for me. Every time I entered the building, they waved me off immediately. They didn't want to do it, for fear that it would ruin the machinery. In the end, I bought noodles made without kansui and aged them in order to get my desired texture. I was flying by the seat of my pants.

Help finally arrived in the form of Joaquin "Quino" Baca, who responded to an ad I'd placed on Monster.com. A family friend had mentioned that the Cheesecake Factory where he worked in Tysons Corner lured all their cooks through Monster, so I'd posted on the site and promptly forgotten about it. Thankfully, Quino's girlfriend came across my job listing and passed it on.

We had the interview at Lucy's. Quino had most recently been in New Mexico, but he'd lived all over the place as the son of diplomats. (I used to joke that his parents worked for the CIA, since their tenures

---

*Information was much harder won back then. I know it's almost impossible to imagine a pre-Google world, but nothing was as simple as looking it up on your phone. Believe me, I wish it had been. In the hopes of getting a glimpse at something remotely relevant to my quest, I staged at a sushi restaurant in New York that served ramen and worked at a noodle bar in an Atlantic City hotel-casino. In my free time, I'd research by eating. While I was still working at Craft, I found a place serving Hakata-style ramen (rich pork-bone broth and thin noodles) that I thought was pretty good. I went dozens of times and watched the cooks' every move, wondering what kind of magical elixir they were simmering in the gigantic cauldron on the back stove. When I finally worked up the courage to ask what went in the pot, the cook responded, "It's just water." Turns out their broth was nothing more than water mixed with premade flavor concentrates. You might think that I found this deflating, but what it told me was that contemporary Japanese ramen was so far ahead of New York. I began to think that what I wanted to do simply didn't exist yet.

around the world always seemed to coincide with a coup d'état.) He'd come to New York hoping to find a spot at Bouley, a French fine-dining temple in Tribeca, but the job he'd been offered wasn't what he'd been hoping for. It left him with a chip on his shoulder and no choice but to answer my call.

What made him a top candidate was that he was a candidate at all. Quino was handsome, like a less beefy Latin version of Vin Diesel. I had not seen him cook, but he was comfortable with himself to an enviable degree. Although I cannot prove this, I'm convinced that any chef in Manhattan who got a tattoo in the mid-2000s did so because they saw the sick sleeve of art Quino came into town wearing on his arm.

After our interview, we went together to clean the walk-in I'd inherited. It was still full of rotting chicken.

On Being Addicted to Work

MY FRIEND THE ARTIST DAVID CHOE SUMMARIZED IT BEST FOR ME: work is the last socially acceptable addiction.

I agree. The term *workaholic* is a silly name for a very real, very intense thing. Chefs often talk about the rush of opening a restaurant. It's not only a rush to me. It's heroin. I know I'm not alone. I received a message recently from a young woman named Joanna who listens to my podcast, and asked for her permission to share part of it with you:

What stuck with me was the way you describe your addiction to work. I've been so used to hearing of depression as something that forces you to do absolutely nothing. But pushing my limits became my drug. It was essentially a form of masochism. 18 years old and I found myself working nonstop for 20 hours a day. I didn't socialize. I major in computer engineering and spent my day in front of a laptop. I wear glasses now from staring at screens so much. Getting things done let me avoid taking care of myself. I was just "too busy." 96% of the things you focused on relating to your struggles have caused me to think, "Oh my gosh, it's not just me!" Frankly, you helped me realize working so hard was a side effect of my depression, a source of control, and not just something other people who didn't know what was up admired me for.

When I set out to open Momofuku, I remember being paralyzed by each and every task ahead of me. *How do I get a permit? How do I get an air-conditioning system? How do we make noodles? Where can I buy a pasta cooker? Why the fuck doesn't anybody want to work with me?* Every problem was an impossibility. The sensation of gritting my teeth, bearing down, and somehow doing what needed doing gave me a primal high.

I crave that resistance, whether it comes from the city, my land-lord, my staff, or my own shortcomings. It's not just helpful, it's nec-essary. You think a salmon really wants to swim upstream and die? They have no choice. That's how I feel, too.

I hated work when I was younger. I was a poor student, a poor employee. But the kitchen was different. I found meaning in the repetitive tasks, as long as I did them with intent and purpose. All that peeling, plucking, slicing, and chopping could seem frivolous, but only if I let myself think that way. When everything else felt out of control, cooking was my North Star. It wouldn't let me down. Putting something on a plate is a finite task. I could see the mise en place in front of me and the customer waiting in the dining room. I saw the pan, the stove, and the process that needed to be accom-plished for the dish to make it into the dining room and onto the table. I saw sales numbers. I saw reviews. Each step provided a tan-gible point of contact. And with success came validation—not only of the work but of myself. One morning I had this simple idea to serve a pork bun—pork belly, hoisin, pickles, steamed bread—as an accompaniment to our ramen, and then we sold a thousand of them in a week. It's an addictive feeling.

As with any addiction, the deeper I got, the higher the dosage I needed. Drug addicts don't get the same pleasure that a random party kid gets from doing a bump in a bathroom stall. They need much more. Sex addicts continually need to up the stakes of their pursuits—more partners, multiple partners, married partners. Marathon runners graduate to ultramarathons and Ironman competitions. It's no different for workaholics.

For instance, I contrast those early impossible-feeling days of opening Momofuku with my schedule as I write this. We've taken on outside investment, which means we've been opening a new restaurant every few months for the past two years, including one this week. Two of my best chefs have put in their notice while I'm simultaneously dealing with a crisis at our L.A. restaurant. There are TV shows to shoot and podcasts to record. I've got a new son at home and I'm locked in trying to write this book. The anxiety and dread are as vivid as when I first felt them. I describe it to Dr. Eliot this way: I used to want to learn how to juggle two balls. Now I'm tossing around motorcycles, chain saws, and babies.

When I'm able to take a step back, I realize that I've created my own prison. I physically cannot take on any more responsibilities. There's no room to do more, and I'm afraid of what that means for my addiction. I want so much to quit and walk away, but I don't know that I have the courage to give it all up. Recovering alcoholics talk about needing to hit rock bottom before they are able to climb out. The paradox for the workaholic is that rock bottom is the top of whatever profession they're in.

4

TRUST EXERCISE

"My husband really knows ramen, and this is not ramen."

The woman approached me one night a few months into Momofuku Noodle Bar's existence. She didn't give her name. She introduced herself as *Let me tell you* and plowed straight ahead: "I'm in the industry, my husband is Japanese, and he and I have spent many years eating around the world together."

I nodded my head and pursed my lips. I tried to communicate telepathically: *Okay, say your piece, so we can both get on with our lives.*

She took my silence as an invitation to continue.

"The noodles are awful. Nothing like real ramen or any noodles I've had in Asia. If you think you're making Japanese food, I'm sorry, you're sorely mistaken. Actually, I have to ask you: have you ever even been to Japan? How can you charge people for this?"

She couldn't stand the loud music or the uncomfortable stools or the unfriendly service, either.

"Does anyone actually enjoy this?" she asked me.

Sadly, she represented the consensus among customers during Noodle Bar's first few months. I had set out to open a restaurant where someone who was accustomed to spending significant coin for a fancy dinner would feel just as good or better after dining at our bare-bones place, having paid only a fraction of the price. I wanted to shock people who thought ramen was nothing more than a cheap and dirty means to fill their belly. That was the big idea: leave everyone walking out the door of Momofuku happy and surprised and glad to have spent their money.

We weren't even close.

On our opening menu were gyoza, a few noodle soups, some snacks, and nothing that could be mistaken for a distinct point of view. Guests filled out sheets of paper with their orders. This was not an affectation but a necessity. Until Quino arrived one week before our opening, I didn't know that I would have anyone on staff, so I needed to make sure the restaurant could work with only one person, the way ramen shops do it in Japan. Only I wasn't in Japan and I wasn't a ramen chef. Were it not for Quino, I'm certain Momofuku would have been dead and buried in the wake of any one of the countless disasters that befell us in those first months. It was a never-ending, real-life version of the Universal Studios tram tour, careening from one calamity to the next.

One night the tenant directly above us got drunk and passed out in his tub with the water running; it took us a month to recover from the flood. On another occasion, in the early hours of the morning, the thermostat broke on our convection oven while we were slow-cooking a batch of pork overnight. Fortunately, someone somehow came to my apartment to alert me that the entire place was going up in smoke.

The risk of catastrophic fire was constant. The electricity would short when the weather was hot and the A/C was running, sending sparks from the circuit board onto the garbage bags lined up against the wall, as well as the grease trap. We shared a sump pump with our neighbors, and we had to clean it out regularly unless we wanted to see the restaurant get flooded with sewage. It was depressing work—worse if it had been raining—but it was necessary.*

I also found an unexpected adversary in a tree around the block that bloomed a cottonlike substance I had never encountered before opening my own restaurant. I didn't know what it was, only that it did not agree with our air-conditioning system. Every day I'd have to climb a ladder and then make my way over the gap between two buildings to get to the air conditioner's compressor and clean the vents. That tree was the bane of my existence.

Then there was the end of service one night, when a man came in asking if we were still open. We weren't. He walked right up to Quino and clocked him in the face. I chased the perp down First Avenue for a few blocks until I finally caught up to him. My brief high school wrestling career ended with me making a mistake that put our star player out for the season, so I wish my former teammates could have seen me perform a flawless suplex on Quino's assailant in the middle of traffic. Blood pooled on the white lines of the crosswalk. Quino followed shortly after with a stool held over his head like a WWE superstar taking the brawl outside the ring. The cops showed up. Bambi, my apartment landlord from across the street, spoke to the police on my behalf and convinced them not to arrest me or the perpetrator, who had just been released on parole.

For months, Quino and I survived on Stromboli Pizza and Popeye's. We simply didn't have the time to make a family meal. I'll never forget the day we finally cooked something for ourselves. It felt like the greatest accomplishment of my life. It took so much just to pull it off once.

---

*In case a member of the New York City Health Department is reading this, we fixed all these issues.

I had been seeing Dr. Eliot three times a week, but I stopped because I didn't have the time and it was getting too damn expensive. I wasn't paying myself a salary, and the healthcare plan we'd signed up for covered only a limited number of sessions. So self-medication took the place of therapy. I'd sit alone in my apartment for hours drinking bourbon and seething. I suspected that we were indistinguishable from any other Asian restaurant around town. We were buying frozen dumplings and serving ice cream sandwiches from the corner bodega for dessert—the former because we couldn't find the time to make them from scratch, the latter because we had no idea what kind of restaurant we were trying to be.

• • •

On many nights, Quino handled dinner service himself, because I was so bad at interacting with our customers. Meanwhile, I'd stay downstairs doing prep or agonizing over our piss-poor numbers. Quino was also great for other, thankless jobs, like sniffing out where we could find our next used appliance. It was nice to have someone in the trenches with me. When I wasn't drinking alone, I'd drink with him.

We usually stuck to the neighborhood, but with Noodle Bar clinging to life and our money all but gone, we decided one night to spend a significant portion of what we had left on giving ourselves a respite. We headed to a new restaurant that everyone was going wild over. Our dinner was as much a reconnaissance mission as it was a break.

Quino and I spent the first part of the meal talking about everything but the food in front of us. We were having a great time away from Noodle Bar. I resisted the urge to ask his opinion of the place: assess a meal in the middle of it, and you risk ruining the night before it's over.

Quino apparently did not subscribe to this philosophy. He reached his verdict between the appetizers and mains.

"This really isn't that good."

I wanted to stand up and hug him across the table.

"Yeah, this sucks!" I yelled over the cacophony of first dates sucking down cocktails and waiting on their plates of whatever was trendy that week. It was the sort of disappointment that's doubly frustrating because everyone around us was loving it.

This kind of shit-talking typically does not serve any purpose— it's sport for cooks—but Quino ended up putting a productive point on it.

"Come on, we can smoke these fools."

I grabbed Quino before he got in a cab and told him that Noodle Bar needed to have a pulse.

In the following weeks, we made some decisions. We had been cash-only from the start because I didn't want to deal with the extra paperwork to take credit cards. It was time to let go of silly decisions made in the name of pragmatism. We arranged to buy a used Aloha POS system, a device I originally thought would be superfluous for a noodle bar with no waitstaff. Speaking of which, we agreed to look for servers. We drove out to Jersey to buy sturdier flatware that wouldn't crack at the faintest touch. We would be left penniless, but we were dead anyway, so what was the point in conserving cash?

Maybe that meal was actually better than we thought or maybe we were just making ourselves feel better by shitting on it. Whatever it was, we saw what we needed to see. Noodle Bar was going out of business because I was letting myself get pulled in every direction but the most important one. It was as though I were running around, yanking my hair out on purpose so that I wouldn't have a free second to stop and face the more difficult questions.

For instance: what the hell is this food we're serving?

• • •

We had been holding back. The concept of a noodle bar didn't yet exist in the minds of most Americans, yet we were cooking as though diners were coming to our restaurant with expectations. We put dumplings on the menu because I thought people would be looking for dumplings. But that wasn't true. They weren't asking for dumplings and I didn't want to make them, which meant that nobody was really satisfied.

The reason we were still alive was that cooks liked us. Our only regulars were the crews from Per Se, Jean-Georges, and Daniel Boulud's various restaurants. They all came in, even the people from Café Boulud who I assumed hated me. After work, they would descend on us and gobble down pork buns—honestly, the only item on our menu I knew to be worth eating.

It puts a lump in my throat to think about all those cooks coming to Noodle Bar. That's the very best part of this business. Deep down, we want to help one another. Daniel would send his dinner guests for lunch, and nearly every other top New York chef dropped in, too, often towing along a member of the New York food cognoscenti.

We were at our best when we were feeding these people who really knew their shit. That realization saved our restaurant. At the last possible moment, we erased the line between what we thought we should be serving our customers and what we wanted to cook for our friends. We threw out anything that smelled of fear, and started shooting from the hip.

I remain apprehensive about spelling out exactly what that means in terms of our cooking because our philosophy is still changing and growing. But I'll try to explain it as best as I can here.

NOBODY KNOWS ANYTHING, SO DO WHAT YOU WANT. The way I grew up eating is more or less the same way as millions of other Asian American kids. A big part of that was hiding our food from white friends out of shame. Of course, I preferred Mom's kimchi jjigae to pot roast or meatloaf, but I suppressed the hell out of that in order to fit in.

But the impulse to blend in was preventing me and Quino—who grew up in a Mexican American home—from distinguishing ourselves as chefs. No more. We would use what made our families different to guide us. And if what our families ate was different from what other Korean or Mexican families ate, so be it. When I was a kid, for example, my grandfather showed me how to crisp up rice cakes in the Japanese style, an improvement on the boiled, Korean method every other Chang espoused. My mom and grandmother would say, "That's not how Korean people eat it," but he liked it crunchy, and so did I. Hence, Momofuku's stir-fried rice cakes with onions, sesame seeds, and gochujang. Our kimchi recipe was my mom's, although I added more sugar than she would, and because of food safety regulations, we couldn't ferment it at room temperature with raw oysters.*

GATHER FROM EVERYWHERE. In my current life, I have the blessing of getting to eat more broadly than almost anyone else on earth. It's a hugely unfair advantage as a chef. But back then, I hadn't seen too much more than your average twenty-something American cook. The difference is that I was willing to recognize the value in everything, even places I despised. I was also readily willing to admit to loving lowbrow foods that other people wrote off as beneath them. I wanted to know *why* people liked what they liked.

I wasn't afraid to cite references from across the culinary universe and adjust them to my taste. I added vegetables and vinegar to our rip-off of Great NY Noodletown's ginger-scallion noodles. I put slow-poached eggs (onsen tamago) in our ramen in place of hard-boiled ones, because I had once watched enviously as a woman

---

*Years later, with a little basic chemistry and microbiology under my belt, I would come to understand that the seafood in kimchi has nothing to do with the fermentation process. Fermentation, by the way, is something that would prove vital to Momofuku's cooking as well.

cracked a perfect soft egg into her bowl of ramen while taking in a flick at a movie house in Tokyo. As I mentioned, we learned to appropriate from our own families and cultures, too. Anything that helped us survive or gave us a competitive advantage. If I were better at making terrines and soufflés, I'd be doing that. It just so happened that I'm Asian and have a better view into Asian food.

I have no hesitation in admitting to these inspirations, because I give credit wherever I can. My advice to chefs is to be transparent about your ignorance and always honor the source material.

THE DINING ROOM IS YOUR CLASSROOM. Our first summer, we began serving a dish of corn sautéed with miso and Benton's bacon. From my place in our open kitchen, I had a front-row seat on humanity, and I would notice different reactions from our diners throughout the season. I learned to see ingredients as living entities. To keep up, I had to adapt recipes on the fly. As the corn became starchier and less sweet, I would see fewer people devouring it with zeal. *Maybe it needs more butter or more miso, which means it could use more pepper. Maybe it could use less bacon and more pork stock. Maybe I should reduce the sauce more. Maybe I should add pickled red onion. Oh, that works! People are eating it up.* More important, I learned something about the value of acidity in a dish like this. *Now how far can I push it? What's the right level? Maybe I can incorporate even more acidity if I up the fat? But now I need chili pepper.* I'd have these conversations with myself all the time. Over the course of a week or even a single day, a dish might evolve into something completely different.

At Noodle Bar, I also learned that Asian people drank the ramen broth. White people only ate the noodles. If we served the soup luke-warm, Asian customers would complain. If it was too hot, the white people wouldn't touch it until it cooled down. By then, the noodles would be soggy. As a cook, you're in a never-ending dance with your diners.

FORGET EVERYTHING YOU THINK AND EMBRACE WHAT YOU SEE. Quino and I also made improvements to the menu that were grounded as much in chance as in creativity. We'd been braising pork in stock as we'd been taught to do, but it took ages and wasn't all that good. One day I made the error of blasting the pork belly at 500°F. It ended up nicely browned on the outside, but undercooked and swimming in rendered fat. I lowered the temperature and let it continue to cook in the oil, like a confit. The process was quicker and the result was far superior. You simply can't rely on common wisdom in the kitchen. Most of it is built on half-truths and outdated assumptions. Be open to every idea.

MERGE. By and large, the most interesting cooking at Momofuku comes from bridging seemingly different worlds. Our restaurant became a place where we would try to replicate the natural merging of ideas, flavors, and techniques that happens when immigrants first arrive in a new place. It wasn't much of a stretch to see Quino and myself as fresh arrivals encountering one another in the Noodle Bar kitchen. Our goal was to encourage the dishes we knew from our childhoods to evolve with new ingredients and interactions.

Quino ate hominy and fried eggs as a kid, while I was accustomed to eating grits. His Mexican forebears ate tamales in the morning, and mine liked jook. The result of our conversations was a dish of shrimp and grits that looked like something you'd find in Charleston, but upon first bite, it only made sense at Noodle Bar. We used dashi as a flavor base but made it with ham instead of the traditional katsuobushi (dried bonito flakes), because I had been reminded of the latter when I first smelled the intoxicating waft of Benton's smoked pork in the kitchen at Craft. On another day, the collision of acidity with richness in a classic caprese salad became a dish of cherry tomatoes, soft tofu, and sesame vinaigrette. We realized that everything can be Korean or Mexican or Japanese or Italian, and that American

food can be anything. Nothing we cooked was authentic. It was neither here nor there, which made it ours.

Obviously we didn't come up with the idea to mix cuisines, but
during that era in American kitchens, whenever a chef tried to mingle
Asian and European culinary ideas, one of two things tended to happen. If a French-trained chef added a stalk of lemongrass to a soup,
the result would be deemed "French food with an Asian accent." In
the reverse case, whenever a little thyme made its way into an Asian
dish, it was called "fusion." I hated the way that the Asian side was
always subsumed by the Western one.

"YOU'LL ALWAYS LOSE WHEN YOU PLAY SOMEONE ELSE'S
GAME." Speaking of Allan Benton, not only was his bacon the cata-
lyst for many of the culinary epiphanies we had at Momofuku, he
also personally bestowed me with this nugget of wisdom. And once
he said it, I realized Momofuku couldn't tell anyone else's story. We
got rid of the dumplings and everything else that wasn't ours. We
dedicated ourselves to making people play our game instead.

By the time we started writing the *Momofuku* cookbook, other
restaurants were already copying our recipes. I was shocked, both
by the fact that people were taking our cooking seriously and also
that anyone would choose imitation as a strategy—a surefire path to
mediocrity. I knew that doing a cookbook would accelerate the process, so I took the opportunity to mess with any potential copycats. In
Momofuku, there's a recipe for the aforementioned roasted rice cakes,
tossed in what is essentially gochujang (fermented chili sauce)—only
we don't call it gochujang. In the book, it has the absolutely awful and
ridiculous name "red dragon sauce." I knew that lazy people would
copy the recipe without bothering to check whether "red dragon
sauce" was a real thing. To this day, I'll see it show up on menus from
time to time. It always makes me laugh.

5

CUTTING THE LINE

ONE NIGHT, QUINO AND I WERE AT A PARTY HONORING SEVERAL OF MY mentors. The event was taking place at a restaurant/club in Flatiron where all the tables were beds. It was called—no joke—Duvet. But there was free booze, so we were all in.

A year had passed since Noodle Bar had been born and nearly died. Our last-ditch rush to the ER kept it alive. More than alive, really. Suddenly, everyone wanted to eat at the restaurant and everyone in the media wanted to write about it.

After helping ourselves to the open bar, we approached a woman standing alone. She was attractive and we were meatheads. I introduced myself as Dave and said I was a cook. We launched into the usual restaurant-people small talk about "what you're liking these days." She was more interested in discussing what she was disliking.

"Have you guys been to Momofuku?"

Yes, we're familiar with it.

"I think it's so overrated. It's total bullshit and everyone is just eating it up. It's not just annoying, it's offensive. David Chang? Give me a break. He's just some kid with no credibility, no history, and no respect. There are so many chefs in the city doing better work. He's just the flavor of the month."

Quino asked if she'd actually eaten at Noodle Bar.

"Yeah, although I wish I hadn't. My boss Maria Johanna—do you know her?—told me it wasn't worth it, but everyone has been talking about it. I should have just trusted her. Her husband is Japanese."

Of course. The woman who had given me that degrading lecture in the early days wasn't lying when she said she was in the industry. Johanna ran a trade organization that hosts a yearly conference in New York City; they fly chefs into town to demonstrate their coolest new dishes to an audience of insiders. I didn't really know about her business at the time. I've since learned about all the restaurant-adjacent entities that promise to put you in front of the public through events and media connections, in exchange for your time and, sometimes, money. Even if you're not paying them directly, chefs often go out of pocket in order to honor their commitments to these conferences. The organization offers lodging and a flight, while the chefs foot the bill for ingredients and extra staff to join them, leaving their restaurants shorthanded. We say yes for fear that saying no could mean upsetting the wrong people or passing up valuable exposure for our businesses.

A good chef never forgets that this is a business. All the extra-curricular shit we do outside the restaurant* should be in service of

---

*Writing this book, for instance.

putting asses in seats. When we do events for the sake of ego, we usually pay the price in cash money. (A good chef also never forgets that awards and events organizations are businesses, too, and that their first concern is their own bottom line.) But that night, we were exhausted. Our defenses were down. Ego won out. Quino and I were 100 percent certain that the woman had never actually eaten at Noodle Bar. She was doing the rounds at industry events, trash-talking us based on something her boss told her. In fact, she was doing it so often and with such glee that she didn't even realize whom she had stumbled into.

"You know what? *Fuck* you. We're on the line cooking every single night at Noodle Bar and you've never been there. And I don't give a fuck if you don't like my restaurant, because it's not for you. We don't cook for people like you."

Our voices were loud enough to attract the attention of the entire room.

"Fuck you."

We piled on. She began to cry. Everyone was focused on us, including Johanna, who was also in attendance. I turned around and delivered the same speech to her, only this time I used my middle finger to illustrate the point. It was an ugly scene—the two of us brutishly picking on this person—but I couldn't pull myself back.

Security ushered me and Quino out of the party and onto the street.

• • •

We'd struck a nerve.

On the one hand, I was far from convinced that the good buzz around us was warranted. On the other, I spent a lot of time thinking about all the shit people were talking about us.

But with our backs against the wall of a space ill suited for delivering culinary excellence, Quino and I were coming up with dish after dish of pure magic. We were in a mind meld. I became a ruthless editor, coaxing out Quino's and my best work while shutting down our less coherent dishes. Ideas collided until we found their tightest and most delicious synthesis.

My belief in Momofuku had been based on two suspicions: (1) The way people ate in train stations, shopping malls, back alleys, and strip malls in Asia was superior to the way we ate in upscale New York restaurants; and (2) cooking was a job that rewarded repetition and grit more than natural talent. Now I had some proof of both. Maybe, I began to think, it was everyone else who was crazy.

I'd never been an overtly competitive person in the kitchen— losing, after all, makes you humble—but with a few hard-won victories under my belt, I felt confident enough to give some credit to our philosophy. We were in a groove, and I didn't want to risk losing our rhythm. Every day for me was do or die. I expected the same of the team, which by this point included a few new members. A cook named Kevin Pemoulie came aboard. He arrived in the East Village an hour early to stop by the bank before his first shift. His start date happened to coincide with our biggest lunch rush to date. I called him up screaming for him to get his ass to Noodle Bar. In his telling of the story, he could hear my voice from a block away before it reached him on the phone.

"PUT FUCKING MIRIN IN IT!" I instructed Pemoulie after throwing him onto the line. He had no idea what mirin was or where it was supposed to go. I'm sure he considered walking out right then and there, but he stuck around. Down the road, he wound up in charge of Noodle Bar.

I didn't know how to teach or lead this team, but I was getting good results. My method, if you can even call it that, was a dangerous, shortsighted combination of fear and fury. My staff was at the mercy of my emotional swings. One second, we were on top of the world. The next, I would be screaming and banging my fists on the counter. I sought out and thrived on conflict. My arrogance was in conflict with my insecurity. Our restaurant was in conflict with the world.

Before we even opened, City Hall didn't want to let me name our restaurant Momofuku, because they thought it sounded lewd. I spent days building a case by gathering a list of all the existing businesses in New York with Asian names that could be misinterpreted as swear-words in English. The EPA tried to shut us down because they were getting complaints of pork smells emanating from the restaurant, which is not an uncommon grievance leveled against Asian establishments in gentrifying neighborhoods. PETA picketed the restaurant on the few occasions that we served foie gras. When we started getting complaints about the noisiness of our HVAC unit, I swear it was the vegans trying to bleed us dry. We spent thousands changing the fan belt and proving that the noises coming from the exhaust were inaudible to human ears.

We were often in conflict with our own customers, as well. A man came in one afternoon and ordered a crawfish special. A minute or two after the dish landed on his table, he asked for the bill. As he signed it, he told Eugene,* one of our first waiters and still the general manager of Noodle Bar, that we should serve the crustaceans without the shells.

"It'd be much more appealing if you did that," he said.

Eugene delivered the feedback to the kitchen, and Quino instructed him on how to respond. Genie chased after the customer down the street and said in his bone-dry-but-always-cordial tone, "Sir, the kitchen doesn't appreciate your comments. Furthermore, they kindly ask you to go fuck yourself."

Conflict was fuel, and Momofuku was a gas-guzzling SUV. Let's say, for instance, I'd eaten somewhere new and enjoyed it. I'd come

---

*Eugene Lee remains the beating heart of Momofuku Noodle Bar.

back the following morning and tell the crew that the meal I'd had made us all look like amateurs, knowing full well that the cooks couldn't possibly work any harder. Or maybe I'd read about an interesting technique—Andoni Luis Aduriz's edible stones, for instance—and if the guys didn't already know about it,* I'd lay into them rather than take the time to explain the concept.**

I never resolved any conflicts between staff. On the contrary, if I heard that two cooks weren't getting along, I'd see to it that they worked together more closely. That was one surefire method, I told myself, to ensure that the place had a pulse. You could feel our anger the second you walked through the door, and that was exactly how I wanted it.

• • •

Why would anybody get so mad about food? It's worth stopping for a second to ask the question.

On one of those lonely nights when I was living on a futon and working at Café Boulud, I was reading about the French chef Fernand Point. At the end of each service at his restaurant La Pyramide, in Lyon, Point would instruct his staff to throw out every ingredient and pour every sauce into the sink, so that they would have no choice but to start completely fresh the following morning. Nothing would be repurposed, no matter what. Considering this was 1930s France, I'd imagine that this was a great deal of sauce.

—————

*Don't tell me that you don't know about Andoni's stones, either.

**Fine, here: The amuse bouche at Andoni's restaurant Mugaritz is a pile of smooth gray rocks that look exactly like the inedible ones you'd find in a stream in Spain's Basque country. Many diners hesitate to take a bite, fearing that they'll shatter a tooth. But the stones are actually boiled potatoes coated in a clay called kaolin, and you eat them with garlic aioli.

Stories about chefs and their capricious ways are a dime a dozen. The Point detail isn't even *that* outlandish, but the gesture stuck with me. At the time, I thought it was badass how far he was willing to go to be the best. But take the thought a little further down the road and you wonder what else Point was throwing down the drain in his fanatical pursuit of perfection. It wasn't just sauce. It was the time and energy of his cooks, time they would otherwise be spending outside the kitchen. It was time taken from their outside lives. It *was* their lives.

To this day, most Western kitchens function in a brigade system developed by Point's mentor, Auguste Escoffier. In devising the ideal structure for a kitchen, Escoffier drew on his time in the army. La Brigade applies a military chain of command to the kitchen, with a discrete delegation of roles aimed at encouraging efficiency, precision, and an air of absolutely unrelenting urgency.

The stress level in a restaurant is already outrageously high without the severe framework of the brigade system forcing everyone to think they're at war. Statistics show that most restaurants fail within a year. You've probably heard this before. In order to survive, you need to tame and harness the mercurial beast that is creativity, while also appeasing the one or two people or entities that can make or break you. I can't help but think of the chef Bernard Loiseau, who killed himself in 2003 after hearing it was *possible* that his restaurant would lose one of its three Michelin stars.

I don't want to sensationalize the cooking profession or draw comparisons to all the other very difficult jobs in the world, but as a cook in an ambitious restaurant, you are expected both to make an enormous time commitment and exert intense physical effort every day. The result of your labor—the thing you take so much pride in— is shit. Literally, shit. Your work is something that the customer will later flush down a toilet. You may as well be a Tibetan monk who spends weeks constructing an elaborate sand mandala only to sweep it away immediately. (Unfortunately, cooking will not provide you with any of the same spiritual rewards.)

To keep going, you must buy into codes that give meaning to your existence: *You are part of a centuries-old continuum that you must honor and preserve at all costs. Every action in a kitchen, every job, every recipe, is the next line in a story that connects back to the previous dinner service, and to the chef who used to work your same station, and to another chef across the ocean, probably long dead, who was the first to figure out how to slice that vegetable in the manner you are now called upon to re-create. Every service is an opportunity to respect that previous contribution and expression and to potentially interpret it in your own way, adding a new pattern to the fabric of culinary history.*

You have this in mind as you work while your friends play, as you miss birthdays and decline wedding invitations. You have few relationships outside your job. You don't have time for reflection or exercise or doctor appointments. You may not even have the time to study the material that would improve the quality of your work.

In the best cases, all this pressure can lead to decent behavior, to professionalism. In many other instances, it encourages unchecked insanity and abuse. All manner of hazing is fair game when it's done in the name of making sure the person next to you is part of the same fellowship. There's physical punishment—impossible assignments, sabotaging mise en place, kidney punches—and there is psychological torture. Astute chefs keep a running log of all the insecurities they detect in a subordinate, so that they can exploit them later. In a calm, unthreatening voice, they'll say, "Hey, I don't understand what's going on with you. I've seen a lot of less talented people do better at this station." Or, more bluntly, "Don't tell anyone you work for me."

They cut into your heart and brain, and if you ask them later why they did it, they will say that it was for your own good. They were breaking you down to build you back up. Because they care about you. Because it's how they were taught. Critical thinking, calm communication, rationality, levelheadedness: none of these traits has traditionally been valued in a kitchen. Or maybe they were, but we weren't listening. It's not so different from a locker room, where viciousness and anger are glamorized as part of a winning culture.

Personally, I don't know whether this behavior actually pushes others to do their best, or if it's purely the release valve for a broken system. All that stress and fear and negativity have to go somewhere.

Either way, as a cook, you absorb it. "Make it happen" is the standing order, and "Yes, chef" is the only response.

For the person who is able to withstand the emotional pummeling—or who just can't find any other work—it can end up being a manageable environment. You learn the language and thrive. I did. Two decades of being scolded and shouted at by parents, teachers, and coaches prepared me reasonably well for restaurant life. But if you're very young and impressionable, as most who enter the profession are, it's easy to spend five or ten years in that basement ecosystem thinking there is honor and dignity in working under these conditions, only to find out later that your growth has been stunted and that there is no promise of success at the end of the road.

So let me ask again: why would anybody get so mad about food?

Because it *is* just food. And when your co-workers are lazy or inconsiderate or don't seem to care as much as you—when they treat food as *just food*—they call your entire worldview into question. They make you feel foolish for believing.

When you were young, did you care deeply about a job, a project, a person, a writer, a band, a sports team? Did you ever have someone laugh in your face and tell you that that thing you loved was dumb? *It's just a game—why do you care so much?* You wanted to punch them in the face, right? It's something like that, multiplied by a thousand.

I'm telling you this and I believe it to be true, but it doesn't really explain me.

I came from a decent family and had the benefit of a college education. For the most part, I was trained by mentors who were even-keeled, forgiving, and invested in my growth. I also walked away from the cycle early to do something in opposition to tradition. Yet throughout my career, I've always been angry. Once I had my own restaurant, the slightest error or show of carelessness from a cook could turn me into a convulsing, raging mass. The only thing that could snap me out of my fits was punching a wall or a steel counter-top, anything to cause me some kind of physical pain.

I'm tempted to blame han. Throughout this book, I will argue against the validity of various cultural truths, but I believe in han. There's no perfect English-language equivalent for this Korean emotion, but it's some combination of strife or unease, sadness, and resentment, born from the many historical injustices and indignities endured by our people. It's a term that came into use in the twenti-eth century after the Japanese occupation of Korea, and it describes this characteristic sorrow and bitterness that Koreans seem to possess wherever they are in the world.* It is transmitted from generation to generation and defines much of the art, literature, and cinema that comes out of Korean culture.

I will not deny that there are benefits to being part of what is often described as a "white-adjacent" or "model" minority. I grew up trying my damnedest to integrate into white society. But among the many problems with the myth of the model minority is that it erases the nuances of the Asian American experience. It also sows division, both within our community and with others. Now, if you will for-give a little bit of self-directed racial discrimination, I am what you might call a "twinkie." Yellow on the outside, white on the inside. There are various factions within the Asian American population, and I definitely reside in the one that looks Asian but lives like a white person. When I visited Korea as part of a program with students from multiple colleges, I found myself excluded from all of the Korean-born, Korean-speaking, and generally more Korean social groups

---

*It was almost too perfect when Marvel comics announced in 2015 that a Korean American man named Amadeus Cho would succeed Bruce Banner as The Hulk.

that formed. Then, once we landed in Seoul, the locals knew immediately from my size that I was a gyopo, or foreign-born Korean, so
I gravitated to the other twinkies. I didn't yet know how to embrace
my Korean heritage, which, ironically, only deepened my experience
of han.

This all leads me to question whether kitchen custom created
my personal brand of rage. I think the job—the fear, the stress, the
habits I'd learned, the culture—unlocked what was already roiling
inside me.

· · ·

Opening Noodle Bar had been a last-gasp attempt at finding my
place in the world before giving in to darker impulses. What I hadn't
considered was what I would do if things worked out. The restaurant was a success. I felt like one of those doomsday crazies who predict the apocalypse, only to watch the appointed day come and go.
With lines forming every day outside 163 First Avenue, the pressure
mounted to open a second location, a facsimile, but I couldn't bring
myself to do it. I still saw myself on a one-way street, and my only
option was to drive faster and more recklessly.

I secured a loan for a million dollars to open a new concept, leveraging Noodle Bar and everything I had.

Between the loan and my new rent, I would have a total monthly
responsibility of $47,000. I'm not a financial whiz, so whenever I
open a restaurant, I try to stick to a general rule of thumb: if I can
cover my loans and rent with the revenue from a typical Monday or
Tuesday dinner service, it will be fine. Forty-seven thousand dollars
was *impossible*. I was done before we opened the doors.

I can now say with complete certainty that I was trying to sabotage my own career. Not a day went by without my asking, *How do
I make this all stop?* At the same time, I can also say that I absolutely
wanted the second restaurant to work. I wanted it to make money

and to ensure that I didn't drag any of my family down into financial ruin with me. I know that these two aims seem incompatible, but they were both equally true. The only solution to the contradiction was to back myself into a corner. I would have no choice but to work as hard as humanly possible to climb out of an impossible situation.

But the day I met with the loan officer to sign the paperwork I noticed a discrepancy. The monthly payment had dropped to $14,000. I asked the officer—a business associate of my dad's—why the amount had decreased by more than $30,000. He told me that my father had taken a lien out on his own businesses to lower my payments. He did it without telling me. Dad stepped in front of the train.

And how was I planning to pay him back? With a restaurant idea that I can effectively describe in two words: Asian Chipotle.

I was never interested in doing anything fancy. Even Noodle Bar was dangerously close to being too refined for my taste. What Steve Ells, Chipotle's founder, was doing to bring higher-quality food to the masses was almost more impressive to me than Ferran Adrià's innovations at elBulli. A business like Chipotle touches many, many more people than a little restaurant overlooking a Catalonian cliff (and makes much more money). I worship Ferran, but I was never going to be an Adrià. But if a guy like Ells could change how the world eats by making Mexican food for white people, I wanted to give it a try myself. I mean, literally, I wanted to serve burritos.

Momofuku Ssäm Bar, I always tell friends, is the craziest restaurant to happen in the history of the world. They don't believe it and surely you won't, either, but here's one example of how improbable this restaurant was. After signing the lease for 207 Second Avenue, I discovered that the building did not have a certificate of occupancy. The city told me that there was no record on file, meaning that to the City of New York, our restaurant was not legally occupiable. The building had been constructed in the late nineteenth century as a carriage house and, in its most recent incarnation, had pulled double duty as a Chinese takeout spot and a basement brothel. The previous tenant was unresponsive to my many emails and calls asking for their occupancy paperwork.

I went down to the Department of Buildings and found the filing office, a brown, dusty space that reminded me of an evidence locker. Behind the desk was an older woman who looked friendly but was not friendly.

"If I can't get my hands on the permit, I can't open this restaurant," I pleaded. "If I can't open this restaurant, I'm going to lose all my money. I have a lot of people who are depending on me."

That wasn't an exaggeration. The money was spent. I was paying cooks, construction was under way. And all of it was leveraged against my dad's lifework.* The clerk gestured behind her toward the endless stacks of filing cabinets. Somewhere in that imposing mass of unsorted paperwork was the key to my salvation. Maybe.

"I can't find it in my records," she said. "It might be here, but you tell me how I'm supposed to get it."

I left, but returned the next morning.

She was there again and waved me off immediately, a PTSD flashback to the brothers at Canton Noodle Corporation shooing me away whenever I stumbled into their business looking for kansui like a harried gorilla.

I went back the day after, and it was no different.

When I walked into her office on the fourth consecutive day, it was because there was nowhere else for me to be and nothing else to be done. It was a special kind of dejection. I held out a minuscule hope that the woman would be gone, replaced by a fresh face with some new idea of how to help me. Or better yet, a digital

---

*I'm looking through all these old emails right now—loan documents and bank statements—and I'm overwhelmed. It's as though I'm looking at a different person, and I want so badly to tell him that it's okay—life will go on, even if he fails at this. What pains me most, though, is that I don't know if I really believe that. I'm better equipped now to deal with the bullshit of opening restaurants, but I still find myself risking too much too often.

kiosk holding a catalog of every building record in New York City history.

There she sat. Before I could speak, she walked over to the cabinets and, annoyed, grabbed a random piece of paper.

"What do you want me to do? Just pull it out of nowhere for you?"

She handed me the paper and I flipped it over. I was stunned. She was stunned.

It was a certificate of occupancy for my building.

6

THE MAGIC HOUR

ssäm (Korean for wrap)

Step 1: Choose ssäm or bowl

1. **Flour Pancake Ssäm**   **$9**
2. **Bibb Lettuce Ssäm** (with rice bowl)   **$12**
3. **Toasted Nori Ssäm** (with rice bowl)   **$11**
4. **Rice Bowl**   **$9**
5. **Chap Chae Bowl**   **$9**

Step 2: Choose protein

- Berkshire Pork
- Organic Chicken
- Angus Beef Brisket
- Braised Tofu

Step 3: Choose extras

- bacon black beans
- red azuki beans
- kewpie slaw
- red kimchi puree
- white kimchi puree
- roasted onions
- pickled shiitake
- edamame
- bean sprouts
- whipped tofu

SSAM IN KOREAN MEANS "WRAPPED." THERE ARE ENDLESS VARIATIONS, but if you've ever been to a Korean barbecue restaurant, you understand the basic concept: take a leaf of lettuce or perilla (a relative of shiso), fold it around some meat, vegetables, and maybe some rice, then top with ssamjang (literally "wrap sauce"). That's the whole idea. Conceptually it's almost identical to a tortilla filled with carnitas, beans, rice, and salsa.

Our opening menu at Ssäm Bar owed as much to Korean and Mexican tradition as it did to a late-night takeout habit I'd developed. Whenever I ordered Chinese food to my apartment, I'd be sure to get mushu pork, and then I'd use the pancakes to wrap everything—noodles, rice, stir-fries. Who doesn't love wrapping food in other food?

The idea of authenticity comes up a lot in the culinary world, both as an ideal and as a criticism. In this conversation, there are usually more questions than answers. What makes something authentic? Is it always better to be authentic? Is authenticity the enemy of innovation? Honestly, having heard these questions asked ad nauseam, I'm bored by the whole topic. Not because it isn't important. It is. But whenever someone starts talking about authenticity and cultural appropriation, my mind begins to wander. I ask myself, *What if my ancestors had traded places and pantries with yours? What would modern Korean food look like if a generation of Changs and Kims and Parks had arrived in Mexico five hundred years ago? What would Mexican food look like?* I imagine both cuisines would be even more delicious, and I bet they'd still be wrapping meat and vegetables in tortillas and leaves. We humans are more alike in our tastes than we think. Even with completely different tools and ingredients, we're bound to arrive at the same conclusions.

I know this isn't an airtight idea, politically speaking. It can be taken as license to do whatever you want without consideration for the source material. But as an Asian chef, I tend to get away with posing such scenarios more than I would if I were a white guy explaining why his Nashville hot chicken doughnut is actually an homage to black cooks. Yellow privilege, baby! It's one of the few perks of being Asian that makes up for, you know, your skin color being referred to as "yellow."

Anyway, as a creative engine in the kitchen, it's a powerful thought exercise.*

At Ssäm, we would have the same setup as Chipotle. The diners would see all their options arranged in front of them and customize their meal as they made their way from one end of the line to the cash register. They'd be served by legitimate chefs, sit in a decently appointed dining room, and listen to good music while enjoying affordable and carefully prepared food before heading back to work.

How could we lose?

We were a flop. People were not ready to follow us on our foray into fast food. Diners, it seemed, still wanted dining to feel special. I couldn't convince them that this wasn't just a cynical cash grab, or that we were trying to make food better at all levels.

Sometimes we would have colossal lines out the door, but far more days were spent scrubbing down the kitchen one extra time just to have something to do. For all practical purposes, we were dead. Forget about feeding the masses; we could barely count on Noodle Bar regulars to drop by once a week.

Thankfully, no major critics came. Why would they have bothered? We'd probably be out of business before their reviews came out.

• • •

"Just wait and hopefully people will come around" was my uninspiring take on Kevin Costner's mantra in *Field of Dreams*.

---

* I often fantasize about a computer that could come up with all the possible combinations and permutations of ingredients and test them against what we know about human taste. Is that too calculating?

As confusing as Ssäm Bar was to patrons, it was equally dispirit-
ing for my chefs. Thanks to the storm of press for Noodle Bar, more
reputable cooks had joined us. They had shown up to grind it out and
cook exciting food but ended up intermittently scooping carnitas.

I'd promised them that entering the Momofuku universe meant
no systems or hierarchies. They could cut the line, just as I had. I used
to tell them, "We don't have titles, because if you don't know what
you're supposed to be doing, you don't belong here." It's the sort of
off-brand Confucian saying that covered up my own lack of clarity.
I do believe that putting too much stock in titles and org charts can
stifle a company. At the same time, not everyone thrives in an environment without structure or direction or a clear chain of command.

The cooks at Ssäm didn't have enough to do, and there wasn't
room at Noodle Bar to accommodate any more bodies. Chief among
the underutilized at Ssäm was Tien Ho, whom I'd met at Café Boulud. He could cook circles around me but still agreed to join as Ssäm's
opening chef. Momofuku attracted a certain type of person who considered themselves underdogs in some respect—the kind of people
who got off on hearing their colleagues tell them it was career suicide
to throw their lot in with ours. That was Tien, for sure. It was also a
fitting description for Cory Lane, who, contrary to my earlier decree
about not issuing titles, was the first person to ever hold the position
of "manager" at Momofuku. Every fast-food place needs a manager,
right?

Tien, Peter Serpico, Tim Maslow—these guys were the real deal.
I'd prepared them to be busy. I bought two Alto-Shaams—the kind
of combination steam oven that cruise ships purchase to feed thousands of people a night.

In my head, there was a clear road map to success: build a fast-
food restaurant that serves high-quality food, and people will notice.
They'll line up for it across the country. Give it some time and they
won't even be able to see the seams between cultures in a Korean bur-
rito. It will seem as natural as a hamburger.

But the proof was in the flour pancakes that sat on a shelf growing stale. It was evident in the bored looks on everyone's faces. Thankfully, the crew was detached from the emotion I felt for my fast-food idea. With nothing to lose and nothing better to do, they woke me up to the truth. We had skill and a nice, big space. We were doing nothing meaningful with any of it. By not admitting defeat and changing course, I was wasting everyone's time and putting both restaurants in danger. My accountant told me we had sixty days of capital left.

So we started cooking again and we fixed it. I eventually paid my dad back to become fully independent, and Ssäm Bar became solvent. It's as simple as that. I know this is a cop-out, but the Ssäm Bar turnaround story sounds more or less identical to the narrative you already read about Noodle Bar. The long and short of it is that we began serving a late-night menu of dishes we knew chefs would want to eat after work.

Roll your eyes all you want. God knows it sounds clichéd. But at that time most chefs in America were giving their customers different food than they were eating themselves. What we ate after service was uglier, spicier, louder. Stuff you want to devour as you pound beer and wine with your friends. It was the off bits that nobody else wanted and the little secret pieces you saved for yourself as a reward for slogging it out in a sweaty kitchen for sixteen hours. It's the stuff we didn't trust the dining public to order or understand: a crispy fritter made from pig's head, garnished with pickled cherries; thin slices of country ham* with a coffee-infused mayo inspired by Southern redeye gravy. My favorite breakthrough never made the cookbook: whipped tofu with tapioca folded in, topped with a fat pile of uni. So

---

*Dave Arnold, the mad-scientist chef and inventor, deserves credit for helping to revive American country hams. He was the one who first suggested we put them on the menu at Momofuku when few other people even knew what they were. Americans still only had eyes for Italian prosciutto when we first started serving paper-thin slices of smoked pork made in Tennessee, Kentucky, and Virginia from purveyors like Benton's, Broadbent, Colonel Newsom's, and Edwards.

fresh, so cold, so clean, and so far outside of our comfort zone. There were so many ideas on the menu that we'd never seen or tried before. The only unifying thread was that we were nervous about every single dish we served.

Like I said, it was essentially the same philosophy that had saved us at Noodle Bar, but with an added layer of thoughtfulness and refinement. The important thing to take away is this: no idea was so bad that we shouldn't try it. If someone on the team was passionate about something, we were all ears. We had to be.

We started charging for bread and butter, because we were serving better bread and butter than you were getting elsewhere. It was a decision that was not only antithetical to common restaurant sense, it's actually illegal in parts of France.

Another seemingly dumb idea we embraced was not making enough food for everyone. The seeds for this notion were planted back when I was working for Jonathan Benno at Craft. I was responsible for making the uber-amuse for VIPs—a flight of oysters and other raw seafood with all the accoutrements, served in giant ice-filled copper pots. Whenever I was called upon to construct one of these, it worried me to no end, because as soon as this plateau of seafood went parading through the dining room, every head in the restaurant would turn. I knew I'd have to make ten more.

It's the velvet-rope effect. If something seems exclusive, nobody wants to feel excluded. We tried to tap into that emotion at Ssäm Bar. While our namesake burritos eventually disappeared from the menu, the pork shoulder we filled them with was too delicious to let go. In its new incarnation, we chose to serve it whole rather than shredding it, with all the fixings needed to make little handheld wraps: rice, lettuce, kimchi, sauces, and fresh oysters. It was our spin on a Korean bo ssam. At first, we just gave it away to friends. Right in the thick of the dinner rush, we'd drop this monstrosity on a table in the middle of the dining room.

Just like that, we started hearing the exact question I was hoping for: *How do I get that?*

"Oh, by reservation, and it's only available at five-thirty or ten-thirty."

And that's how we filled our restaurant during off-peak hours.*

None of this is what I had in mind for Ssäm Bar, but I won't complain about the steady, enthusiastic business that followed. I rolled with it, although, as always, I was constantly vacillating between extreme confidence and paralyzing self-doubt. I was comforted by the revelation that coming up against failure head-on is a powerful motivating tool. It means you've already stared the worst-case scenario in the face. It also means that you have more data than everyone else, freeing you up to take risks others won't. By confronting failure, you take fear out of the equation. You stop shying away from ideas just because they seem like they may not work. You start asking whether an idea is "bad" because it's actually bad or because the common wisdom says so. You begin to thrive when you're not supposed to. You just have to be comfortable with instability, change, and a great deal of stress.

Here's how I describe it to my cooks: we can spend twenty-three hours of the day wringing our hands, talking about possible new recipes. In that span of time, we will be able to make enough unwise and arbitrary decisions to jeopardize our motivation to take another stab at it in the morning. But in the moment of greatest need, in that

---

*The ancillary benefit to this bit of shrewd business was that I got to wedge in my interpretation of Korean bo ssam before most people in America knew better. If you were to order bo ssam from a real Korean restaurant, ninety-nine times out of a hundred, you'd get a dozen oysters and a platter of thick-sliced boiled pork belly. Ours was completely inauthentic. It gives me no small amount of pleasure to think of all the people who have since gone into a Korean restaurant after eating at Momofuku, expecting brown-sugar-glazed pork shoulder and being greeted with chewy, room-temperature pork belly instead.

final hour, we will see what needs to happen and put it into motion immediately.

I don't mean this as a metaphor. I've found that the best moment to start working on a new dish is the hour before doors open, when everyone on staff is rushing to shovel food into their mouths and finish their mise en place; every kind of distraction is sure to present itself. On paper, it's the worst possible time to try to be creative, but for that exact reason you end up with no choice but to make decisions and stick to them. You print the dish description on the menu and then you make it work. You can refine it later, but the only way to shut out all the unnecessary doubts in your head is to impose a deadline, and five-thirty p.m. is as good a time as any.

• • •

I thought I had unlocked the big secret, and now I wanted to bottle it. There were new voices in our organization and much more noise from the outside to tune out. We needed to record and examine what worked for us. At least that's how I would put it now. This is how I explained it to the staff in May 2007:

Hi All,

Starting today, at the end of each service for both restaurants, a kitchen manager must send an email to this email list. The email should cover anything that happened in service or prep, and in addition to the prep list for the kitchen, we should use this as way to commicate notes on dishes, food stuff, etc.*******AGAIN THIS IS HAPPENING EVERYDAY, EVERY SERVICE, SOMEONE WRITES A FUCKING EMAIL!!!!

Everyone has access to email now, so there is no excuse for everyone not to be on the same page in terms of what's happening in the restaurant. There are lots of

different faces and different ideas, we need to do this
to be more efficient in communicating with each other,
so please check emails every morning and night

***Those of you who desire a blackberry like device, we
will be more than willing to cover all costs for the
phone, including monthly payments. I will not force you
to do so, but highly encourage you to do so. So if you
don't check emails daily, fuck you.

***FOR real—I did call Jon at Baldor, and was unware
about the snow peas, so he promised to get us nice petit
pois, there is a standing order for two cases tues, and
thursdays, this cal always changes.

Examples Kitchen Log emails—write some shit like this

Noodle Bar—Sunday, May 13th, 12:00 am
Dinner service was great today, Ace Frehley from Kiss
came in and Tim Maslow sent him a pickle plate. Quino
worked on new dish and it tastes great, we used ramp
leaves and made a sauce out of it. Scott, can you please
makesure that the chicken legs get deboned first thing
in the morning so we can get them on brine and smoke
them for chicken and eggs, because we only have 4 orders
in house.It should be enought to get you through lunch
service, but you definately need to get them going first
so we have enough for dinner.

Noodle Bar—Monday, May 14th, 4:56 pm
Service was smooth, but the pilot kept on going out
on the right oven, called KRS and they fixed it during
service.German kicked ass, but Jeffery had head up ass.
Passion Fruit from Baldor was shit again!!! so I talked
to Kevin and Quino and we decided that for the time
being to switch to kiwi fruit until Baldor gets their
shit straight.I told dave about the problem and he gave
me the number to Jon, the head honcho at Baldor,

and so on. . . .

The Roundtable, as the email list came to be known, grew
to include as many as ten participants and encompass all kinds of

discussions. On top of sharing sales numbers and information on ingredients, we'd give play-by-plays of memorable meals we'd eaten around town or talk about cooks whom we might want to bring into the fold. Mentions of hangovers were frequent. Quino and I made an effort to be as open as possible about any opportunities we were feeling out. I could throw my craziest ideas out there and put them to a vote. For instance:

```
I realize that serving something like tamales would be
absurd, but it's so crazy it might work. Plus it's really
a ssam
```

This digital brain trust was nothing like the top-down systems you'd see at most places, where the leader usually keeps only a few trusted operatives aware of what's truly going on. The emails allowed us to pause at the end of a crazy night and reset for the following day, equipped with new goals. The ceaseless chain of messages—if you slept in, you'd have to go through at least fifty replies—exemplified the aforementioned philosophy that there's no idea we won't consider. Everything is a data point we can use. TMI for most people is never enough for me.*

The staff were giving everything they had to being better, to making Momofuku better. I felt an obligation to them. I devised

---

*It takes most of my new colleagues a while to catch on, but I'm not exaggerating when I say I want to hear all the information. People have a tendency to want to filter things out in the name of "sparing" me the hassle of too many emails or too much detail. To them I say, "Don't filter anything. I'll decide when it's too much information." Without fail, I will continue to be left off emails and calls that are deemed a waste of my time. I will say again, louder, "Don't fucking filter *anything.*" Once they finally get the idea and my inbox is packed with reports and invites to conference calls and conversations about menial details, I breathe a little sigh of relief.

what I hoped would be an alternative to the brigade system, a setup devoid of bullshit and hazing, with clear lines of communication that would allow us to grow without too much pain. I proposed breaking the company into subgroups—seven teams of about four people—each consisting of a leader, a veteran, a rookie, and a prep cook:

```
- Every group should try to meet up once a week or go
out for beers, etc. Discuss what's happening in the
restaurant and ways that we can make things better.
Basically instant access to employee feedback. Good or
bad news should be shared. As we grow larger in size,
hopefully this makes it easier for someone to fit in and
not feel so lost within the restaurant.

- I think the most important aspect to this new
organization is cross training, everyone will be able to
show and explain or at least have a better understanding
of what everyone does at the restaurant. Some of
you have group memebers that don't speak English
fluently . . . please take advantage of this situation
and make it a positive one.

- Lastly, like most things we do, we will probably
really suck at this, but let's be patient. Quino
mentioned that a great way to promote this concept is
for competition. . . . like new menu ideas get a money
for booze, whatever.

- Please explain this to the members in you're group,
I know this whole thing sounds silly and absurd, but I
really think that it will promote teamwork.
```

Momofuku turned into something between a committee and a commune. The Roundtable was an assembly of yellers and poor spellers—my frequent mistake was referring to green beans as "haircoverts"—where everyone's opinion was not simply welcomed but mandatory. I may have been the most prolific contributor, because I valued the feedback so much.

From: dave chang
Date: Fri, Jun 8, 2007 at 6:58 AM
Subject: Food Notes

Hi all,

thanks for doing such a great job with the rountable
discussion, the volume has been healthy and there is
constant communication between the two restaurants as
well bridging the gap with different work crews. But I
think that the element that is missing in our emails
is a more detailed description of food stuff and menu
evolution. So take five more minutes and devote a little
more to the food and ideas concerning food.

take note of certain patterns—poularde has historically
been a bad selling item, which is why we are constantly
changing the dish. try and help out with this dish, we
need you're input:

At the moment we want to pair it with summer corn
and nori puree, Tien made a bad ass farce and made a
ballontine of the chicken. My concern with the dish is
that the farce is too grayish green, but it is quite
delicious witht the nori center.

Debone Chicken, I think that tien used a robo coupe
for the leg meat and folded in the nori puree that we
have been using. Toque into torchon, and steam in combi
at 165 degrees, I think that we should do it at 160
degrees, do you guys think that is too low? Tien wants
to serve it pan-fried in panko, but I think that if
we aggresively season the chicken and gently cook the
poularde it can be served cold, thoughts? need opinions
because I think that we have a potential winner on our
hands.

BTW, the lamb belly dish is sexy with the chard and
lemon.

The squid dish v. 2.2—i think it is a bad ass dish—squid
charred and cooked like before. Inspired by meals at
Grand Sichuan. Tien made it with celery noodles, chilled
in ice water and using the veg peeler to create strips

that curl up in ice water. We made a comprimse with the
use of radishes, Tien seems to really like XMAS colors
and wants red and green, if I see sliced radishes as
garnish on another dish I'm going to lose my mind. The
squid is tossed with celery, chili oil (puręe of dried
red chilies and toasted sichuan peppers, grapeseed
oil, salt) I made an oil last week and it's too fucking
spicy. We need to find the right ratio for this chili
oil / paste. But plate with the oil, celery and squid,
in small oval bowl. Garnish with celery leaves and some
dried red chlies. It's fucking spicy but we thought it
worked real well, Julie and I liked it lots The celery
does an amazing job of balancing out the heat. It's
real important to have the sichuan peppers as the litte
buggers numb the tongue so you can eat something that
spicy. My concerns are that customers are going to eat
something that they cannont handle, and it will kill
their palate for the entire meal . . . but I sort of
could care less. Servers will have to warn people that
it is violently spicy, thoughts?

Scallop Dish v 2.0—we are going to keep the pinepple
thing till we come up with an nice alternative. Serpico
mentioned that the dish might be nice with pea juice
and shiso, etc. After talking with Tien and Julie, a
connsome (WD-50 style) was hatched and would be poured
over sliced scallops and topped with nori chips and
sliced sugar snaps or snow peas. Maybe we infuse shiso
into the consomme. I was thinking later that we puree
the peas with dashi, as I've had a nice dish in Tokyo
with fresh petit pois cooked in a light dashi, that it,
it was fucking delicious. Serpico wanted to juice the
peas in the juicer, but I think that Tien used the Vita
Prep since we were using gelatin. Thoughts, Serpico,
anyone?

I had a nice chat with Tien and Julie on umeboshi . . .
If you don't know . . . I fucking hate the stuff. It
has a time and place in Japanese cuisine. But it is too
strong to pair with food. It's fine with booze or as a
candy/snack, but paired with food I think it is vile.
Seriously when's the last time you ate seafood or sushi
and fish was paired with umeboshi? never, exactly. I'm
all for new flavor combinations. But if we want to pair

```
fish with plums, lets wait til July and use real local
plums. I think that might work with scallops, nice dark
skinned plums, tart and sweet.

Everyday, we try to get a little bit better, love

dc
```

                                    • • •

I wish I could remember half of the inside jokes from these emails. Nevertheless, it brings me joy to reread them. Pemoulie:

```
Just talked to two of my best friends from nj.
Apparently brown liquor is good. And rubber sheets
are fine. X-mas this year is gonna be fun for me and
my moustache. I wish you all a happy and a merry and
a stache-worthy holiday. Listen to neil diamond's
christmas album and just take bong rips (Q and scotty)
and then order chinese (pete) and bathe in eggrolls.
Fuck you all and i'll see yous tomorrow.

My moustache wrote this. It wasnt me.

Kp
```

No one knew when work ended or began. We were part of something we couldn't appreciate until much later. Together, we were building a world, and while that task could be overwhelming, I realize now what a privilege it was to be able to focus all of our attention on it. The older I get, the more distractions get in the way—the more I'm drawn from the stove and the thing I'm best at. To this day, whenever I get together with Quino to catch up over dinner or a beer, we always say that the beginning of Momofuku was the best time of our lives. Nostalgia is funny that way. I don't want to put words in everyone else's mouths, but I hope they all look back on this period as fondly as I do.

We were winging it. We had thrown out our original plans for

Ssäm in January and received validation of the course correction from *The New York Times* with a two-star review less than two months later. (The following year, the same critic, Frank Bruni, upgraded Ssäm to three stars, putting it on par with restaurants like Gramercy Tavern and . . . Café Boulud.) That first review saved the business and launched us into the stratosphere. I woke up one morning in March to learn that we had been nominated for two James Beard Awards: Rising Star Chef (me, for the second time) and Best New Restaurant (Ssäm).

For all my bluster, I was scared shitless. Writing about the facts of my life here, it seems like a logical progression. This happened and then that happened and I slowly learned this and by the time this moment came I was ready. But in between every triumph or epiphany I've described in this book, there were five hundred moments of doubt. There were embarrassments and mistakes, people I pissed off or disappointed, chances I squandered. There were dishes that sucked and services that made me want to tear my eyeballs out. And there was the constant thrum of depression in the back of my skull.

The accolades felt like they were coming out of nowhere. I've always had a knack for getting the best out of others, but it took me years to appreciate that as a skill. In the moment, it seemed as though I was sucking up all the credit for what was a team effort. When Dana Cowin called to inform me that I was one of *Food & Wine*'s Best New Chefs, I tried my best to decline. Ask her, if you don't believe me. I kept waiting for someone to flip a switch in my brain that would make me think, *You deserve this, Dave. You're one of the best. Forget everything else.* But it never came.

If there was one moment that was supposed to do it, it was the Beards. Being nominated for a Beard Award was the signal that I'd arrived, but it only generated more anxiety. I felt like I was hiding a shameful secret—that I didn't deserve to be in the same company as my mentors, some of whom had been passed over for years by the Beards. The only coping strategy in my repertoire was to laugh it off. Or, as I suggested to the team, we'd just get too drunk to worry about winning or losing. They seemed on board.

• • •

Over the past thirty years, there has been no more important event for American restaurants than the James Beard Awards. For a massive industry that isn't synonymous with high fashion or red carpets or classy behavior, the annual ceremony is a nice opportunity to play dress-up and be taken seriously. It's black tie and, for a long time, was held in New York at the Marriott Marquis and later Avery Fisher Hall, where the Philharmonic plays. It is an aspirational and intensely ceremonial event, and with good reason: a Beard Award is the highest honor you can receive as a chef or restaurateur; joining the class of winners or even nominees can change a career.

People take it very seriously. I respected the awards deeply, I just didn't respect myself, which made it all the more difficult to picture myself in a tux, strutting past those pretty fountains in Lincoln Center Plaza and into the room where Simon and Garfunkel, Miles Davis, and Leonard Bernstein had performed—not to mention thousands of extremely talented classical musicians. I wasn't especially looking forward to chitchatting with all my highly respected peers from around the country. Everybody goes to the Beards.

But bailing would have been worse, so I channeled my anxiety into planning a night the team wouldn't soon forget. Most people who come to town for the Beards try to hit the restaurants of the moment or pay their respects to established local chefs. It's one of the coolest parts of the tradition. There are also a bunch of pre- and after-parties, hosted by restaurant groups and liquor companies and magazines. Our goal would be to minimize our exposure to small talk. It would be a set of activities designed to shield us from the gravity of the situation.

I secured a party bus, complete with disco lights, a smoke machine, and very shoddy leather seating. It was also outfitted with a stripper pole, which was a complete surprise to me. It was probably the first time the vehicle had been used to transport anybody other than horny bachelors. It also happened to be cheaper than any other available limo. I'd never gone to prom, but I imagined this wasn't far off.

That evening in May, the whole gang and a few plus-ones got dressed to the nines and boarded the Momobus, which was pointed due northwest. I'd rented out Daisy May's, Adam Perry Lang's fine spot for smoked meat in Hell's Kitchen. We were going to have some barbecue. When we arrived, we put on plastic aprons and rubber gloves, and wrapped our forearms with garbage bags to avoid getting our clothes dirty. We drank beer and liquor from red Solo cups. We served ourselves from aluminum platters filled with pulled pork, ribs, Texas toast, and coleslaw.

Our good mood lasted us through the event, which went by in a blur. Ssäm didn't get the award, but I did, which made me want to blow things out even more ridiculously during the ride around town later that night. The pictures from the rest of the evening suggest we did a pretty good job of that.

I got some feedback in the aftermath that gave me the impression that other attendees found our behavior to be disrespectful. That's a fair way of seeing it. But the truth is, it was one of the nicest things we'd ever done together as a family.

7

HOT WATER

IN MY TYPICAL TELLING OF THIS STORY, WINNING A BEARD AWARD IS THE moment we decided to mature as a restaurant group. We would relocate Noodle Bar to a larger space up the block. Taking its place would be a tasting-menu restaurant called Ko (which means "son of" in Japanese). In opening Ko, we would ask to be measured against the finest restaurants in the country. When I say it like that, it sounds like a pretty solid plan.

What I usually neglect to mention is the major creative influence of the New York City Department of Health and Mental Hygiene.

I cannot overstate how not in control we actually were. The infrastructure at Noodle Bar had begun to burst apart years earlier. We'd gotten pretty good at keeping pace with the relentless succession of malfunctions and mini-emergencies posed by the pipes, ventilation, drainage system, and general anatomy of 163 First Avenue, but the space could no longer handle the number of people eating and working in there. I'd get messages from Quino saying that the plumber had to come by again because there was "doodoo water" coming out of one of the sinks. There were little things all the time and big things more often than a reputable business owner should accept.

Here's Quino in an email to the Roundtable during that era:

```
Today was mostly plumbing with a dash of elctricity.
First expo sink burst at the base of the drain and
required some new parts ( nathan ran to the sotre for
me 6:00), then dish sink started overflowing because
there was a folded up plastic lid jammed in the drain
pipe (just a little finger action 7:00), then slop
sink downstairs pulled a ditto from the sink upstairs
and started spooging all over the compressors ( some
tightening and tape 10:00) for good measure the upstairs
big lowboy crapped out three times during service
because of the loose plug (i replaced the outlet and
wrapped the whole damn thing in plastic).
```

For the most part, we took it in stride. We tried not to fret over our deficiencies in money, space, and infrastructure. Viewed pessimistically, these were all complications working against us, but they could also inspire creativity. For example, I wanted to serve chicken wings at Noodle Bar, but without a fryer, we needed to come up with another way to cook them. *Maybe we could griddle them,* I thought. *But we can't griddle them from raw. I guess we can try to smoke them, then confit them first. Where are we going to get all the fat for confit? Well, the pork belly gives off a ton of fat—I don't see why we can't use that. Hmm, the confit process yields all this smoky, meaty, gelatinous liquid as a by-product. Perfect, we'll throw it in the tare for the ramen.*

If you looked at our menu, you might easily mistake what we were doing as being bold or visionary, but in fact almost all of it was informed purely by necessity. That dynamic extended beyond menu creation, too. The most significant infrastructure problem at Noodle

Bar was that by late 2006, the restaurant had become so popular that we often ran out of electricity for our water heaters. ConEd did not heed our requests for more juice; they didn't believe that a restaurant of our size could feed as many people as it did. The obvious solution would have been a gas heater. No chance it would fit, and no way to run the necessary gas pipes to our side of the building. As a consequence, and in the most unscientific manner, we figured out when exactly to turn on and shut off certain appliances to make sure we'd have enough charge to survive. We were like a family hiding out in a boarded-up house during the zombie apocalypse, staying ever mindful of the emergency generator.

We managed for months, tempting a power far worse than zombies. It's hard to express just how frustrating it is to deal with the DOH. Here's how an inspection works: an agent comes in unannounced and without the slightest regard for whether it's convenient—say, in the middle of a crammed service with people waiting out the door for a seat. The person on staff with a food-safety certificate must drop everything to accompany the inspector as they check every nook and cranny of the restaurant. They accept no excuses. At the conclusion of the visit, they'll pull out their laptop right in the middle of the dining room to file a report.

Any violation is counted as "points" against you. I don't think it's an exaggeration to say that most restaurateurs are baffled by the arbitrary nature of the point system and how much is left to the inspector's discretion. An empty paper towel dispenser over the hand sink is ten points, yet rodent droppings are only a five-point deduction. (What qualifies as a piece of mouse shit, by the way, is completely up to the inspector's mood.)

The specific regulations regarding hot water are laid out in their Byzantine code: *"Hot water used for sanitizing must be heated to and maintained at or above 170 degrees Fahrenheit (76.6 degrees Celsius). A numerically scaled, indicating or digital thermometer calibrated to be accurate to plus or minus 2 degrees Fahrenheit (1.1 degrees Celsius) must be used to measure water temperature. Items must be wholly immersed for at least 30 seconds to destroy surface pathogens."*

Without hot water, you can't wash dishes or hands properly or kill potential pathogens. I don't disagree with the idea. Not having enough hot water was a big reason why I let myself get completely fleeced by the owner of the restaurant at 171 First Avenue so we could take over his lease and move Noodle Bar a few doors away. (It sucks negotiating from a position of need, and I was begging for my life. He fucked me accordingly.) It's also why we decided not to turn 163 into a Mexican restaurant where Quino's cooking could take center stage. We bounced the idea around for a while, but we couldn't solve the water issue. Any restaurant that intended to serve as many people as Noodle Bar was going to face the same struggle.

So, as nice a story as it would have been, we didn't decide to open Ko so that we could challenge what it meant to serve a tasting menu in America. We did it because we were backed into a corner by a meddling bureaucracy and had to find a way to make money serving far fewer people each night. Momofuku Ko wasn't a stroke of great ambition or business genius. It was the only option.

• • •

While we waited for our new home to be ready, Noodle Bar would have to dodge the DOH's wrath for a few more months. Any shred of confidence I had in our chances of making it out unscathed was rooted in one factor: Christina Tosi. But in order to get to Tosi, first I need to talk about Wylie.

In the late 1990s, Wylie Dufresne did the unheard-of: he opened a serious restaurant on the Lower East Side, at a period in the city's history when you'd literally have to mind broken glass and other unsavory detritus as you walked down the sidewalk to dinner there. More radical than opening on the pre-gentrification Lower East Side was the unapologetic, forward-thinking creativity of Wylie's cooking. He wasn't concerned with pleasing everyone, a form of courage almost completely absent from New York kitchens at the time. His restaurant was called 71 Clinton Fresh Food, and the meals I had there while I was in culinary school changed how I think about food. It was my favorite place to eat in New York.

Wylie spent two or three years at 71 before leaving to open a more polished project. He didn't leave the block. His next restaurant, wd~50, was another spot that flew over the heads of far too many people who claim to know what they're talking about. He stuck it out for more than a decade, inventing countless new techniques in the service of dishes as delicious as they were clever. You'd read the descriptions and think, *That sounds bizarre,* and then eat the food and immediately wonder, *Where has this been all my life?* I get goose bumps remembering the deep-fried eggs Benedict, shrimp cannelloni (as in pasta made from shrimp) with Thai basil and chorizo paste, aerated foie gras with pickled beet gelée, and mind-bending desserts from pastry chefs Sam Mason and Alex Stupak. It's agonizing that I can't taste any of it anymore.

Wylie never compromised his vision for the sake of publicity or even business. His persistence did earn him more praise, but it didn't keep the operation going for as long as it should have. He is New York's culinary Prometheus. If people—I'm looking at you, food media—had taken the time to understand what he was doing, New York would be a completely different place to eat.

Before I ever knew him, Wylie was an inspiration—teaching me from afar not to be afraid to fight convention. Over the years, we've developed a close friendship, during which he has bestowed many gifts. None was more welcome or needed than an introduction to Christina Sylvia Tosi.

As Wylie and I got better acquainted with one another, I'd complain to him about how our infrastructural headaches were taking our focus away from making delicious food. Floods, leaks, fires, and inspections—plus our ignorance of how to deal with these various catastrophes—were eating up most of our energy. I told Wylie about a recent day when the DOH came by and found that we were storing food in vacuum-sealed bags. I had organized the whole walk-in and Cryovac'd everything from pickles to raw pork belly to a massive shipment of country hams and bacon that had just come in from Allan Benton—probably $10,000 worth of the world's best smoked pork products. I was incredibly proud of how tight and clean it all looked.

The inspector saw it differently. Apparently, any establishment that uses vacuum bags must develop, implement, and maintain a detailed set of plans for any potentially problematic phases of food production. It's called a Hazard Analysis and Critical Control Point (HACCP) plan, and we didn't have one.

The inspector opened all our bags and made me pour bleach over everything, regardless of whether it was shelf stable. It felt like he was telling me to shoot my own kids. I called him a "Nazi."

Wylie told me that one of his most talented pastry cooks had also done a great job putting HACCP plans in place for him and a bunch of other restaurants and suggested I hire her. Tosi needed no time to begin work on our refuge for buffoons. She made herself valuable instantly, fixing a whole lot more than how we documented our pork belly storage. She built out our first office. She helped me organize English classes for staff members who couldn't speak the language. (Bridging the gap between me and Momofuku's Hispanic and Latino cooks was foundational in establishing our company's culture and values.) She identified potential problems in almost every aspect of the operation long before everyone else, and she was never shy about pointing them out. She once ordered new phones for us at Noodle Bar, preloaded with an accompanying message: "You guys need to take care of these new phones better than you do your own busted fucking asses."

Tosi was a total asset for a staff made of people who were more doers than thinkers. She was also, lest I forget, one of the world's great pastry chefs.

. . .

I was juggling two restaurants with a third on the way. The problem was, my formula for winning was based on a simple but bleak-sounding bit of logic: if everything is meaningless, then you have nothing to lose. With nothing to lose, you're free to risk everything all the time. I attributed our success to this approach. I would triple-down on it by laying everything on the line again for Ko.

I became even more of a neurotic mess. I'd have panic attacks at work and try my best to hide them from the staff. I experienced the nightmare that is shingles and a bunch of other psychosomatic crap. The activities that had always chilled me out—massages and haircuts, mainly—began to trigger episodes of crippling anxiety. Any time that I had to sit still, including when I was at my therapist's office, I felt a weight on my chest. I couldn't seem to get enough oxygen, no matter how deeply I inhaled.

"Everything is so crazy right now" is how I started kicking off sessions with Dr. Eliot, whom I started visiting again. "I really mean it this time, this is so fucking crazy, you have to believe me, I think I might break." He put me on Klonopin for when I was feeling anxious and propranolol for when I was calmer. I didn't much care for the propranolol, because I couldn't feel it chilling me out, but I took it anyway. I preferred the Klonopin, at least at first.

In theory I knew how to treat myself without medication. It's almost too obvious to state: adjust my diet, exercise, find meaningful companionship, slow down, don't drink more Pappy than water. (And I did try. I started working with a yoga instructor, for instance, but I was still drinking my face off.) I could have taken stock of how much had changed in three years. There was more data for reassurance than any single person should ever need: *Look at everything that's happened. One in a billion.*

But that's not how it works. Momofuku was my identity and it was born of my depression. I couldn't separate a failure in the kitchen, no matter how small, from a failure of the self. I'd actually come to depend on the emotional and mental instability. I wasn't beating my illness, or even trying to, really. I had subdued it by redirecting its energy into my own productivity. We were locked together like two judo opponents. It was always there, waiting for me to loosen my grip so that it could flip me over and pin me to the ground.

So I never lightened the load. It may not have been my life's dream to have a tasting-menu restaurant, but once I decided to open Ko, I knew it would consume me. Noodle Bar and Ssäm wouldn't lose any of my attention, either. I'd just have to sleep less. More growth, more strain, no stopping.

It fucking hurt, but I started to see the pain as no different from the feeling of soreness you get after working out. It was a good hurt.

• • •

When I first started exploring options to finance and build Ko in early 2007, I wrote to one of my contacts at the bank with an explanation of what I thought the restaurant would be. I described it as a "higher-end concept serving contemporary European cuisine."

I didn't have any fully fleshed-out plans, so this was the most succinct way to communicate the vision to a person who didn't care about food. I've never been able to label the food at Momofuku, but whenever I'm cornered for an answer, I fall back on "American" as the best adjective for what we do. Second choice is "Asian." Begrudgingly.

I've never rejected Europe, though. Yes, in order to start Momofuku, I turned my back on restaurants that descended from a

European lineage, but I am also a classicist at heart. I didn't have the chance to work in a European kitchen and was very much obsessed with them. I used to rant about how every serious cook, no matter the cuisine they wanted to focus on, needed to have a classical French foundation. I spoke longingly about Marc Veyrat, Alain Passard, Michel Bras, and Marco Pierre White. We had photos of these legends posted on the walls of both kitchens, so that in the unlikely event that they ever stopped in, we'd recognize them and break our no-comps policy to give them everything for free.

At Ko, we were adopting a format most people would associate with fine dining—the tasting menu—and planning to work with foie gras, caviar, and more butter than you'd find at any nominally Asian restaurant. Just as before, we'd be cooking in front of our guests, but this time, they'd see a lot fewer boiling pots and less frantic movements. We'd also incorporate more ideas pioneered by chefs like Heston Blumenthal, the Adriàs, and Wylie. No one could dismiss it as "slinging noodles."

But I wanted people to eat at Ko and detect a coherent, explosive marriage of influences that could only exist at Momofuku. If you came to Ko and ate a dish you could find at Jean-Georges or Per Se or anywhere else on earth, it would be our failure. The food needed to build on what we'd started at Noodle and Ssäm. More of that je ne sais quoi, but even slicker.

The person I tapped to be Ko's chef was well suited to the task. Peter Serpico had worked under David Bouley, the Tribeca chef known for his nuanced marriage of French and Japanese influences. Serpico and I set about framing our approach. At Ssäm and Noodle, guests chose haphazardly from categories that didn't follow the typical appetizer-main-dessert organization. They ordered a mix of stuff without much guidance, and the food would arrive as it was ready; if the guests ordered well and we happened to be doing our jobs right, the meal would make sense. At Ko, we'd have to orchestrate a more deliberate progression. We'd have to consider flow. We'd be taking you on a ride and dictating the stops, mixing quiet moments with louder ones. It couldn't drag on, like so many of those special-occasion meals that end up feeling more like an examination than a celebration. Every move needed to count. Each dish needed to be a hit on its own but work in the service of the greater goal: offering a seamless experience where the pleasures blur together and you remember not the particulars but the whole, like a good set list.

Our contractor and designer, Swee Phuah and Hiromi Tsuruta, were going to update the space from a casual noodle joint to a more refined experience, but the stools and general absence of ornamentation would remain. We were never going to hang a chandelier in 163. I characterized the look we were chasing as "wooden box." We would continue our chef-centric approach, using as few servers as possible and putting most of the onus of explaining and serving dishes on the cooks. (I originally wanted no servers at all, until I realized that was both stupid and impossible.) Because the cooks would work inches from the diners, they wouldn't be the only ones feeling the heat of the stoves. The guests would feel it, too, sometimes to the point of discomfort. As ever, we would implement no dress code.

We would strip away as much unnecessary shit as possible so we could deliver value and make a statement: we hide behind nothing here.

· · ·

Later in the summer there were two significant developments. The new Noodle Bar was going to be delayed, and the DOH and DEP—the Department of Environmental Protection—were now really on our case. We finally got cited for a critical violation because of the insufficient hot water. If they were to find the same problem the next time they came through, it could put us out of business.

From: dave chang
Date: Wed, Aug 15, 2007 at 5:35 PM
Subject: D. HEALTH SUPER IMPORTANT

For Noodle Bar:

The most important thing for Noodle Bar inspection
is that we have hot water running through the sinks
upstairs. We need to conserve all hot water until we get
inspected. Please no hot water usage by cooks or prep
cooks. The water tanks need to be full so we have hot
water. PLEASE TELL DISHWASHERS NOT TO SPRAY DISHES WITH
HOTWATER.

**If we get in busted for lack of hot water WE WILL BE
SHUT DOWN. As we have been cited for lack of running hot
water before. A critical violation that will cause the
DOH to close the restaurant.

please help me from offing myself.

I was overwhelmed by my paranoia, convinced we were too far gone. Knowing that the inspectors were set to make a return visit, I decided to make one big bet before skipping town.

According to health code, your sinks need to run hot for at least thirty seconds. The safe play would have been to rely on the cooks to conserve hot water, but I wanted the inspector to turn on a faucet and witness a deluge like he'd never seen in his life. I had a hunch about which sink he would test, so I told Swee to hire a welder to direct all the hot water to that faucet. Then I left.

I got a room at one of the casinos in Atlantic City. Quino might have come with me. I honestly can't remember. I know you're thinking that this sounds incredibly irresponsible. Why abandon the restaurant at this crucial moment?

Well, I'd made my play. We were going to bet it all on one faucet. There was nothing else to be done, so with our fate entirely in the hands of Lady Luck, I decided to face her head-on at the tables.

I hadn't even made it to New Jersey when I got a call from Tosi.

How did it go?

"It was like Old Faithful," she said.

The inspector picked the right faucet. The stream was forceful and scalding. As far as he was concerned, Momofuku Noodle Bar could run hot water nonstop for weeks. I got to AC, drank and played blackjack for a day, then cut my Jersey exile short to return home and plan a restaurant.

Had the inspector simply picked another faucet, the DOH would have shut down Noodle Bar. But we needed the income from Noodle Bar to fund the construction of the new space. If that went south, we'd also have lost Ko as a result. I'd have had to lay off a bunch of staff. Ssäm Bar would have had to become a huge moneymaker—but even then, the loans needed to be paid off. I needed everything to fall into place in sequence for any of it to work. My apartment was on the line, as well as my dad's businesses. Plus the world would think we were filthy and unprofessional.

I had hit on sixteen with the dealer showing an ace, because it was the only move I could make. The odds dictated that I put my faith in that one sink. The dealer busted.

This kind of deus ex machina moment will likely sound familiar by now. I often have trouble figuring out how much of Momofuku's history really happened the way I remember it. How can things simply work out so often? These escape acts seem too improbable to be luck, but I'm too blasphemous to deserve divine intervention. And when I retell the story, it feels too tidy to be true. It sounds like magical realism.

I often wonder aloud to my friends if I'm living in a computer simulation or cosmic reality show. It honestly sounds more logical than the unbelievable string of luck I've had. Perhaps my memory is editing the most hectic moments of my life so that they're easier to digest. Or maybe I'm just a bullshitter.

8

KO-BOOM

"Be careful with the bloggers."

That was the general sentiment among the industry's veterans. At first, the Internet had been a curiosity to most chefs, who were flattered by the interest from this new, ultra-passionate audience. But once the bloggers started taking a critical stance, flattery turned to extreme suspicion. Chefs that had been playing the publicity game for years did not trust the blogs at all. According to them, the only outlets worthy of respect were the major print ones, organizations with history and journalistic integrity. These chefs had come up when *The New York Times*, *New York* magazine, *Gourmet,* and *Food & Wine* held all of the power in food. To be mentioned, let alone praised, in the printed pages of one of these publications meant everything.

Tuesday night was sacred in the New York restaurant community. That's when you could go to the *Times* building and get your hands on a copy of their weekly food section. When I was at Craft and Café Boulud, the food world moved to the rhythm that the *Times* set every week. If you wanted to know who mattered and what was next, the answer was right there. The night after the first *Times* review of Noodle Bar was published, I had dinner at Casa Mono. Liz Chapman (now Benno), who was cooking there at the time, said, "Your life is about to change." It didn't matter that the review had been in Peter Meehan's $25 and Under column—the paper's de facto "ethnic cheap eats" feature. It was still the *Times*.

On the other end of the spectrum were the websites that most old-school chefs detested. As the Internet supernovaed into the global consciousness, more and more voices were elbowing into the discussion. Communities formed around the subject of restaurants, in primordial corners of the Web where no detail was too small or too dorky to discuss in excruciating detail. Their members had the passion and obsessiveness of cosplayers and Comic Con attendees.*

There were different subsets of the new media: news and gossip blogs, like *Eater;* single-author sites from independently wealthy foodies who spent their time and money flying to restaurants all over the world; and message boards, like eGullet, Mouthfuls, and Opinionated About Dining, where fanatics compared notes about chefs and meals.

While chefs of the previous generation weren't hot on these developments, I was stoked. To be a curious chef had always been a gigantic inconvenience. In order to gather information about the

---

*And chefs have become the exact same kind of celebrity as, say, the stars of the movie *Serenity*: incredibly popular to some, completely unknown to most. Seriously, do you know who Nathan Fillion is? Well, he has 3.5 million Twitter followers.

culinary arts beyond New York City, one had to rely on conversations with people who had worked abroad, or at least traveled more broadly than you. I'd ask friends who were doing stages in Spain or France to send me letters describing their experiences. Some people view it romantically as the last totally analog era. You really had to want the information to get it. But it was also frustrating to be so far behind. Cookbooks were the best resource for an American cook who wanted to know what was happening in Europe. (Good luck if you were interested in Asia or Africa or South America.) Sadly, I can tell you with certainty that cookbooks cannot give you the full picture.

All of a sudden I could stay in my underwear and visit some dude's blog to see pictures of every single dish from the latest menu at Pierre Gagnaire in Paris. Not all of the bloggers knew what they were talking about, but some of them were even more knowledgeable than writers working in the New York bubble. "But the writing is so bad" was a common complaint. So long as there were pictures of the food, it didn't matter to me.* It was a giant leap forward.

eGullet was amazing through and through. I would spend hours on its forums reading about people's experiences at restaurants outside the *Times*'s purview. I read opinions about different writers and trends, browsed ideas for recipes, looked up reviews of kitchen appliances—*everything,* all in one place, organized into discrete categories.

When the bloggers began eating at Momofuku, I didn't mind it in the least.** These proto-foodies were showing intense interest in something that most people found frivolous. I can still go to eGullet

---

*I wasn't the only one. Tom Colicchio was an early adopter, too. He cooked for bloggers when no one else would give them the time of day.

**Though, to be fair, I would go on to have a few feuds.

and see every post about Noodle Bar, Ssäm Bar, and Ko. It's a very strange artifact.

Here's a post that was published a month after we opened Noodle Bar, from a user named snausages2000:

> The cooking at Momofuku is done under your nose at the noodle bar. Every detail of the kitchen's operation is easily appreciated. Last night, the presentation was wildly inappropriate. The culprit was the restaurant's owner, David Chang.
>
> About two minutes after sitting at my stool, I was distracted from reading the menu as Mr. Chang reprimanded his dishwasher, ordering him to speak-up when he passed through the kitchen, to say more loudly, "Behind!" I felt bad for the dishwasher, whose English was broken, and spoke with little confidence, let alone volume. But, fair enough, in a narrow cooking space the staff needs to be vocal to avoid the danger of collision.
>
> After placing our order, the sole line cook began preparing the ramen. Almost immediately Mr. Chang, a large, physically intimidating guy, began to scold the cook, leaning over his shoulder, ordering him to be more on top of things, more efficient, essentially telling him everything he was doing was wrong. Chang was not yelling, but in such a small space every word was audible. Rattled by the public humiliation, the cook went more and more into a shell, and the more he tensed up, the more Chang rode him. Regardless of whether or not Chang's criticisms were valid (we hadn't noticed anything wrong with what the cook was doing and our food was served within 5 minutes of ordering), he brought his cook to the verge of tears, told him he was going to be fired, and thus made it impossible for me or my girlfriend to enjoy ourselves, or the food, the quality of which, ironically, so concerned Chang.
>
> I respect Chang's obsession with his product, and his CIA and Craft background were evident in the kind of

```
attention-to-detail, always-prepared kitchen philosophy
he was dictating, but he demonstrated complete ignorance
in one culinary aspect: the customer's experience.

Chewing out a sub-standard cook may be a necessary
instructional tool in a kitchen, but when diners
are sitting a foot away, and the owner never even
acknowledges the situation, or apologizes to the diners
for the ugly scene, he is showing utter lack of respect
for anyone eating in his restaurant. We left a bit
traumatized, and I was angry at myself for not having
said anything to Chang, but then remembered that it'd be
better to let you, a potential customer, know.
```

I don't recall this person being in the restaurant, and to be clear, I attended the French Culinary Institute, not the CIA. Otherwise, I'm sure his or her account is accurate and could have been written about almost any night I was working service.

We'd built no separation between the kitchen and the dining room at 163 First Avenue—Noodle Bar's original home and Ko's soon-to-be new digs. Everything we did was within full view of anyone who walked in our doors. With the megaphone of the Internet, any mistake we made was a public one.

In the early days of Momofuku, I took pride in our fuck-you attitude toward diners who didn't fit the mold of our ideal customer. I've bragged about it and been celebrated for it. I rejected snausages's criticism for years. What did they know about the pressure I was under or what the restaurants meant to me?

Recently, I've started to see this particular incident for the lesson it was. Blame it on insecurity, depression, bipolar disorder, whatever. The simple fact is that I was contradicting my own belief that the only thing that matters is how the diners feel when they walk out the door. Because we were in such tight quarters, when you came to Momofuku, you were eating dinner with me. And nobody wants to eat dinner with a dick.

. . .

Except for the Deathwatch,* I liked *Eater*. They swam in the minutiae, talking about the industry like it was their favorite sport, and
like most sports fans, they didn't mind prodding their heroes. The
press hated them just as much as many chefs, which was quite an
achievement. By claiming that they were dealing in rumors, *Eater*
could share potential news that hadn't been announced yet. If it was
completely wrong, it didn't matter. By the next day, the story would
be buried under twenty more posts. But if the information was correct, it would mean scooping the *Times* and a food section that had
been developing the story for weeks, in addition to all the investors
and PR reps who were orchestrating a splashier announcement.

For a while, I even wrote a column for them. Well, not me so
much as Meehan. After reviewing us in the *Times,* Meehan kept coming to Noodle Bar and, over time, became an active participant in
all matters Momofuku. He could listen to my ramblings and know
precisely what I wanted to say. (Sometimes he would have to explain
it to me.) I'm not a bad storyteller, but writing is a challenge. I tend
to jump around from thought to thought, and then painstakingly figure out how to piece it all together later. But Peter's prose was full of
whimsy and knowledge; reading his reviews somehow reminded me
of listening to the lo-fi bands we both loved. He contributed to every
column or op-ed with my name on it. He would tune up comments I
sent to journalists and look at memos I wanted to share with the staff.
He adopted a voice for me that was far more lucid and consistent than

---

*Deathwatch was an early *Eater* feature that disgusted a lot of people in the industry: whenever they identified a restaurant that looked like it was on life support,
they would put it on the "Deathwatch" and track every moment of its painful
collapse. People's dreams and livelihoods were being mocked while they were in
hospice.

the real-life version. He gave me swagger. "David Chang" was our culinary Tony Clifton. Whenever he made an appearance in print, nobody could be sure if it was Andy Kaufman or Bob Zmuda under the prosthetics.*

As they did for many restaurant openings, *Eater* implemented a tactic of "flooding the zone" with Ko coverage, posting anything and everything related to the restaurant: a story about our community board meeting, a photo gallery of our storefront completely blanketed in brown paper like a sad Christo and Jeanne-Claude installation, murmurs about the menu.

I said yes to media requests primarily because I was afraid of what would happen to business if I said no. I had no publicist, no social media, no other way to convince people to spend money at Momofuku. I'd like to think that the food itself was our best form of advertisement, but as long as people were interested in me, I would milk it for as much commercial value as it would yield.

In the summer of 2008, Larissa MacFarquhar profiled me for *The New Yorker*. It was a detailed snapshot of the work Serpico and I were doing behind the scenes as we prepared to open Ko, how we planned each dish and debated every possible choice. A profile of a chef in *The New Yorker* was still an anomaly at the time.

Eater reblogged it, to which a commenter responded:

> This is beyond ridiculous—hero worship of a guy who
> serves a few hundred meals a day? How about a press
> blackout for a few months so people can actually get in

---

*The only writing collaborator I ever considered for the Momofuku cookbook was Peter. I was confident we'd be able to produce something great and fresh together, but our publisher, Clarkson Potter, tried to keep us on a tight leash. They wanted cute headnotes and dishes geared toward the home cook; we wanted to move freely between imperial and metric units and break the record for the world's most elaborate chicken-wing recipe. In the end, we got what we wanted. They must have come around as well, given the fact that they're publishing this book, too.

the restaurant and judge it on its merits, not on a cult
of personality build up by the media?

In its early days, the *Eater* comments section was a haven for anybody who thought the other boards were too civilized. You could log
on anonymously and write anything short of a death threat, and it
would stay untouched. I learned quickly that any update on Momofuku would inevitably incite a mini-referendum on me.

Umm Eater, you have chang batter running down your chin
it's time to wipe it off.

i think dc forgot to put "eater.com will be press,
partner of momofuku"

I got to say #29 that is pretty gay. The comment on
D-Chang being best chef in NYC, putting him in the same
catagory as Adria and Gargniere is crazy talk.

It seemed that there was a growing perception that the media was
in Momofuku's pocket. *All right, then,* I thought, *we'll make eating at
Ko as egalitarian as humanly possible.*

Ko had only twenty-four seats—two turns of twelve—available
each night. With all the attention on us, we'd certainly open with
thousands more requests for reservations than we could handle from
civilian diners, friends, family, and press. If we showed any favorit-
ism, we'd be feeding the perception that we were elitist or nepotistic.

I decided early on that we'd build our own bookings portal for
Ko on the Momofuku website. Every morning at ten a.m., reservations would open for the evening one week out. Diners could log in
and see a simple grid of times with green checkmarks denoting available spots and red Xs signaling that all seats had been taken. No special requests. No back doors. Let the people sort it out for themselves.

This would have the added benefit of streamlining the reservation
process and all its bullshit ambiguities. It always struck me as illogi-
cal for restaurants to pay reservationists. I had seen the inefficiencies

firsthand. My first job at Craft, you may remember, had been answering the phones. I suppose it's nice to talk to someone live, but at a busy restaurant, that person's job is basically to say, "No, sorry." I also cringed at the juggling act that restaurant reservationists had to perform to keep seats available every night for surprise VIPs. (When a restaurant says to you, "Sorry, we're fully committed this evening," they mean that while there are technically seats available, they're not for you.) At Ko, if there were no tables, that was it. No conversation necessary, no special treatment—just a red X.

Eater reported on the new reservation system under the all-caps tag *KO-BOOM*. They wrote about the server crashing under the number of requests we were receiving; about tables intermittently popping up; about people scalping tickets; about two women who had secured a four-top and put an ad on Craigslist looking for two potential suitors to join them on a blind date.

Momofuku's magic had always been based on underselling and overdelivering. The risk for Ko was raising expectations too high. It was such a hard seat to get that diners who got lucky would inevitably be let down or, worse, convince themselves that the experience was greater than it actually had been. When people spend a bunch of money on something or go through a prolonged hassle to get it, they tend to do all sorts of mental gymnastics to convince themselves it was worth it. Otherwise, buyer's remorse can sink in and you can't brag about it to your friends.

Instead of talking about the menu, the critics were writing about how they had to enlist legions of interns to try to get them in, and how they still failed. No plan of attack worked. The risk was that if the critics couldn't reliably get into Ko, they might not be able to give the cooking a fair shake. The rule of thumb for food criticism is that you eat at a restaurant three times before assessing it.

Adam Platt, the grumpy critic for *New York* magazine, broke protocol and wrote his review after only one visit. Bruni came in all three times.

They ate it up.

The James Beard Awards Committee nominated Ko for Best New Restaurant, and we won.

You're pretty far into this book now. I haven't been patting myself on the back too much, have I? I think I've been a sufficiently Debbie Downer–like narrator when it comes to my own achievements. Well, listen, I'm not afraid to tell you that I was proud to be right about this one. Not the reviews or the awards, necessarily, but the insurgency of it all. I loved that just when people had decided we were media darlings, we flipped the story to our advantage.

The only benefit to tying your identity, happiness, well-being, and self-worth to your business is that you never stop thinking about it or worrying over what's around the corner. If I have been quick to adapt to the changing restaurant landscape, it is because I have viewed it as a literal matter of survival. I have never allowed myself to coast, or believed that I deserve for life to get easier with success. That's where hubris comes from. The worst version of me was the one who, as a preteen, thought he had what it took to be a pro golfer. I believed my own hype, and I was a snotty little shit about it. The humiliation and pain of having it all slip through my fingers is something I'd rather never feel again. And so, I choose not to hear compliments or allow myself to bask in positive feedback. Instead, I spend every day imagining the many ways in which the wheels might fall off. This book itself is a source of near-constant uneasiness. I'm afraid that the people and restaurants and accomplishments I've commemorated in writing will all have disappeared by the time it's been published. If you hold on too tightly to what you have, it'll only hurt more once it's gone, and from an early age, I've had an overwhelming fear that it can all be taken away. Around every corner is another threat.

9

HE'LL KILL YOU, AND THEN HE'LL GO TO WORK ON YOU

Speaking of threats, the Billionaire was the first person from the world of the power lunch to drag himself downtown for a meal with us at Noodle Bar.

I assumed he wasn't just coming in for the food—guys like the Billionaire are always on the hunt for investment opportunities. I got the sense that he was doing me a favor by checking us out, so at the conclusion of his lunch, I told him it was on the house.

"Son, that's no way to run a business," he said, leaving a hundred bucks on the counter as he walked out the door.

The idea of taking on a large investor had always been a prospect I kept on the far back burner, but it was coming up more and more as Momofuku grew. Thus far, I had said no to anyone who came knocking, out of fear of being screwed. Even a good deal can come with unforeseen complications. So I did the best I could with Dad's input and an accountant on Long Island. I handled all the numbers myself with an unconvincing mix of constant worry and laissez-faire affect. I didn't hesitate to make Quino a partner in Momofuku or give many of the cooks a piece of the restaurants where they worked—not that their equity amounted to anything. Every dollar of profit went straight back into the company.

That's not to say I was uninterested in making money. Money would mean we could plan longer term, open more restaurants, take better care of people. I wasn't ready to yield to the suits in New York, but the one path I'd seen other chefs walk with some degree of success was very appealing to me: Vegas.

The town seemed strangely pure. Nobody disguised their motives: *I want money and I want pleasure and then I want to leave.* It would be an interesting challenge to offer a compelling dining experience in a place no one expected to find one. It would also be a welcome reprieve from the New York slog. *I didn't ask for any of this,* I'd whine to myself. I could be happy in the desert, sitting at the sports book, playing poker every day. I could be like Michael Corleone, moving the family business to Nevada.

Quino and I traveled to Vegas a few times to entertain offers from people on and off the Strip. Because they always showed us a good time, we were inclined to hear them out, but we never took any of it too seriously.

Then the Casino Boss came knocking.

The Casino Boss had done more to draw people to Vegas than Wayne Newton, Siegfried, Roy, and all their white tigers combined. He wanted to talk to us about his new resort. Given the man's stature and legacy, I gave the offer more consideration than all the others.

The Casino Boss flew us in and showed us the over-the-top hospitality we had come to expect. (But honestly, if you've seen one giant suite with floor-to-ceiling windows and TVs built into the mirrors, you've seen them all.) A lackey accompanied us everywhere we went. I found myself holding my pee because I was sure someone was watching me in the bathrooms. Everyone we met spoke incessantly about the Casino Boss and his ways.

At one point I spotted the man himself and raised my hand to wave, but one of his subordinates redirected me toward a tour of the Boss's Ferrari collection.

Over the weekend, we shared some meals with the Casino Boss's brain trust and heard their case for opening a Noodle Bar in Vegas. In conversation, these people all spoke glowingly about their past corporations and ventures as a proxy for talking about themselves. I had the distinct feeling of a cow being fattened up for slaughter.

Another chef who'd worked with the Casino Boss served as one of our ambassadors over the weekend. While in Vegas I'd heard a rumor about this chef and the circumstances under which he'd agreed to open his Vegas restaurant. The story was that he had been flying on a private plane when he heard the sales pitch. Once the flight landed, the chef was not allowed to deplane until he signed the papers.

I thought that in coming to Vegas I'd avoided getting in the water with the sharks, but instead I'd swum right into the path of the biggest alpha predator anyone had ever seen.

On the final night of the trip, the Casino Boss rented out half a nightclub for us. It was astonishingly unnecessary, but I accepted the extra-ness of it all.

I was sitting on a couch by myself when the chef-ambassador approached. He whispered something in my ear. I couldn't make out what he was saying over the music, but I heard a message very clearly in my head:

"Don't do this deal."

• • •

At one point, I almost sold Momofuku to a giant fast-food chain. Let me do my best to tell you the story within the confines of my nondis-closure agreement.

They are a big company. We were a small company that wanted to go big. I was very happy. For reasons, it didn't work out. I ███████ ███ that company.

• • •

Here's another one that almost got me.

I had dinner with the Developer at a gaudy Japanese restaurant. Over the course of our meal, three different women joined us at dif-ferent times. They ordered drinks but left without eating. None of their visits overlapped.

"I apologize for the interruptions," said the Developer. "But I'm fucking all three of them."

He told me he had spent years racked with guilt—not about the philandering, necessarily, but because all the travel kept him from seeing his kids.

"That's one of the reasons I don't think I'll ever be a good par-ent," I told him, trying to relate. "I'm married to my work."

"But you know what I did, Dave? Do you know what hap-pened?"

He milked the silence for dramatic effect.

"One day I decided I was no longer going to feel guilt. And you know what? My life has never been better."

I suspected he was a sociopath before we met. Now I was sure of it.

The Developer wanted me to take over a small space on an exclu-sive piece of real estate in one of the hottest markets in the United States.

"I don't care what you do, Dave. I trust you. Just make sure there's a burger and eggs Benedict on the menu," the Developer said. "And serve them at all hours. That's what people want to eat after they fuck."

Despite my reservations about his character, the Developer had a record of excellence and a preternatural skill for creating attractive spaces. I agreed to team up with him, and recruited a husband-and-wife pair of chefs I knew and admired to come onboard. They leapt at the chance to run an intimate restaurant that would cater to rich and famous people from around the world. Negotiations with the Developer went on for months. In the meantime, I took a trip to Northern California to do some work at the Culinary Institute of America's Greystone campus. I was staying at the home of my friend Dr. Larry Turley, the proprietor of Turley Wine Cellars, a former ER doctor, and the father of Ko's first sommelier, Christina Turley. Whenever I saw him, Larry would insist that I come to the vineyard and take some time off. I was obliging him.

Standing outside one morning, looking over a ridge onto the green expanses of Napa Valley, I got a call from my lawyer.

"They want to add a provision about the other property."

As part of our agreement, I had committed to take over the food and beverage operations at another of the Developer's spots. It was an amazing space, but not much had been done to it since the late 1990s. The whole building smelled like a pool changing room. Nevertheless, I'd agreed to tackle the project.

My lawyer explained that there was a last-minute amendment that had nearly escaped his notice: "In the event there's any damage to the structure caused by the restaurant, you would assume responsibility."

Under most circumstances, I wouldn't mind being held responsible if my negligence destroyed someone's building. But I had serious doubts that the restaurant space had ever been brought up to code. I'd seen exposed wood framing in the ceiling that screamed "fire hazard." I was inheriting a house of cards and being told that if it fell, it would be on me. The Developer was trying to fuck me, too. I ran away from him as fast as I could.

I don't think I was being paranoid. I speak to younger chefs about this all the time these days. Think about it. Where were all these people before you were successful? Why would they suddenly be so eager to get into business with you? They're trying to exploit you, confuse you, bum-rush you with deals you don't understand. I know from experience.

10

THANK YOU, SIR, MAY I
HAVE ANOTHER?

IN THE FALL OF 2008, I SIGNED UP TO COOK FOR AN OBAMA CAMPAIGN
fundraiser.

It was going to be an intimate affair, a high-priced function at
someone's loft in SoHo. The senator would not be in attendance, but
I was still very excited. In case you've forgotten, that first election
was a sight to behold. The mere thought of Obama's candidacy could
turn me into the sunniest person on the block.

Our politics aligned on civil liberties, the environment, and a general sense of responsibility to the world, but what really spoke to me
about Obama was the promise he represented. It wasn't only a promise
of middle-class tax relief or campaign reform or universal healthcare.
It was a promise of purpose. Built into the slogans HOPE and CHANGE
was the notion that things *could* get better, as long as we got up and

chased it. I had my doubts about whether plates of sous-vide eggs with caviar and onion soubise—our signature dish at Ko—would make a difference at the ballot box, but that was what I could offer.*

While fervor built around the upcoming election, there was another, far less meaningful contest on the horizon. Chatter was picking up about who would win Michelin stars that year. The Michelin Guide had begun appraising restaurants in New York only a few years earlier, and the local press had never warmed to them. They argued that Michelin was out of step with the dining culture and lacked transparency. No one knew who the anonymous inspectors were or what protocols they followed. To Michelin's critics, the flaws were reflected in their haphazard selections; some restaurants with high ratings from the *Times* and elsewhere were totally blanked by Michelin, while other spots that weren't part of the local conversation were winning one or even two stars. To almost all of the New York food writers, the tire company was an outsider doing a poor job of recognizing legitimate quality.

I admired Michelin's history too much to dismiss it. For all its misfires and shiftiness, the organization and its stars had been the standard of excellence in European kitchens for most of the past century. Michelin stars are among the first prizes you learn to respect and aspire to as a cook—or even a diner. I'd be lying through my teeth if I told you that earning a star wasn't a huge honor.

That, however, does not mean I thought we were in the running. Momofuku restaurants were textbook candidates for a Bib Gourmand—the unstarred recognition that Michelin bestows on

---

*A decade later, chefs are still figuring out how best to use our platform to support the causes we believe in. It's tricky because of all the ways that restaurants can serve the greater good, perhaps the most important is being a space where people come together. My big dream for Momofuku has always been to emulate the classless dining I'd experienced in Asia, where if you want to eat, you have to be comfortable rubbing elbows with people from all walks of life. As a restaurateur, I aim to feed everyone, even those I disagree with. Within reason, of course.

"friendly establishments that serve good food at moderate prices" and describes on their website as "most definitely not a consolation prize."* Bib Gourmand restaurants are something between "cheap eats" and "upscale ethnic spots." I wasn't complaining. The restaurants to which I feel the most kinship are Bib Gourmands. Ssäm had been listed in the category the previous year, and it was great.

It had been less than seven months since we'd opened Ko. My thinking was that Michelin would not be able to look past the cramped quarters and lack of polish in our dining experience, even if they state flat out that their inspectors only care about the food. If we were lucky, they would maybe give us one star in a few years. As the announcement neared, cooks and friends asked if I was excited. I was actually zen about it.

At the Obama dinner, everything went smoothly. The guests were excited to get a peek at what we were serving at our restaurant, where it was still annoyingly difficult to get a reservation. I befriended people who do very good work for others. It was a nice break from the insularity of the food world—an insularity that might be best summed up by the hundreds of hours people were spending speculating about a guide that they'd all agreed sucks.

The cooks were cleaning up at the end of the night when I ducked into a spacious broom closet, took a seat on an overturned bucket, and caught up on emails. I scrolled to a message from Ben Leventhal, the co-founder of *Eater*.

Dude, you got two, he wrote.

What are you talking about?

Michelin. I saw an early copy. Congratulations, sir.

---

*If your only idea of the Michelin Guide comes from the movie *Burnt,* here's a quick primer: it was originally developed as a tool for motorists traveling through the French countryside. (This would be the reason why a tire company is involved with food at all.) The official guidelines describe a one-star restaurant as "high quality cooking, worth a stop." Two stars is "excellent cooking, worth a detour." And three is "exceptional cooking, worth a special journey."

Ko was among the seven restaurants in the city that had earned two stars. Only four establishments—Per Se, Masa, Jean-Georges, and Le Bernardin—had received the full three.

I stayed seated in the closet for another few minutes, not quite sure how to describe the feeling in my stomach.

Looking back, I know what it was.

Dread.

• • •

"You know, we have never awarded a restaurant two stars that I haven't visited myself."

"It's very surreal for us. This is such an honor, sir."

"Never to a restaurant in its first year, either."

Jean-Luc Naret, the director of Michelin at the time, came to check out Ko for himself. It was a couple of months after the announcement, and we were ready for his visit. He did not use aliases. His job was to be the face of Michelin and its anonymous platoon. Although I had heard about chefs in Europe developing relationships with local directors, getting lunch together, eliciting regular feedback, I didn't feel comfortable going any deeper than pleasantries.

"Chef," he continued. "I must ask: do you desire the third star?"

I mumbled something about how I didn't know how to answer that question and how we were thrilled with what we had. I shrank back into the kitchen.

I glanced over at Naret and his companion as often as I could during their meal. I noticed that they were only picking at the food. They seemed pleased but not euphoric. They weren't exactly devouring a dish of hand-torn pasta with chicken-and-snail farce, fines herbes, butter, and a nice little chicken-skin crisp on top—one of Serpico's classic dishes. How could we be a two-star restaurant if we couldn't get the Michelin director to lick his plate clean?

It was such a good dish and I wanted so badly for him to like it.

I was upset, not because we'd failed as a kitchen but because of how much his approval meant to me. This is the power of organizations like Michelin or the World's 50 Best, and it's the reason why chefs loathe and curse them behind closed doors.

You'll observe that a lot of chefs who win a Michelin star say something like, "This is a tremendous honor, but we try not to be driven by awards." They say this because they're simultaneously worried about losing their stars and terrified of the power that these awards possess. It's not just the fact that Michelin can make or break your business, it's the control they have over how you approach or even enjoy your work.

So do I want a third star? Absolutely. Do I want my team to feel the elation of reaching the very top of the food world? Of course I do.

I also fear it.

I fear the inevitable fall from the top. More than that, I fear what it means for people to think they've reached the pinnacle of their profession. What happens to a cook's motivation when the job becomes about maintenance and not improvement?

With a third star, you do everything you can to avoid disturbing the delicate balance you've created. No grind. No friction. You're trapped by your own self-confidence, scared to abandon what you know already works.

I know that not everyone benefits from this kind of emphasis on perpetual struggle, but a lot of people in the culinary world do. You know why Noma continues to be the best restaurant in the world? I'm fairly sure it's because they've never gotten three stars. To me, it's actually a blessing.

To thrive in this business, we need the promise of purpose—a reason to tackle the prep list every morning and push to come up with something new and extraordinary.

We need hope.

— 11 —

THE EUROPEANS

THE MEN FROM DENMARK SPENT MOST OF THE WEEKEND COLLECTING
shells on the freezing shores of Normandy.

"What the hell are they doing, Tosi?"

"Why don't you go ask them?"

"I, uh, don't want to disturb their process. If I trip on a pebble,
I'll fall and crush them and their precious shells."

In February 2008 Tosi and I traveled to the seaside town of Deau-
ville, France, for a conference called Omnivore, where chefs demo
new dishes and talk about their ideas. This sort of gathering became
common after the astonishing rise of elBulli.

elBulli was only a restaurant for half the year. The rest of the time
it was a full-on research-and-development program and dedicated
culinary lab. The chef-brothers behind elBulli, Ferran and Albert

Adrià, would close up shop for six months of the year and move into
a workshop in Barcelona to come up with an entirely new menu for
the following season. People often reduced what elBulli did to the
term *molecular gastronomy,* which I think is a bit of marketing mumbo
jumbo that unfairly paints their approach as somehow unnatural.
It also misses the point. At elBulli, Ferran and Albert called every
assumption about cooking into question. While other chefs were
more or less convinced that everything under the sun had already
been done, the Adriàs unlocked astounding new methods of cooking and serving food year after year. All that science was a means to a
much greater artistic end.

The Adriàs' charisma made it so that every chef of the era felt
that they needed their own stage on which to perform in front of
an audience. Pretty soon there was a full-blown circuit of festivals,
sort of like fashion week for food freaks.* If they wanted to, chefs
could spend the entire year away from their restaurants, attending
gatherings and cooking collaborative dinners, usually on the local
tourism board's dime. There was Madrid Fusión and Gastronomika
in Spain. Identità Golose in Italy. Omnivore in France. A lot of
these events were about making money through corporate spon-
sors. As chefs grew wiser to the scheme, they would hand the cooking responsibility over to their assistants. The quality of talent got
worse. Chefs cried out for something smaller and smarter. Hence,

------

*These things can be a slog. Here's my patented approach to event cooking: shoot
for 70 percent. My philosophy is based on an apocryphal story I've heard about
how a large financial services firm used to choose their new analysts. They didn't
hire people who scored 100 on their Series 7 exam. They wanted people who
purposely aimed for 70, because it meant you knew the material so well that you
could confidently shoot for a C-minus and get it. That's where you want to be
when you're cooking for events. Not the worst and not the best. Whether it's a
cooking demo or a collaborative dinner, trying to impress people is a fool's errand.
You can either fail spectacularly or you can succeed, which only means people
will expect more from you. Be smart enough not to break your back over these
one-off get-togethers.

more intimate gatherings like Cook It Raw, MAD, and Gelinaz! These days, everyone just wants a Netflix show. If I sound jaded, it's because I am.

But this was my first rodeo, and Europe was still an enigma to me. The coolest shit was happening over there. The chefs had an impenetrable air of disaffected intellectualism. I imagined them discussing Descartes after service, with a cigarette burning in one hand and a glass of cloudy *vin jaune* in the other.

The two men on the beach were René Redzepi and his sous-chef, Christian Puglisi, from Noma, which had been climbing the ranks of the World's 50 Best Restaurants list. They opened in Copenhagen the same year as Noodle Bar, and the buzz around Redzepi had spread to New York. We'd met once, briefly, when he dropped into Ssäm Bar, but mostly I went off rumors. Redzepi had been cooking since his late teens and had been a star pupil at the French Laundry and elBulli. I'd heard a little bit about the food he was making. I had his very first cookbook, *Noma: Nordic Cuisine,* in my collection. His thing at Noma, as I understood it, was foraging. Eating stuff from the ground.

True to form, Redzepi was gnawing on a leaf while he scavenged the beach. He would pick up a shell, hold it up to the light, and turn it over, as if he were inspecting a champagne glass for smudges.

The next day I made kimchi on stage. Needless to say, live demos are not my forte, but it was perfectly fine. I talked about history and deceptive simplicity. I talked about my cross-cultural background, living and working in America, my unique perspective.

With my task complete, I joined the crowd to enjoy the rest of the program. A pig in shit, I fixed my attention on Pierre Gagnaire, Michel Bras, Jean-François Piège, Andoni Luis Aduriz, and several other chef heroes I'd never seen in the flesh.

Redzepi and Puglisi walked onto the stage holding a big, black foam box. They switched off the lights in the hall and began playing a video that opened with scenes from the chilly Copenhagen harbor

and the centuries-old waterfront warehouse that contained their restaurant. The event had a wine sponsor—one of those super oxidative
whites that someone had proudly described as smelling like a jackass.
The soundtrack for Redzepi's presentation was Beck's "Jack-Ass."

"What if all the inspiration we need is right in our backyard?"
began Redzepi's live narration, which I'll now piece together for you
from memory.

His delivery was gentle but confident.

"When we first began Noma, most people didn't understand our
approach. They called us 'seal fuckers.'"

In the video, Redzepi travels to a castle outside the city to visit
with one of his farmers and pluck gorgeous produce straight from the
ground.

"That's Søren Wiuff. He makes the most stunning carrot you
could ever imagine. We have him age some of them for us. You
would be shocked by the flavor. Basted in butter, it's better than any
steak."

Onscreen, Redzepi notices shattered seashells buried in the same
soil where the vegetables grow. The angle widens, revealing the coast
off in the distance.

"The unspoken rule in Copenhagen was that a nice restaurant
had to serve caviar, foie gras, and wines from Bordeaux in order to
be taken seriously. But why give diners what they could find a short
flight away, where it would no doubt be better?"

We watched the produce being delivered to Noma's kitchen,
where they packed it into a big, black foam box. Redzepi reached the
end of his scripted speech just as this was playing out onscreen.

"At Noma, our mission is to dig deeper than ever before, to discover what our own terroir has to offer. I can tell you that we have
only scratched the surface."

With that, we heard the sound of a donkey hee-hawing. The
lights in the auditorium came back on. The screen transitioned to
a live, overhead shot of the counter, the stove, and the black box.

Puglisi removed the lid. In the case were the same vegetables that had appeared in the video, arranged exactly as we had seen seconds earlier. These two were not fucking around.

They started cooking. Puglisi prepped the pile of vegetables and Redzepi made a beurre monté. Puglisi whipped out the bucket of shells from the beach. He pulverized them in batches, handing the powder to Redzepi, who added it to the butter and strained the mixture into a container.

Redzepi went on to make five different vegetable dishes using that shell butter. The presentation concluded right as the clock on stage ran out. Fifteen minutes. They got the only standing ovation of the weekend.

"I'm glad I didn't have to follow them," I said to Tosi as we clapped.

"Don't sell yourself short," she teased. "Showing everyone how to open a jar of kimchi was pretty cool."

• • •

At the afterparty I almost knocked over two people as I bulldozed through the crowd to shake Redzepi's hand.

"Hi, René, I'm Dave from Momofuku in New York, you ate at my restaurant last year. I just wanted to say that what you did earlier today was one of the most amazing things I've ever seen."

"I know who you are, chef," he laughed. "When are you going to come visit us in Copenhagen? It's amazing in the summer."

"Oh, yeah?"

That was the last question I got to ask him. Redzepi spent the rest of our chat casually grilling me about the restaurants, my upbringing, New York, the state of my romantic life. René can give off a supremely chill vibe, but I could tell he was absorbing and processing everything I said. Naïve journalists would often wonder how such a stereotypically calm and happy Dane could make it in the kitchen, but I could see that he was not like other Danes. In fact, he was born in the former Yugoslavia. His family fled the war. In Copenhagen, his dad found work as a cabdriver, his mother as a cleaner. As a young boy, René was mocked for being not so tall and not so Scandinavian. He started working in kitchens when he was fifteen and never stopped.

"What are you doing later tonight?" he asked.

I downplayed whatever dinner plans I had.

"Why don't you come for a snack around eleven-thirty? Ask one of the staff to show you into the kitchen in the back."

I took a nap and returned to the hall, where the crew was almost finished breaking down the stage. I asked a volunteer if they could show me to the kitchen.

"The festival is over, sir."

"Oh. René Redzepi said to meet him there."

"Oh, you are here with the chefs? Of course!"

He escorted me to the catering kitchen in the basement. Redzepi spotted me walking down the stairs and came to the door.

I held his handshake for too long, distracted by the scene behind him: Michel Bras, the humble master craftsman, wearing jeans and tournéeing carrots with his Laguiole pocketknife; Franck Cerutti, Alain Ducasse's longtime right-hand man, filleting fish; and a large man with a squiggly mass of black hair who was wearing an apron but otherwise looked ready for the aperitivo hour with his fancy slippers, pristine blue dress shirt, and scarf wrapped around his neck. This third man looked agitated. He was screaming in Italian.

"That's Fulvio, I think you know. He's a little upset. They lost his arugula."

I wasn't familiar with Fulvio Pierangelini, but I liked him immediately. He was freaking out over family meal, which made him a legend in my book.

"What can I help with, René?"

"No, chef, don't worry. Have a glass of wine."

And then some of the greatest chefs in the world stood around a steel prep table and ate dinner together. I don't speak French or Italian and there were no subtitles. I remember risotto, salad, wine, and cheese. Jean-Yves Bordier, the master butter maker from Brittany, was there with his rosy cheeks and twenty pounds of his products. I've never eaten so much butter in my life.

I tried to blend into the wall and absorb the feeling into my bones.

• • •

I made it to Copenhagen a year later. René put in the good word and I was invited to participate in Cook It Raw, which was something between a culinary jam session and a Boy Scout retreat. The idea was that every year ten or so chefs would visit a different region of the world together to gain inspiration, shoot the shit, and cook. The trip would culminate in a collaborative dinner inspired by the location. In its early editions, Cook It Raw was one of the purest of all the chef gatherings.

The lineup in Copenhagen was impressive. For one thing, they'd booked Albert Adrià, who, in addition to being one of the most innovative pastry chefs of all time, ran R&D for elBulli. He and his brother, Ferran, had recently closed the restaurant, and Albert was coming out of semi-retirement to join us. Then there was Pascal Barbot, whose cooking at l'Astrance in Paris was a direct inspiration for Ko; Daniel Patterson, the most forward-thinking chef in San Francisco; Massimo Bottura, who was agitating the establishment in his country by messing with classic Italian food; and several others, including René, our host.

We all stayed at the Admiral Hotel, a nautical-themed spot on the water. The morning of the dinner I rode my bike through town to Noma. It was spring. The city was perfect. All the beautiful people of Denmark were happy.

Inside Noma, not so much.

The dinner was thematically linked to an ongoing climate sum-mit, and our task was to cook dinner using minimal electricity. I was one of only a few chefs who adhered to the proscription. My course was a savory broken buttermilk panna cotta surrounded by an apple dashi and herbs. I was pretty proud of it, until I started seeing what everyone else was making.

My eyes were locked on Barbot, whom I idolized. One of the most polished chefs in the world, he was also a great improviser. Every night at l'Astrance, he risked his three Michelin stars to come up with new dishes on the fly. Here at Noma, he was layering slices of marinated mackerel in a dainty espresso cup with eel, Frangelico, and mushroom purée.

Meanwhile, René was pacing around, asking everyone the same question.

"Where the fuck is Iñaki? Has anyone heard from him?"

Iñaki Aizpitarte didn't have a fancy restaurant. He hadn't gone to culinary school. He didn't train at any Michelin-starred palaces of gastronomy. He was a dishwasher who taught himself how to cook. He owned a bistro in Paris that was turning heads all over Europe.

"It's like this every fucking time." René sighed. "Every fucking time."

The last anyone had seen of Iñaki was the previous night. We'd had some drinks in town after spending the day foraging in the sub-urbs. Around one a.m., everyone returned to the hotel to get some rest. Iñaki stayed out to polish off the second magnum of wine.

"Don't be angry wiz me, René. I love you," Iñaki said when he finally surfaced, giving Redzepi a kiss on both cheeks. "Ah, Dah-vid Chang? A pleasure again to see you. It's very nice here in Copen-agen, no?"

Iñaki settled in to work next to Barbot. I asked him what he was going to make.

"I will see now."

Iñaki began pulling ingredients from Barbot's garbage. From a pile of mushroom and eel scraps, he made a consommé, then Cryovac'd it with pieces of raw lobster, putting the package through the vacuum sealer multiple times to force flavor into the shellfish. He grated pistachios and mixed them with orange zest and a handful of sea salt to produce what seemed to me a psychedelic furikake. He puréed squab liver and sliced the lobster into thin medallions. He hit the consommé with a squeeze of lemon. He put it all together.

It was one of the most outrageously good dishes I have ever tasted, and I would bet almost anything that if you asked him today, Iñaki would have zero clue what he cooked that night. People sometimes ask if you can be born a great chef. If Iñaki didn't exist, my answer would be no, but the guy is a natural culinary genius.

After the last course was cleared, an impromptu conga line broke out in the dining room. Everyone was riding high. We headed out to celebrate at a bar that René's wife, Nadine, had rented out for us. It was supposed to be a small gathering for the chefs, but everybody at the dinner came along. Everybody who heard about it came along. I watched Massimo mix cocktails using his credit card as a spoon. Iñaki held court in a booth. Even René, king of the Irish goodbye, stayed out for most of the night.

The sun was shining by the time I headed back to the Admiral. In my memory, bodies were lining the path home—the world's top food critics and chefs asleep on the sidewalk—but that can't be right. What I did see without question, however, was Iñaki passed out in the elevator. Or rather, halfway in the elevator. His torso had made it in; his legs were still in the lobby. Every few seconds the doors would close on him, briefly lifting him off the ground. Neither the sensation of being rotisseried nor the sound of the elevator alarm could rouse him.

It was the best weekend a chef could ever imagine, and every three or four months for the next few years, I'd hang out with different iterations of that crew. New members joined up. Quique Dacosta. Magnus Nilsson. Alex Atala. People from both inside and outside the restaurant community often ask me with a mixture of wonder and resentment about being in the cool chefs club. The company line is that there's no such thing.

Well, the fact is there *was* a club.* And yes, for years, we were a boys' club. There's no use in denying that. We didn't look around and ask ourselves where the women were. It's abundantly clear to me now why people viewed our little clique with distaste. Looking back, I do, too. It was only the latest in a long line of male-centric inflection points in modern chef history. Moreover, a lot of the material we presented at these gatherings was bullshit. In the new millennium, chefs began to see themselves as evangelists. People asked and we freely offered our thoughts on science, creativity, the environment, politics, art. At the same time, it wasn't a bad thing for a high school dropout to have the chance to hear Harold McGee speak, or for a culinary student to see that their work wouldn't necessarily be dismissed as a minor form of culture, or for a chef from Peru to find a spiritual sibling living in the northernmost stretch of Sweden.

In our separate corners of the world, we were all wrestling with the same issues. There was no one else who understood the staggering weirdness of the opportunities being presented to us. We were the last generation to live through a time before all of this and simultaneously the last generation to benefit from it. In the coming decade,

---

*Some scenes from Cook It Raw in Lapland: Immersion circulators cooking reindeer tongues in Bottura's bathtub. Yoshihiro Narisawa and his kimono-clad wife, Yuko, breaking down a whole bear. I made reindeer-milk dashi to accompany fish I was slow-cooking in a wood-burning sauna. When I went to check on the fish, I found my chef-partner, Davide Scabin, and his wife lying naked under a bearskin blanket. He'd built the fire up to a huge inferno. My fish was literally on fire. What an incredible shitshow.

food would become more democratic. More restaurants, more knowledge, less attention span. It would be harder for a chef to stand out as
a singular figure.

Of course, that may only be what I'm telling myself because I
don't know where the party is anymore.

PART TWO

DOWN AND
BACK AGAIN

*Abandoning the chronological telling of this story to explore subjects
I've yet to fully process with Dr. Eliot: mania; some armchair
philosophizing and shameless artistic comparisons; the limits of
anger; racist chicken; the joy of pushing the boulder back up the hill.*

12

FIGS ON A PLATE

I'VE HAD A LOT OF PRACTICE TELLING THE STORIES FROM THE FIRST HALF of this book. I have less experience talking about what comes next.

I suppose I may as well start where my last book left off.

Leading up to the release of *Momofuku* in 2009, Tony Bourdain had invited me to join him as part of the New York Wine and Food Festival. I hated public speaking, but the publisher had impressed upon me the importance of doing promotional events. The title of our talk was "I Call Bullshit." The organizers wanted us to rant.

It was the first time Tony and I had ever appeared onstage together. As a matter of fact, I'm not sure whether or not we had even met when our mutual book agent, Kim Witherspoon, got Tony to blurb the *Momofuku* cookbook. He was already becoming a mythic figure in food, but the truth is, it took me a while to come around.

When *Kitchen Confidential* came out, I was cooking at Craft. Cooks and chefs had yet to become cool or even normalized, and honestly we were all skeptical about this chef of a not-great restaurant in New York writing a tell-all about our business.

Tony never worked in the upper echelon of restaurants. That gave many of us in the industry reason to thumb our noses at him, but it's also exactly what made him remarkable. He was a lifelong line cook—the kind of guy who never aspires to climb the ladder of fancy restaurants. He represented the majority of cooks, and he wrote about our world with extraordinary intelligence and empathy.

When he visited The French Laundry for *A Cook's Tour,* the full weight of Tony's genius dawned on me. Maybe he couldn't keep up with a chef like Thomas Keller in the kitchen, but he understood what made Keller special and he masterfully communicated it to his audience. He was the guy you wanted to hang out with because he was, first and foremost, a fan of food and restaurants. Many of the stories he championed in his writing and television shows were the ones that chefs care about: camaraderie, honesty, creativity, and the Latin American cooks who prop up the whole business. The person who may have done the most to legitimize our profession was the one we originally didn't think had the chops.

The more time Tony and I spent together, the more I came to love him. We shared a lot in common, but we also filled in the holes in our respective perspectives. I know that sounds vague, but it's impossible to pinpoint the ways in which he impacted my life. It's like trying to explain why you love a sibling. All I can say is that he was always there.

In the green room before the event, he barely touched the beer he'd cracked open. I tore through every last can in the ice bucket before transitioning to bourbon.

"Sure you don't want any?" I asked.

"I'm good, but by all means, go to town."

The stage had been made up to look like a living area in an

IKEA showroom, and more beers were waiting for us when we walked out.

Tony lobbed me a softball to start.

"What do you think of all this Momofuku hype?"

I talked about how we were overrated, and the self-flagellation went over well. As the night continued, we zeroed in on mutual objects of scorn: Guy Fieri's hair. Cupcakes. Paula Deen. Safe targets. We also spoke about what we loved: taco trucks and underappreciated chefs like Gray Kunz and Christian Delouvrier. More easy points.

We waded into rougher waters when Tony referred to Alice Waters as "Pol Pot in a muumuu." I didn't share his view. I admired Alice and what she had created at Chez Panisse. I loved dining at the restaurant. Plus, the couple of times we'd met, Alice had been warm and generous, and treated me like her own kin. I didn't think she was the chosen one or anything, but I also didn't think she deserved our wrath.

"She means well," I said, deflecting.

I could sense that the audience was thirsty for more blood. Not wanting to disappoint them, I offered a consolation: "I *will* call bullshit on San Francisco, though."

"Okay. What's wrong with San Francisco?"

"There's only a handful of restaurants out there manipulating food."

"What does that mean?"

"Fucking every restaurant in San Francisco is serving figs on a plate with nothing on it. *Do something* with your food."

The Bay Area has the best produce in the country, which had given rise to a culinary approach that prioritized ingredients above all else. A San Francisco chef's only job was to amplify the intrinsic qualities of what they found at the market or harvested from the garden.

That's great, but come on—it was getting ridiculous. Single-minded fanaticism about farm-to-table cooking was ruining Bay Area restaurants. Rinsing under water had come to qualify as cooking. I'd once ordered persimmons for dessert in San Francisco, and that's exactly what I got: a plate of whole, unsliced persimmons. No honey, no salt, nothing. These hippies didn't know what it really meant to cook. In my opinion, the only restaurants in Northern California with a distinct point of view were run by chefs who had left New York City.

New York was where real cooking happened. We might have inferior ingredients, but we made do, putting them through multiple stages of enhancement before reaching the plate. Everyone in the Bay Area was relying on their crutch. I wasn't the only person saying this. Years earlier, Daniel Patterson—one of the only chefs I could cite as doing any proper cooking in San Francisco—made a similar observation in a *New York Times* op-ed, and he was vilified for it. This part of the world that had embraced so many forward-thinking movements—from the Summer of Love, to the beatniks, to the Grateful Dead, to Harvey Milk, to the tech boom—was set in its boring foodways.

I was confident that I explained my reasoning onstage. I gave context. The crowd seemed pleased with my assessment. I didn't give it another thought.

• • •

I was set to promote the book in San Francisco the following month. The publisher stacked my schedule with readings, Q&As, panel discussions, signings, and demos. I still wonder what the scene must have looked like in the publicity department as they saw my figs-on-a-plate comment spread across the Internet like a horrifying fungus.

My peers in the Bay Area didn't take my ribbing lightly. They were enraged. I couldn't grasp why they cared what a New York chef thought about their city. The ordeal only grew more disastrous when a local SF blog asked me to make my case. I took the bait and suggested that everybody in San Francisco needed to smoke more weed.

The Asia Society, which had signed on to host a big book event, pulled the plug when an anonymous local chef complained. A spokesperson issued a statement: "This wasn't just a barstool conversation. It was for the public record, in front of hundreds of people. I understand bad boy talk, but you can't do that in public."

The public record. Good Lord.

We trudged on with the remaining events. For our final night in town, we planned a party at a bar in North Beach. I invited everyone I knew and anyone I came across. I'm not exaggerating. During a book signing at the Google campus, I told each and every person that they should come out for drinks later. On me.

That night, I set up shop at a corner table. The bar was selling a beer I'd never seen before: little seven-ounce pony bottles of Miller High Life. I thought they were adorable and ingenious. With their minuscule size, the watery brew within would be long gone before it had a chance to warm up in your hand. I ordered every single bottle in the house—120 beers—and waited for the people I'd met to start showing up.

Only one of them did: Chris Ying, a former cook turned book editor and evidently the last member of San Francisco's food circle whom I hadn't alienated. Had he and three or four of his friends not come, I would have undoubtedly found myself in the ER getting my stomach pumped. As it was, our little group finished every last beer. At the end of the night, I leaned out a second-story window to get some air and went crashing to the sidewalk below. Ying was standing outside and started to rush over to help but stopped when he saw me tumble into a crouched position like an oversized Korean Simone Biles. According to his account, I started tying my shoe like nothing had happened.

That's the person I remember being. Following the book tour, I detected a shift in how other people saw me. There was more scrutiny, more attention. Part of it was due to the continued success of my restaurants, but food media was also expanding. *Eater* was now a full-fledged national operation. Their strategy for meeting the requirements of a twenty-four-hour news cycle included publishing every offhand remark I made in the vicinity of one of their reporters. Beyond that, it seemed that whenever anyone needed a comment on a story vaguely related to the culinary world, they called me. A writer could be doing an exploration of Peruvian corn varietals and think to herself, *What this article needs is a quote from David Chang.* Figs on a plate did not die, either. Almost a year later, a website published a roundup of restaurants in San Francisco that were serving cheeky variations on the dish—the city's chefs were making hay out of my affront.

This was the period when I felt the weight of public attention at its most crushing. I was unnerved by the number of people writing about me and talking to me. It'd be a lie to say I didn't I enjoy the attention, but chefs, generally speaking, are about as well equipped to deal with fame as child actors, which is to say, not at all. I was stressing out, questioning what was real. Later on, I'd ask Dr. Eliot if there was a chance that I was schizophrenic, which he assured me I was not. That was a disappointment. What an easier explanation that would have been.

There would be more reverberations. I did a cameo on *Treme,* David Simon's follow-up to *The Wire.* I started doing segments on *Jimmy Fallon.* I showed up on *Letterman. Time* chose me for its annual list of the 100 most influential people of 2010, along with Barack Obama, Ben Stiller, Serena Williams, Steve Jobs, Alice Munro, Zaha Hadid, and ninety-three others, in whose company I felt like a total phony.

Later they gave me a TV show, and then another one. They gave me a podcast. They asked me to write *another* book.

Most of the time, I feel like I'm barely holding on.

13

KEEPING IT TOGETHER

THE ONLY PIECE OF ART HANGING AT NOODLE BAR IS A MASSIVE FRAMED
photo of The Band taken in 1968 by Elliott Landy, when they were
recording *Music from Big Pink*. People waiting in front of our host
stand always brush up against the photo as they shuffle around to let
fellow diners in and out the door.

I have the same picture hanging in my house. I love it so much.
It captures their rugged humility perfectly: nothing more than five
hairy dudes standing on a misty hill in Woodstock. I've always considered The Band to be the platonic ideal of a group. There was no
obvious front man; everybody took turns singing. They weren't the
best-looking bunch and they didn't ham it up. Several members could
play more than one instrument. There were honest cracks in the

music they made; some of their recordings are great precisely because they feel like a train that's about to go off the tracks. Far as I could tell, they only cared about playing music and laughing. They were simply The Band.

I wanted Momofuku to be the same kind of imperfect collaborative organism. I tried to avoid putting anyone into a neatly defined role, because that would suck the energy from the company. People had their home bases—Quino and Pemoulie at Noodle Bar, Tien Ho at Ssäm, and Serpico at Ko—but those outposts could never exist discretely. For my part, there were periods when I was cooking every day—that was definitely the case when we were getting Ko off the ground—and many others when I wanted to be off the line. I'd focus on the business side, tossing ideas for dishes to the team.

For a long time, it was understood that The Band's decision to call it quits was amicable. They planned their last show and filmed it. Directed by Martin Scorsese, *The Last Waltz* is one of the greatest concert films ever made. Exits don't get any more pure than that.

Of course, it would later emerge that The Band's dissolution was much more complicated, a mess of hurt feelings and clashing egos. There are no clean breakups.

• • •

In the spring of 2009, I got a letter from the people behind the World's 50 Best Restaurants list alerting me that Ssäm Bar had made it onto their annual rankings. They invited me to the ceremony in London. I got the core team tickets and we flew to England in April.

We entered the list at number 31. According to this peculiar voting body of "leaders in the restaurant industry," our restaurant—and its not one but two framed posters of John McEnroe—was better than Alain Ducasse's Le Louis XV in Monaco (number 43). There's a lot I can say about the World's 50 Best, but all that really stands out from that trip is that we all slept in the same hotel room—and that Quino wasn't with us. He was a month away from opening his own restaurant.

We'd officially decided on the split only a few weeks earlier, though we had been parting company for some time.

Quino was never excited about Ko. He wasn't interested in chasing anything fancy, while I'd come around to the idea. He had his style and interests and they didn't extend to making Riesling gelées and dishes that referenced Alain Passard. Quino was focused on pursuits like perfecting the art of cooking over open fire.

Noodle Bar had worked because his flavors naturally complemented my own, despite the fact that they were rooted in different traditions. But the balance of our dynamic was imperfect. Alan Richman wrote an article in 2007 that mentioned a joke we had in the kitchen: if Momofuku ever opened Quino's Mexican restaurant, the press headline would read *David Chang has discovered his Mexican roots.*

Quino was the person you would see cooking if you came into the restaurant. As I've said before, my greatest strength is in creating environments for other people to grow and succeed. I love teams. This sounds like lip service, but I really tried to dispel the notion that Momofuku was all about me. Nevertheless, everyone was laboring in my shadow. All anyone heard in the vicinity of the restaurants was my name. Diners imagined me personally executing every single aspect of their experience. It didn't matter if I wasn't even in the building, I could still suck the air out of a room.

It was probably a bitter pill to swallow, but Quino never forced the issue, not out loud anyway. And I didn't want to address the unsaid. So we punted.

As the news trickled out that he was leaving, I started to panic. I didn't want to cut ties with the person who'd saved me before we even opened. He was part of Momofuku's DNA. He'd stood by my side when there was zero promise of success. He'd compensated for my critical failings, and he was a hell of a cook. I'll say it again: he was my family.

I'm bad at letting people go, whether by their choice or mine. I scream and shout a lot—too much—but I always have a hard time firing anyone. I like knowing that everybody is around. I yearn for the acceptance and comfort of friends and family. I hate the idea that they'll leave me. It drags up all manner of old hurts. I feel foolish for trusting that they ever cared about me or Momofuku.

At least in this case the ending was amicable. I did what I could to help Quino get his awesome Williamsburg restaurant, the Brooklyn Star, off the ground.

He was gone and we'd convinced ourselves that it was the natural evolution, but I couldn't shake the feeling that I'd taken him for granted or used him for my gain. Had I really done everything I could to give him the shine he deserved? Why hadn't we opened the taco place, really? Perhaps I was fooling myself into thinking I was an honorable person when, in fact, I'd have no problem leaving behind a trail of bodies as I forged ahead. Was my loyalty to the staff dependent on their own fealty to me? I didn't want to believe it. I thought there was plenty of room for all of us to succeed together, but maybe that was a lie, too.

They would all leave sooner or later—some for greener pastures; others burned out. Success is hard. Communication was poor. I tried my best to keep the band together with duct tape and string. I felt each departure like a puncture wound, but my outward response was always the same: *Fuck it.** We'll be better for it.*

• • •

---

*Or, more often than not, *Fuck them.*

"When do you think they're finally going to show up and tell us that our time is up?"

Tosi asked me this during one of our regular pre-service walks around the neighborhood. Our impending doom was a frequent subject of our chats. Neither of us could believe our luck. In a couple of short years she's gone from reluctant pastry chef at Ko to presiding over a burgeoning business of her own in Milk Bar. In many ways she was better at handling success than I was.

People who had completely written me off were coming out of the woodwork. One day I got a call from a few former classmates who would have sooner pushed me down a flight of stairs than spoken to me in high school. These were the same guys who had said things like "I need to take a shower to wash the gook off" after hooking up with Asian girls in school. Now there was a class reunion coming up and they were inviting me to hang out. That sort of interaction really screwed with my head. I didn't become famous for being handsome or athletic or musically gifted. I was just a cook.

Speaking of deceptive appearances, on the surface, Tosi was this *Brady Bunch*–looking character who knit scarves for regulars, but underneath she was a massively creative cook—gifted but never too self-serious. While the rest of us at Momofuku raged and roared, she was an assassin.

Her ascent began at Ko. I had always viewed dessert as gratuitous, an incongruous moment where the pastry chef would inevitably interrupt the story you'd been trying to tell through the menu. But the desserts Tosi developed for Ko greatly enhanced our effort. The opening menu culminated with a McDonald's-inspired fried apple pie that could bring the Hamburglar to his knees, and a panna cotta that tasted exactly like the milk that's left at the bottom of the bowl when you finish all the cornflakes. If "cereal milk" seems like a cliché flavor today, it's only because she fucking invented it.

Most people found Tosi's dishes to be charming and clever. I thought they were among the most subversive creations in the history of American dining. Tosi grew up in a suburban household in Virginia, feeding her limitless energy with horrendous amounts of Dairy Queen and junk food. While so many pastry chefs devote themselves to mastering the European standards, Tosi did not shun what had shaped her. It helped her stand out. She developed her fluency in Americana into a cheery rebellion at Milk Bar, which started out as a bakery in the back room of Ssäm Bar selling confections like birthday cake truffles and "Compost Cookies." There were no canelés, macarons, or mille-feuilles on the premises. The point of Milk Bar was to challenge the notion that a great pastry chef had to be a French-trained dude. People caught onto Tosi's brilliance quickly.

As we walked back to the restaurant after another one of our frequent strolls, we received news that a recent hire who had gone to the hospital with a bad tummy ache had returned with a hepatitis A diagnosis.

Hep A is not life-threatening, but it may as well be to a restaurant owner. The disease is transmitted through the consumption of liquids or foods that have come into contact with the fecal matter of an infected person. I learned this by searching "hep A" on my phone. It took a while to type out those four letters because my hands were shaking so much.

My business was in danger. By extension, Tosi's business was in danger, too. We had no idea how many staff and customers could have been infected during Cook Zero's incubation period, when he didn't yet know he had fallen under the Hep's mighty spell. We wouldn't know unless others got sick. I was scared shitless, but Tosi had schooled me in thoroughness. We alerted the Department of Health and Mental Hygiene immediately. We learned that the DOH waits a week before closing down a business that's had a hep A scare. I didn't want to sit in a holding pattern. I closed down Ssäm

Bar and sent every single member of the team to get tested and vaccinated.

A day later, we were all clear.

I began to think an awful thought. People were going to be our downfall. Unpredictable, sick, uncaring people.

14

CARPETBAGGING

BETWEEN THE STAFF DEPARTURES, THE UNRELENTING SPOTLIGHT, AND MY increasing paranoia about all of it falling apart, I fell back on my base instincts: I decided I needed to run as far away as possible.

In order to do so, I finally signed a partnership deal. The first Momofuku restaurant outside Manhattan would be located in a casino ten thousand miles away.

Anytime someone at HQ asked about my new commute, I'd pull up Google Maps and measure the distance between New York and Sydney with my thumb and index finger.

"See? It's not so bad."

Distance aside, the move didn't seem like a huge stretch. Most management deals are transactional. A property—say, a hotel or a new shopping center—pays a well-known chef to come in and set up a restaurant with their name and a menu of greatest hits. The chef flies in for the grand opening, walks around glad-handing diners in his whites, and departs a few days later, leaving a lieutenant behind. The contract stipulates the minimum number of appearances the chef has to make each year, usually not a heavy lift.

Management deals are the bread and butter of many global restaurateurs. The true masters of expansion are able to bottle the formulas to their success and consistently maintain a certain vibe and level of quality across vast empires. Nobu Matsuhisa can fly around in a private jet and open three massive sushi restaurants in the same weekend. Joël Robuchon earned three Michelin stars inside the MGM Grand in Vegas.

The restaurant we signed on to open was part of the revitalization of a twenty-year-old casino. I'd met the development team when I was exploring a move to Vegas. Now they were working on a hotel-casino in Australia, and promised me I could choose any space on the property and design it however I liked. They would enable me with anything I needed—in fact, they insisted I buy the most expensive kitchen equipment possible. I jumped onboard without giving it a second thought.

On its face, the project was far from the most attractive opportunity we'd come across. The original architect of the hotel once described the development as the most hideous set of structures his firm ever conceived. In the daylight it looks like three airport Radissons having sex with a riverwalk mall. Locals hate it. No money could really fix the Star. This appealed to me for the same reason Vegas had: I loved the thought of giving people something awesome in the last place they would look for it.

Although we weren't planning to reinvent the wheel at Momofuku Seiōbo, we weren't going to settle for Chang's House of Noods and Buns, either. I wanted to innovate within the ostensibly limited framework of a management deal. The odds had to be completely stacked against us for it to succeed. That's when we do our best work.

With that in mind, when the developers told us we could open anywhere in the complex, I chose the one space they didn't even bother showing me. I noticed it one night when I was trying to find the bathrooms: an awkward black box far away from the main gaming floor in a lost corner of a reviled casino in a country I barely knew.

•   •   •

In the restaurant business, you show your respect for peers by sharing insights that will help them acclimate to a new territory: *What do diners like? Who's the best seafood supplier? How do I find good cooks? What do the critics look like?*

The aid was slow to come in Sydney. Australia has tall poppy syndrome—they don't love people who stick out—so you can imagine how they took to an intrusion by a loudmouth know-it-all from New York. I avoided going to restaurants owned by the famous chefs in the city and stuck to my favorite late-night Cantonese seafood spot, Golden Century. The rest of the time I lived in the casino, where I barked orders and stomped around the kitchen during working hours and gambled in my free time.

An American cowboy parachuting into Australia to open a hotel restaurant was never going to go over well. And so, without alerting anyone back home, I made the decision to move fully into the Star. I'd been traveling back and forth to New York, but now I wasn't going anywhere. The locals would have to get used to it.

Our plan was to lean into the country's bounty, rather than fall back on European ideals. (Ben Shewry was pioneering this approach in Melbourne, but generally speaking, Australian chefs still seemed uncomfortable embracing how special their country is.) We would eschew luxury products from around the globe in favor of local and native ingredients. We were going to show people a good time by unraveling everything they thought to be true about fine dining, including the kind of dishes that are worthy of serving on a tasting menu. Australia is home to some of the finest Chinese, Thai, Malaysian, and Vietnamese restaurants in the world and has a knowledgeable dining public that appreciates them. What better place to upend people's preconceptions about fine dining? It would be a big heartfelt love letter to their country, with a little fuck-you on the side. The imaginary dialogue I had with the city went like this: *You think you're Australian? I'll show you the most Australian restaurant ever built.*

At Seiōbo we assembled one of the finest restaurant teams I've seen anywhere in the world. Serpico was still around, for one thing, as well as three new hires with whom I couldn't wait to get down to business. Chase Lovecky had trained at Jean-Georges and served as chef de partie at Ko; Serpico thought he had great potential. Clayton Wells, the lone Aussie, had put in time for local legend Tetsuya Wakuda. I'd met Ben Greeno while he was still at Noma. We tapped him to be executive chef.

We had a stacked crew, a shiny new kitchen, exciting ingredients to play with, and the full backing of the hotel. We were fully prepared to crush it on the culinary side of things, and . . . we weren't that good.

All restaurants need time. Out the gate things weren't clicking for us in the kitchen. And while Greeno would eventually find his sea legs, what kept us together in those first few months was the front of house.

Earlier in this book, I mentioned how I originally didn't want to employ any waiters at Ko. I'd always felt there was a huge imbalance in the way that servers were compensated with tips while cooks were not. It was my opinion that the kitchen made the only truly essential contribution. Wine lists and waitstaffs were affectations of Western dining. I fully believed that a restaurant with good enough food could win without any of that junk.

In Sydney, I lucked into an all-star service team: Richard

Hargreave, a Brit, had won several top sommelier awards work-ing for renowned Sydney restaurants. I still didn't understand what a sommelier really did, but I'd watch him chatting up guests who would inevitably buy whatever he suggested, and I'd think, *How did he just do that?* Charles Leong, who also helped set up our wine pro-gram, was like Buddha incarnate. He brought calm and serenity to the room whenever he walked in.

Su Wong Ruiz was a Sydney native who had cooked at various spots in New York before transitioning to the dining room. Serpico knew her from his time at a restaurant called Sumile. She agreed to move back to Australia for the project. I'd worked with many tal-ented FOH staff already, but nobody quite like Su and her seemingly infinite reserve of stubbornness.

Right away she clicked with the back of house. Every morning in Sydney, Su and Greeno would have coffee to analyze the previous day and brainstorm. Their rapport inspired the kitchen and the dining room to form the kind of bond that's rare in restaurants, where it can sometimes feel as if there are two opposing teams working toward the same goal. At Seiōbo, the servers had the trust of the cooks to convey the stories behind the food to the dining room. The cooks, in turn, became more eager to engage with guests and to connect with their colleagues across the aisle.

With Su at the helm, Seiōbo—a casino restaurant opened as part of a management deal that critics suspected of being a cash grab—took home the award for best new restaurant in Australia from the country's most prestigious dining guide.*

---

*What Su planted in Sydney was so strong, it lasted into the next generation. Years later, after she and the rest of the opening team moved on, Kylie Javier Ashton took over the front of the house and Paul Carmichael assumed the reins in the kitchen. Paul and Kylie managed to win best restaurant a second time, with a com-pletely new menu and vision of service but the same deep connection between the two. Frankly, I think it's an even more fun place to eat now—probably the closest we've ever gotten to my ideal vision of what a restaurant can be.

The year or so I spent in Australia was an extremely turbulent time, but it wasn't without its breakthroughs. Understanding the importance of a strong relationship between front and back of house—and how dumb I was to write off hospitality before—was chief among them.

• • •

As I mentioned, Greeno would eventually right the ship in the kitchen. He and the team made food you could eat with your fingers, all produced with supertechnical cooking, but never at the expense of deliciousness. For instance, we took inspiration from a classic Joël Robuchon dish of pastry-wrapped langoustine, and filled delicate cylinders of brik pastry with smoked eel and apple puree, and topped it with freeze-dried apple. The menu was full of surprises. We lifted underloved dishes and ingredients out of their context and deployed them in delightful new ways.

In fact, everything we served on the tasting menu at Seiōbo turned out to be completely new, save for two courses. First, we had to give people our pork buns. Every goddamn article about the restaurant mentioned them. The second was our bo ssam. We'd already learned to harness the hypnotic appeal of a whole pork shoulder at Ssäm Bar. At Seiōbo, we added a new twist.

My only job during service was to take care of the bo ssam. The pork luxuriated in a combi (combination steam-and-convection) oven, where I'd glaze it with brown sugar and its own juices every five or ten minutes. With the right combination of fat, temperature, sugar, and attention, a roast pork shoulder can take on a glow more brilliant than the sheen of a perfectly tanned Peking duck. Two-thirds of the way through the menu, just as the fish course was being served, I'd move the pork to a counter that was in full view of the dining room. The direct overhead lighting made it look like a prized museum artifact begging to be stolen.

"What is *that*?" asked nearly every diner who was seated at the chef's counter.

The waiters would deflect the question. "Oh, that's our staff meal. Just some pork for later."

Dessert would come. Guests would ask for the bill.

"You've still got one more course, actually. Hope you don't mind."

By then, the pork shoulder was jiggly-tender with a crunchy-sweet bark. We pulled chunks off with tongs and presented them as is. No condiments, no sides.

"Chef recommends you eat this with your hands." The waiters smiled. "And let me know if you want more."

Every night at the end of service, we took the pork fat that had collected at the bottom of the pan and turned it into little caramels. At La Maison Seiōbo, these were the mignardises.

Much of what we've done at Momofuku has been described as rebellious or as some kind of counterpoint to the rigidity and refinement of the dining establishment. I would argue that it's a little more nuanced than that.

I definitely wasn't thinking about it back then, but I've since come to understand Momofuku through a book I read in college. I'll spare you too much of my amateur philosophical analysis, but here's the top line of what Friedrich Nietzsche is saying in *The Birth of Tragedy:* all great art is based on the coupling of the Apollonian and the Dionysian. The Apollonian represents order, beauty, truth, perfection. In culinary terms, it's a tasting menu. The Dionysian is the unpredictable, the uncontrollable, the extremes of ecstasy and suffering. More like a pig roast or crawfish boil. You don't fully appreciate one without the other. Order is beautiful because of the underlying chaos in the world. Conversely, works of a wild and unexpected nature are awe-inspiring or tragic or moving because they defy our sense of order. A moment of messy, porky joy like the one at Seiōbo is only meaningful because it's happening at the end of a linear tasting menu at a casino restaurant. We are trying to show you both the Apollonian and the Dionysian at the same time.*

Of course, none of the reviews of Seiōbo put it like that, but I was happy with the reception nonetheless. Pat Nourse, Australia's most important critic, loved it. In his review, he wrote exactly what I'd hoped he would: Seiōbo was the last thing you'd expect to find in a casino. Like I said, the big annual ranking, the *Good Food Guide,* named us the best new restaurant of the year. They rate on a scale of one to three hats. Before we showed up, no restaurant in Australia had ever received three in its first year.

In the months spent getting Seiōbo up and running, I fell out of touch with life in the States. I flew back to America as little as possible, which still left me in a state of constant jet lag. Everybody was right. It really is far. And there, on the other side of the world, beyond the view of anyone I knew, I could give in to my worst impulses.

---

*Proper Nietzsche scholars will likely roll their eyes at my applying the Apollonian/Dionysian mechanism to food, as it's usually discussed in terms of music or visual arts.

15

THIRTY-FIVE

SOMETIME DURING SEIŌBO'S FIRST YEAR, I TURNED THIRTY-FIVE, AN AGE that marked an incredible, unbroken streak of personal and professional horrors that brought out the worst in me. I look back on that time with sorrow, regret, terror. I thought I'd be fine revisiting the period for this book, but I find myself pissed that I have to rehash it. I'm completely stuck. I risk looking unsympathetic if I share what I was truly thinking at the time, but it's revisionist history if I change it. All I want is to edit this period of my life—not just for you, but for myself. I wish I could have seen and experienced it all differently. I ~~wish I could~~ am going to rewrite this whole chapter.

• • •

As Momofuku Seiōbo approached its opening date, we needed one more capable line cook. The first candidate arrived for his trail and almost immediately asked what time he would be able to leave. ~~I told him he could leave right then and there. One of the first things another applicant mentioned to me was that if he worked for us, the schedule couldn't interfere with his surfing. He would need Mondays and Fridays off. I said he could have as many days off as he needed, because he would not be working for us.~~ It didn't matter to me what your personal needs were. Any needs were indicative of frailty and I was of the mind that there was no place for weakness in our company. I convinced myself that basic human needs were selfish; ergo, if you needed something beyond the work, you were a bad person. I had conflated my own selfishness with selflessness. I was miserable to work for.

The third candidate was waiting for us when we arrived, and turned out to be one of the best trails I've ever seen. He had great flow and worked clean. He watched everything closely, asked the right questions, took notes. His knives were sharp. Around two a.m., as I was getting ready to leave, he was still wiping down one of the counters. I offered him the job.

He said he appreciated my time but that it didn't seem like a good fit. He was recently married and wanted to have some balance in his life. He politely declined.

I walked in the opposite direction.

~~"Fuck that guy,"~~ "It kills me when they do this. I feel these rejections like a physical attack. I know it sounds irrational. I will spend years trying to understand it. I don't actually begrudge him wanting to see his family. I don't have any reason to hate him. I'm just jealous of him," I told our chef, tossing my apron into the hamper.

• • •

The maintenance man strolled into the restaurant yet again, whistling his tune like Bilbo fucking Baggins, interrupting our ~~serious~~ self-important world with his joy~~ful obliviousness. I stormed toward him like a drill instructor~~.

I can't actually recall anything about what came next. I was literally out of my mind. My staff tells me I screamed at the man. Threatened him. They said I had been slicing something on a cutting board and was now gesticulating wildly with the knife. They said it could easily have been interpreted as a weapon. I'm not excusing myself—I simply can't remember. It doesn't matter. The guy felt threatened. I should never have come close to scaring him.

The ensuing report to HR nearly got me deported from Australia. It didn't help my case that he was the most beloved, popular employee in the whole casino. I wrote an apology, ~~but I didn't really mean it~~ but I didn't truly know how to apologize. No one took it lightly. I was punished severely, but again, it doesn't matter. I have lost control too many times and frightened too many people over the years. I will never be able to explain how much I hate this, the spiral I enter whenever it happens, or how desperately I work to change it.

• • •

In Sydney, tucked in a hidden corner of a hotel, far from the real world, from Momofuku, from Dr. Eliot, I was free to be terrible. When I wasn't at work, I'd drink, gamble, and ~~entertain and rub elbows with~~ distract myself by hanging out with the celebs that visited the casino.

Their favorite spot was a club inside the hotel that played the worst music I have ever heard in my life. I drank myself to oblivion every time we visited.

"This is fucking crazy," I yelled to one former heartthrob turned A-lister over the *untz-untz-untz*. "You're as old as me and I get exhausted just watching you. How can you possibly work in the morning? Aren't you tired?"

I'm not sure how much he heard, but he turned toward me, exhaling a trail of smoke.

"How could I ever get tired of this?"

The following morning I woke up in the janitor's closet of a restaurant on Bondi. It may as well have been a dumpster.

. . .

With the success of the restaurants, women became more interested in dating ~~me~~ celebrity chef David Chang. I was a terrible companion to all of them. I was ~~suddenly desirable~~ immature, selfish, narcissistic, undeserving.

For the most part, I avoided flings. Deep down, I wanted companionship and I gravitated toward smart, sociable, super ambitious women. But none of my relationships made it past six months. It's not that I didn't want it—I just couldn't bring myself to grow up enough to be with someone.

One failed romance in particular really broke my heart. Without giving it much thought at all, I dove deep into another relationship with the next woman I started dating. ~~We got engaged.~~ Asking her to marry me would have been a huge mistake—selfish and unfair to her. I knew we weren't right for each other. I knew I would be putting her through immense pain for my own benefit, but I was running on autopilot.

At its worst, our brief relationship was unbelievably painful, dramatic, disastrous, actually terrifying. It ended, too.

. . .

I was on an airplane when I opened an email from one of my siblings. Mom had gone for her annual checkup and found out that she had a tumor in her brain. She'd already dealt with bone and breast cancers.

The same day, Dad's doctor told him that he had liver cancer.

That month, my friend Alex Calderwood, the founder of the Ace Hotel, died of an overdose.

Then my friend Peggy died in childbirth in Philadelphia.

• • •

The core family I had at Momofuku began to leave.

It required my attention, but I still couldn't stand being in New York. I couldn't stand any of it.

• • •

The cook was seventeen when his parents dropped him off on our doorstep, ~~like an orphan~~. In my mind, he was like an orphan, but that's not true. In certain restaurants, the hierarchical structure and the extremely close quarters—combined with the fact that cooks have traditionally been a bunch of outsiders longing for some kind of acceptance—can approximate the sensation of a family. Young people come into the kitchen in need of guidance and structure, and chefs are all too happy to assume the role of parental surrogate. With him, I relished the opportunity. He was as bright as they come.

I took him on as my mentee, a person for whom I had big plans. I wanted him to take over the kitchen at Noodle Bar.

I was invested in him because right away I could see the promise not only in his abilities but his attitude. He never had an excuse. He cared so much—to his own detriment, sometimes. He was funny, smart, loyal.

I set him up with a stage with Sean Brock at McCrady's in Charleston when it was the hottest restaurant in the South. I arranged for him to spend a season working with Andoni Luis Aduriz of Mugaritz so he could see the most interesting food in the world up close and personal. He came back from each experience energized and grateful.

But now, for the life of me, I could not understand the succession of complaints I was getting from the team. He wasn't the same person he'd been. Nobody understood why. I was grooming him, and the team knew how much he meant to me. I could sense that they resented the preferential treatment I showed him.

I was in Toronto when I got a call informing me about his most recent episode. I called to scold him and said we'd speak in person when I got back to New York. At the end of the week, I got another call. The police had found him dead in his apartment.

His parents flew up on Saturday. We met in the office of Má Pêche, our restaurant in Midtown. Talking to them about how he'd died—how we'd failed him—was unequivocally the most difficult thing I've ever done.

His mom told me he loved working for me. He loved me.

I loved him with all my heart, I said. ~~I told them that I would dedicate myself to making Momofuku a testament to their son and what he meant to me.~~ I'm a father myself now. I know that whatever I said was meaningless.

. . .

I was always good at noticing when cooks were struggling in their private lives. I could sniff out drug use—no problem. I didn't fire people for it, either. I just wanted to know what they were doing, so I could make sure that *they* knew what they were doing.

He died of an accidental overdose.* For a while, I put the blame on

---

*I'm glad to see binge drinking becoming less of a problem in kitchens these days, but I'm terrified to see it being replaced by pills.

the team at Momofuku. I was so pissed at them. They were supposed to care about each other, to dig deeper when they sensed something wrong with their brother. ~~We were a thoughtful company—the kind that would be able to recognize a co-worker in need. But we weren't good enough.~~ The fact is, he died on my watch.

I had spent my career obsessing over my own mortality and how suicidal thoughts had led to a breakthrough in the form of Momofuku. I talked constantly about this business as life and death. My head had gone so far up my ass.

I won't tell you any more about his death. It's disrespectful to his memory. I'd give anything to be writing instead about all the great things he's achieved with us.

In the months that followed, I put on fifty pounds. I stopped drinking and smoking pot, but I'd order pizza at three a.m. and eat the whole pie by myself. I couldn't fall asleep unless my stomach hurt, and I couldn't exercise because of a back injury. I was immobilized.

Before my mentee's death, my visits to therapy had mostly been a release. Now I was searching frantically for a way to make things right. We devoted all of our time to discussing his death.

It was a clear line in my head. I was his boss and a big-brother figure and I'd told him he had failed me.

For years, Dr. Eliot worked to convince me that this was an egotistical outlook. He told me that my treatment of my mentee's mistake had been unpleasant, aggressive, and unconstructive, but that it was not the cause of his death. To think I had the power to kill him meant that I had the power to save him, which was also not true. He didn't die because of me, but he didn't die *for* me, either. He deserves more than to be defined by our relationship. He meant much more to this world than what he was to me.

I'm not supposed to blame myself, but not a day goes by when I don't think about him or wonder what would have been if I'd gotten on a plane and shown up at his door earlier.

If anyone was supposed to die, it was me. When I signed the

ten-year lease for the very first restaurant, I was twenty-six years old. My broker offered an additional five-year option at the same rate, but I declined. I was certain I would be dead within a decade.

Now I was thirty-five and alive. None of it was supposed to matter. I needed to figure out what to do with all this extra life.

16

THE MAGAZINE BUSINESS

Okay, here's the pitch.

We visit small farms all across America, the ones that supply your restaurants. Then you see all the things they're doing wrong. They're not getting the most out of the land, which means you're not getting the best possible products. You start yelling at the farmers and . . .

THAT WAS AN ACTUAL SHOW THAT A PRODUCER TRIED TO MAKE WITH ME. Dave Chang yelling at farmers.

People were coming from all directions, trying to get me to be on television. Occasionally, if a friend was involved, I'd agree to a guest appearance. Martha Stewart, for instance, was among the early patron saints of Momofuku. (When she first came in, she waited in line outside with everyone else.) She invited me onto her show, and we had a blast. I did *Top Chef*, too. I'm pretty sure that in order to get me on camera saying something as simple as "Everything lookin' good, Tom?" they must have had to splice together syllables from eight or ten different takes.

I didn't feel like I was in any kind of shape to be on TV regularly. I ultimately caved in order to put more asses in seats at the restaurants. Anything for the business. And so, I began taking meetings with every production outfit that had culinary ambitions, including the Food Network. I didn't make much of an effort to hide my distaste for their programming. I told them how much I thought they sucked, and they never called again.

I tried to think of chefs who had successfully branched into television without tarnishing their credibility. I reached out to the ones I knew to ask how they'd avoided becoming dancing monkeys. From their answers, I cobbled together a set of criteria for considering media projects:

1. It must be educational.
2. It must fund the creative efforts of the restaurants.
3. It must reflect what I stand for and depict the industry in a fair light.

These remain my yardsticks to this day.

• • •

After publishing *Momofuku* together, Peter Meehan and I didn't take a break between projects. The two of us set out to find someone to make the TV show we wanted to see, and the one place that was interested in working with us was Bourdain's company, Zero Point Zero, which produced *No Reservations*. Rather than a traditional show, they proposed we develop a mobile app that would allow users to explore the world of food through video, photography, essays, and interactive features. It was 2010, iPads were new, and everybody under the sun wanted a piece of the app market. Of course, nobody knew what that meant or what they were doing.

Together with ZPZ, Meehan and I devised a concept inspired by my brainstorming sessions. When I'm working through an idea or a recipe, I like to scribble on a whiteboard: one thought connects to another, to another, which breeds a new insight, and so on, until you have a meandering, interconnected web of ideas encircling the main subject. In the app, we imagined users taking self-guided tours through an interactive mind map with branches leading off to different video clips and accompanying text. Each "episode" would revolve around a different theme. ZPZ put the money up to film segments for the first couple of themes—Ramen and The Sweet Spot—and we traveled to Japan, the American South, Spain, and California to shoot.

The edited footage and the early iterations of the technology seemed great to me, and the project ticked all three of my requirements. It was so promising that Apple agreed in principle to use the app in their commercials for the next iPad launch.

There was one shortcoming. The app couldn't really allow for long-form writing or accommodate all of the hundreds of hours of footage we'd accumulated. What could we do with all this extra material? Peter suggested a magazine. I loved the idea for one reason: I pictured a reader holding a magazine in one hand and an iPad in the other, frantically looking back and forth in order to get the full experience. This ridiculous image brought me so much happiness.

We called up Chris Ying, who had worked his way from being an intern at the indie publishing house McSweeney's while moonlighting in kitchens to being the publisher of the company. As ambitious and talented as he is, Ying and I have frequently butted heads over the years because he's naturally more risk averse than me. It's frustrating to no end when he's not willing to go all in. But when we called him to propose we make a magazine together, he said yes immediately. I liked that. He and Meehan started digging in right away.

Our third-party software development firm delivered the fruits of their labor. There were concerns. If I remember correctly, most apps at the time were two to four megabytes in size. One episode of our app was four . . . gigabytes. We sent the app over to Apple and received a call from an engineer, who said something to the effect of: "At Apple, we usually consider one memory leak in an application to be too many. At the moment, your app has one hundred fifty-three."

Anyway, the app is called Lucky Peach. It's officially still in beta.

Lucky Peach, the quarterly magazine, released two or three issues before we internally called time of death on the app. I took a meeting with one of the producers at ZPZ. He was freaking out. There was no way for the company to recoup the money they'd spent on producing our footage or the app. He pleaded with me to release what we'd shot to them so they could repurpose it. I agreed to divvy up the rights to what we'd made. I wanted the material out there as much as anyone else. We'd put a lot of brainpower and sweat into it.

A few months later, our show came out on PBS and Netflix with Tony narrating and the title *Mind of a Chef.* It won a James Beard Award, and, to my surprise, was renewed for a second season. It didn't feel great, if I'm being honest, to see our show and ideas continue on TV without us. I guess that's what I get for giving away film and television rights and retaining the written word.

• • •

But making a magazine was so much fun.

Lucky Peach was a hit out of the gate. The late media critic David Carr wrote about it for *The New York Times,* heaping praise on the first issue as though it were the second coming of Gutenberg. We couldn't print copies fast enough. We truly hadn't anticipated any of it, and I don't think we could have mapped it out on paper if we'd tried. Organic growth, I always say, means having absolutely no strategy.

I was in a recklessly creative state, and *Lucky Peach* was the perfect outlet. I could throw anything at the wall—*Guys, let's publish an excerpt of Thomas Bernhard's "Old Masters"*—and it would happen. We could do whatever we wanted. We printed short, meditative stories about fly-fishing from one of my favorite obscure writers, Russell Chatham. Every day there would be a different batshit crazy idea that we almost always managed to execute.

For our third issue, we decided to lampoon the cliché of cooks having butcher diagrams of pigs tattooed on their bodies. Ying brought a pork leg to the local tattoo shop and had them ink a butcher diagram of a human on it. *Boom, that's our cover.* Issue four revolved around "American Food." I suggested we grab a photo of a cow eating hot dogs. (The dogs were vegetarian.) Issue five was "Chinatown," for which the boys wrote an elaborate hoax article based on George Plimpton's famous April Fool's Day prank, "The Curious Case of Sidd Finch." Writing for *Sports Illustrated,* Plimpton created a fake story about an as-yet-undiscovered Tibetan baseball pitcher named Siddhartha "Sidd" Finch, who could throw a 168-mile-per-hour fastball. Our version revolved around an intrepid reporter named Syd Finch, an untraceable Chinese chef, the secretly Asian roots of Italian cooking, and a secluded restaurant that was so creative it made Osteria Francescana look like Olive Garden.

At various points in *Lucky Peach*'s history, we published a play; a booklet tucked inside a pouch made to look like a human stomach; a story about the unheralded gay roots of American cooking; excerpts from two books that would later win Pulitzers; and an article claiming that the three-Michelin-star restaurant Benu was offering an all-you-can-eat fried rice supplement to its tasting menu. We celebrated unsung heroes like Alex Lee and Claudia Fleming and shed light on conversations that chefs had previously only explored in private.

Ying was working from California, where he hired a young fiction writer named Rachel Khong, who would become the spiritual backbone of the magazine. In New York, a group of bright recent college grads—Priya Krishna, Ryan Healey, Brette Warshaw—joined our ragtag band. Adam Krefman, the guy we hired to act as our publisher, was another McSweeney's alum based in Chicago. I looked around and suddenly, without ever writing down a business plan, we had "bureaus" in San Francisco, Chicago, and New York. It was all too ridiculous to believe.

What truly made me happy about *Lucky Peach* was how much harder it made life for everybody else. It wasn't enough to be a chef with a TV show or a cookbook anymore—now you needed a magazine to tell your story properly. And although we never came close to the circulation of *Bon Appétit* or *Food & Wine,* I think we pushed the big brands to be smarter and work harder. Our second year we cleaned up at the James Beard Media Awards. I felt an undeniable schadenfreude in watching our gang of upstarts steal medal after medal.

I can't take much of the credit. After the first few issues, I faded into the background. *Lucky Peach*'s ascent coincided with the rest of my life unraveling. I don't think it bothered the *Lucky Peach* staff one bit, as no one wanted to appear like they were making *Momofuku Monthly*.

While Peter and I had gotten our start on the Momofuku cookbook, I can only imagine how irritating that perception must have been for the staff members who were already established in their own careers. I once heard someone refer to Peter as "the dude who works for David Chang." He never signed up to be a shill for me or our restaurants. I understood very clearly why they removed the name Momofuku from the cover of the second issue. I didn't protest, but I could feel a resentment growing between me and Peter.

The magazine certainly did not suffer from the lack of my presence. It only got stronger. The team championed quality writing at whatever length suited the story, fresh voices from inside and outside the food fold, stirring the pot, and a beautifully unorthodox design aesthetic. Ying brought on an eighteen-year-old kid named Walter Green as art director. Every fourth issue, they completely redesigned the magazine—a signature move inherited from McSweeney's. If you want to understand Walter's impact, just have a look at how other food magazine covers evolved between 2011 and 2017.

Again, let me emphasize that none of this was planned. Spontaneity, foolhardiness, self-indulgence, and DIY jerry-rigging were baked into the magazine's DNA. The photographer who did the *Momofuku* cookbook, Gabriele Stabile—credited in our masthead as *Italian Photographer*—shot 75 percent of the photos for the first few issues. The rest was shot in Meehan's living room.

McSweeney's served as our publisher from the beginning, but we didn't iron out our contract until issue ten. Do the math on a quarterly(-ish) magazine, and that's two and a half years of flying by the seat of our pants. Then, almost as soon as we signed a deal, the feast-or-famine financial reality of running the magazine became too much of a strain on McSweeney's. Putting up huge sums of money to finance and print it, then waiting for months to see any money come back was too much for them to handle. Momofuku essentially took the place of publisher—not that we were any better suited.

But who needs a plan when you've got freedom?

• • •

You can believe me or not, but Momofuku has never been about getting rich. I don't mean we're a nonprofit. What I'm saying is that I'm proud that I've never let the threat of losing everything—or the prospect of making more money—get in the way of doing what I think is right. I've leveraged everything I have for the business. I want to take care of the people who work for Momofuku, in terms of both their well-being and their freedom to be creative, and I have made insanely irresponsible financial choices to do so. I put off making and saving money for myself, so that we could win as a team.

But because *Lucky Peach* folded without an explanation, I will always be pegged as the selfish asshole who shut it down.

I know exactly how it looked. People see Momofuku expanding into shopping malls and sports arenas, and they interpret it as greed. They see me hosting a TV show on Netflix, and they interpret it as vanity. In 2016, Momofuku almost collapsed. You'll read about it later, but the business was slipping and our magic spark was dimming. I didn't want to take on outside money. I had turned down enormous offers from private equity firms in the past. I certainly didn't want to have a physical so that I could personally guarantee a nine-million-dollar loan myself. Those are things I *had* to do. What I would have liked was to start a family and buy an apartment, but the bank told me I was too leveraged to borrow any more money. All of my financial security was baked into the businesses.

This disparity between the reality and perception of Momofuku's and my finances put an immense strain on my relationship with the *Lucky Peach* team. They wanted to grow and expand—hell, I'd told them they should. The more financially sound *Lucky Peach* became, the more freedom they would have to continue pushing the envelope—and the better they could take care of all the brilliant writers that were showing up to push it with them.

The catch, of course, is that making money in the creative world involves risk, compromise, and an extraordinary amount of luck. The potential was certainly there. I fully believe that *Lucky Peach* could have grown and thrived under the right conditions, but it never made money while it was alive, and Momofuku was often treading water.

That posed a problem because Momofuku and *Lucky Peach* were completely twisted up in one another's roots. Each shared in the other's successes as well as its shortcomings. If the magazine fell short of payroll, we would always back them. If they were to fail catastrophically—if print sales dropped, or the leadership mismanaged the business—they would bring Momofuku down with them, and vice versa. It wasn't so different from any of the other individual businesses in our group, which is maybe why we approached *Lucky*

Peach like we were managing a restaurant. That was what we knew best. But *Lucky Peach* was actually something else entirely, and the financial risk was much greater.

For years, Momofuku had no investors. We supported ourselves and we were fortunate enough to never run a negative enterprise. Every last cent of profit went back into the restaurants. We loosened that restriction to help finance *Lucky Peach* and our partnership with Dave Arnold in the experimental bar and equipment company Booker and Dax. But at a certain point, the restaurants weren't performing as strongly as they once had. And without the restaurants bringing in as much cash, we were incredibly vulnerable.

I don't know if any of this information made it to the staff. I don't know if they understood how much I cared about the magazine, or the effort I'd made to keep it alive. That's my fault. I didn't make myself available enough to them. We were a bicoastal operation that may as well have been corresponding by Pony Express. Two of the casualties I especially regret were people I love and admire—Rachel and Ying were both driven out before the end.*

Momofuku and *Lucky Peach* became like a married couple who went to bed angry every night, never sharing our frustrations with one another. It all came to a head at the beginning of 2017. We explored every option to save the magazine. Maybe a larger media company could buy it. Although I was still sore from our experience with *Mind of a Chef,* I agreed to do more TV. The hope was that *Ugly Delicious* (originally called *Lucky Peach*), our Netflix show about culture and food—made with Bourdain's blessing and produced in collaboration with Academy Award winner Morgan Neville—could

---

*Rachel's become a crazy successful novelist, so don't feel too bad. Ryan Healey works for Momofuku now, and I'm working with Priya Krishna on a big project, too. Ying and I reunited last year. In fact, he's helping me write this book as we speak. The only reason his name isn't also on the cover is that I don't want anyone getting any ideas about poaching him. I'm not about to lose him again. We've got too much work to do.

fund the magazine and increase the company's valuation. I offered to surrender my majority ownership and forgive any outstanding debt to Momofuku, in exchange for shifting the future financial liability off Momofuku's books. But we couldn't work it out.

Like I said, when news broke that *Lucky Peach* had folded, speculation about the cause was rampant. None of it reflected well on me. Angry writers and readers sent me messages about how I put a bunch of people out of work without thinking twice—that I had killed the community *Lucky Peach* built while preserving my own hide. The last interaction I had with Jonathan Gold before he died—if you can even call it an interaction—was reading his negative review of our Los Angeles restaurant, Majordomo, in which he flatly declared that he was pissed at me for shutting down the magazine. He referred to me as "Caesar." Gold had been very close with Meehan and a friend and influential figure to me. Do you know how upsetting it is to read in print that your friend thinks so poorly of you, only to realize that you'll never have the chance to fix it?

I'm sorry to let myself get dragged into the muck here, but this project we started with such joy and excitement became a heartache that was only made worse by the people who blame me for its demise. You assholes don't know where my head was and how much this all hurt. You don't know what it felt like to be so horribly lost and be spat on like some kind of villain. I stayed quiet about *Lucky Peach*'s closure because that's the right thing to do in these situations, not to mention I'd promised to it in the form of a non-disparagement agreement. I've spent my life as a petty man, and I'm trying to take the high road. You know what fucking sucks? Taking the high road.

For anybody who thinks I didn't feel a responsibility to the magazine, or that *Lucky Peach* wasn't tied into the very heart of my own identity, let me explain something to you. To this day, it's still something journalists ask me.

You know what the name Momofuku means?

It means "lucky peach."

17

HYUNG

HERE'S ANOTHER LANGUAGE LESSON. IN KOREAN CULTURE, IT'S IMPORtant to address family members and strangers alike with the appropriate honorific based on how old they are. Men call their older brothers 형 (hyung) and older sisters 누나 (noona). Hyung is also used more widely when referring to an elder of the same gender—a mentor type.

As a kid I got on fine with my older brothers, but they were much older than me and, besides the many hours we spent together on the golf course, I never really cared to be taken under Jhoon's or Yong's wing. Neither of them tried to bring me in, so it wasn't a problem. I had professional mentors in kitchens, but I didn't consider anyone to be my hyung.

Then I met Dr. Jim Yong Kim. We were both attending a state

dinner in honor of the Korean president Lee Myung-bak, for which the Obama White House had rounded up any Korean Americans of note. I was on the runway at Sydney Airport when I got the invite. I'd just flown back from another whirlwind to the U.S.; this time to speak to a class at Harvard, then shoot a scene in New Orleans for the show *Treme*. Without unpacking my bags, I got on a plane to Washington, D.C., where I met up with my tuxedo. The Momofuku team had FedEx'd it from NYC.

I'm glad I went. Janelle Monáe performed. I sat next to Ruth Bader Ginsburg.* I took my mom as my date, which was exciting for her, but I think she was even more thrilled when she saw me mixing it up with the coolest Korean American alive. Dr. Kim had been the president of Dartmouth and would go on to serve as president of the World Bank. He was educated at Brown and Harvard. He did transformational work fighting AIDS and curing infectious diseases in third-world countries through his organization, Partners in Health. Whenever I talk about him, the biographic detail I always like to share is that as an undersized Korean immigrant kid in the 1960s, attending high school in Muscatine, Iowa, he fought to become quarterback of the football team *and* starting point guard on the basketball squad.

We kept in touch after the White House event—it helped that he loves food—and when we spoke, I would lay my problems out bare. I didn't have to say much for Dr. Kim to understand my personal predicaments. His father grew up near my father in Korea; he grokked my perspective immediately. He listened empathetically as I told him about the abject shittiness of my thirty-fifth year, which was just barely in my rearview mirror. It also took him about half a second to wrap his head around the professional challenges I was facing. He had

---

*Do you know how to properly address a Supreme Court justice? I certainly didn't. I went with "Judge." None other than Jill Biden corrected me: "It's 'Madam Justice.'"

tangibly improved the lives of thousands of people throughout the world while working within a massive bureaucracy. I couldn't keep a few restaurants afloat without devolving into biweekly crises.

Dr. Kim told me that just as people have trainers to help them get in physical shape, he had a trainer who kept an eye on him at work. What I needed, he said, was an executive coach. He asked if he could recommend that his friend take me on as a client—pro bono.

The big toothy smile of celebrity motivator Tony Robbins came to mind immediately. *Maybe* a coach would make the company run more efficiently, but what sort of company would we be if I started taking advice from gurus and self-help books?

Dr. Kim told me to look up Marshall Goldsmith and get back to him.

To visit Marshall Goldsmith's website is to be assaulted with enthusiasm.* The first image you see is a picture of the old fella himself, bald and beaming, with open arms and a look that says, "You did it! You found me!" It looks like a stock photo, but, no, that's really him. There are charts illustrating the concept of paying it forward; more pictures of Goldsmith smiling; a section on his many books, with titles like *Work Is Love Made Visible* and *What Got You Here Won't Get You There;* and a banner advertising Goldsmith's induction into the Thinkers50 Management Hall of Fame.

Boeing had hired Goldsmith to coach its CEO, Alan Mulally, during the company's post-9/11 nadir. In the same decade, Mulally helped revive another American icon, Ford, after the automotive crisis. By all accounts, Goldsmith was the Michael Jordan of executive coaching. I read the About section and focused in on one line in particular: "I help people understand how our beliefs and the environments we operate in can trigger negative behaviors."

My apprehension about taking Dr. Kim up on his offer came

---

*Go ahead, I'll wait.

down to the same reason I'd initially hesitated to see a therapist. I
didn't want to admit to being flawed or weak. But I certainly wasn't
a better natural leader than Dr. Kim, who was telling me that he'd
personally benefited from a coach. I thought of the other powerful people I'd encountered in my life and how I'd occasionally felt
disadvantaged without the benefit of an education in business and
leadership.

Goldsmith was Dr. Kim's guy. He could have passed him on to
any number of candidates, but he didn't. He chose me.

Okay, I'll give it a whirl.

. . .

Whereas most executive coaches are called in to address a particular deficiency in a leader, Marshall Goldsmith is known for taking a
more personal approach. He considers the human being as a whole,
assessing their values and temperament before prescribing a course of
action. It sounded a lot like therapy.

Unlike my psychiatrist, however, Goldsmith was interested in
more than just my side of the story. His team conducted background
interviews with thirty of my employees, family members, and
friends. They assured everyone that they could speak openly without
fear of retribution. Under no circumstances would Goldsmith reveal
the sources. He'd spent years mastering how to remove any clues
from the transcripts. The process is called *360-degree feedback.*

Marshall and I met for the first time in the same conference room
where I'd spoken with my mentee's parents after his death. Marshall was calm, clear, pleasant, and engaged. I sensed the confidence
of someone walking into a negotiation with all the leverage. He and
his team had spent the past few days reviewing comments from the
people closest to me and organizing them so that I could get a sense of
the major trends.

We would start with the positives. He handed me a manila folder stuffed with paper and left the room. I savored those pages. It was like a spa for my mind. When I got to the end, I wondered if maybe Marshall had concluded I was being too hard on myself. I had so much to be proud of. Marshall asked if I had any questions. I didn't. He encouraged me to sleep on what I'd just read. In the morning we'd review the critical feedback.

The next day, Marshall and his assistant returned with a mountain of documents. It took me more than a day to review their report. I read every single comment. When I finished, he and his team came back in to provide context for the monumental case against me as a leader.

He ripped the Band-Aid right off. "This might be one of the harshest things I can share with someone this early on, but it's important that you hear it: it's incredible to us that so many people have stayed by your side for so long when they can't stand you."

This gentleman, who looked like the Gorton's fisherman, had effortlessly offered an indictment of the whole system I'd built. People were sacrificing themselves for someone they disliked. They were succeeding in spite of me.

"Fuck," I said at last. "I've done so much harm. Do I even have a chance here? I don't know where I would begin."

"That means we're on the right track, Dave."

• • •

I began to develop a more specific understanding of Marshall's coaching philosophy. What he does better than anyone is help assholes realize that they are assholes. He's got a whole arsenal of adages for this:

"Successful people become great leaders when they learn to shift the focus from themselves to others."

"You can continue doing what you're doing for a long time, but you'll never become the person you want to be."

"It's harder to unfuck yourself than it is to fuck yourself."

When he's delivering his assessments, you cannot contradict him. You can swear all you want, but if you try to argue or make excuses with him, he makes you put money in a jar for charity. Yes, he's an executive coach with an exceptionally positive outlook, but Marshall's also a very honest person. He supports his instructions with facts and data. In my raw state, receiving his aphorisms was like studying with the Buddha.

"You have to eat the shit!" he repeated over and over during one of our first sessions. He had the tone and zeal of a boxing trainer. "Shit tastes good!"

"What does that even mean?" I chuckled.

"Don't laugh," he said sternly. Marshall told me that my job wasn't to cook food. It wasn't about looking at numbers or commanding people, either. My company would live or die based on my capacity to eat shit and like it. "I am going to watch you eat as many bowls of shit as our time will allow," he said. We had plenty of time.

Eating shit meant listening. Eating shit meant acknowledging my errors and shortcomings. Eating shit meant facing confrontations that made me uncomfortable. Eating shit meant putting my cell phone away when someone was talking to me. Eating shit meant not fleeing. Eating shit meant being grateful. Eating shit meant controlling myself when people fell short of my expectations. Eating shit meant putting others before myself.

This last detail was important. With Dr. Eliot, I got away with describing my MO as self-destructive—my managerial tendencies were harmful, but only to me. Now, according to Marshall, I was using that assessment as cover for my poor behavior. In my mind, all the people who had left Momofuku were leaving me. When they failed at their jobs, they were betraying me. Marshall pointed out the ugly truth that this belied. I believed that the people at Momofuku were there to serve me.

I had always wielded my dedication to Momofuku with great

arrogance. Friendships could crumble, hearts could break, cooks could fall to their knees and cry: all collateral damage in the noble pursuit of bringing good food to more people. I believed that I was Momofuku and that everything I did was for Momofuku. Therefore, whatever was good for me was good for Momofuku.

Throughout our year together, Marshall kept me on a tight leash; he was my emotional parole officer. If we didn't meet in person, he rang me up. He took me to seminars and dinners with other executives he had advised. He gave me books to read. He asked colleagues how I was doing and, if he didn't like what he heard, I would have to answer for my behavior.

I enthusiastically ate up the insights as they were served to me.

"It feels like I'm making progress, Marshall."

He never took my word for it.

Marshall was a bright light during a pitch-black time. He wasn't the only one who helped. There were probably a dozen men and women in my life who reached out to give me guidance—people like Jim Kim, who made immense gestures of support and love. Tony Bourdain was one of them. He looked out for me, and I became fiercely protective of him, too. The way brothers do. I look back and see that I had many hyung and noona.

If I haven't thanked you enough, thank you.

• • •

I told Dr. Eliot that I wanted to try something new. I had made up my mind to get off the meds.

As in all matters, Dr. Eliot preached thoroughness. We always talked at great length before adjusting our program. At this point, I'd drawn a lot of clarity from working with Marshall. I'd pushed myself out of my comfort zone. I was trying to get healthy.

He noted that it had not broken me.

"Yeah, but I think the next step is getting off the meds. I keep wondering what's underneath the drugs."

He understood, but he pointed out that I was at the tail end of a highly stressful, painful period. The medication had been helping, even if I couldn't tell. The new strategies had given me some confidence, but there would be more pressure ahead. I respect Dr. Eliot immensely, but isn't that what doctors are supposed to say? That their treatments are working? How could I be sure if the medication was still having a positive effect if I didn't know what my baseline was anymore?

"Do you think it would be dangerous?" I asked.

He told me no, it wasn't necessarily dangerous, but it could be detrimental to the goals I'd set. I'd been on medication for nearly a decade, and this wasn't the time to experiment. There could be withdrawals. My mood could plummet.

I felt on the verge of something. I was about to grow, but I couldn't access the best version of myself while I was medicated. I needed the change. Looking back, I see that the depression was tricking me yet again—this time it had convinced me that I was okay.

Dr. Eliot warned me that there would be a risk of manic episodes. He confirmed once again that I was sure about my decision, then gave me instructions for weaning myself off everything I was taking.

18

NOT MYSELF

I DRANK AND SMOKED POT IN HIGH SCHOOL—NOTHING CRAZY OR OF ANY decent quality. The first time I got really drunk was with some class-mates on cheap bottles of Thunderbird when I was fourteen, and I got in a tremendous amount of trouble.

I accidentally smoked PCP on the roof of a house in Chesapeake Bay when I was eighteen. I thought it was pot until I started having vision trails.

I started to abuse Ritalin and Dexadrine in college, just to get through papers. I felt like they gave me superpowers.

My brother Yong told me to steer clear of cocaine and heroin, but I caved senior year of college and bought a few bags of blow. I found that once you're holding, all kinds of skeezy people come out of the woodwork. I also think it messes with your palate. Coke's not for me.

I did acid a couple of times and had incredibly bad trips. I swore it off after that.

I used to do mushrooms whenever I had the chance. I liked the energy of one cap—all the magic without the hallucinations.

I've lost track of the difference between ecstasy, molly, and MDMA, but it used to be that if it was around and I had nothing to do the next day, you could count me in. Antidepressants make the comedown that much harder. It was a small price to pay.

I've taken a lot of Valium and muscle relaxers in my day. Percocet. Klonopin and a glass of wine. Vicodin and a beer. When you pair them, it's like having twenty-five drinks at once. I can say without exaggeration or nostalgia that I should have died on a handful of occasions.

Once, when I was on vacation, someone had a stockpile of shrooms and edibles. I just kept eating and eating. I wanted to be on another planet. I hallucinated tidal waves on a lake and swore I saw two moons in the sky.

Sometimes when I was fucked up, I could be incredibly boisterous and outgoing. I could laugh and socialize and be someone else entirely. That's probably the most fun version of me. Usually, though, I would get incredibly sad and paranoid. I kept doing drugs because I thought that one of those times I was finally going to be able to control them. Drugs remove your sense of reality, and I was convinced that at some point I would be able to dictate where they took me.* For instance, that pot-and-shroom-induced paranoia could be useful, if I could only get a grip on it. As I sat stoned on the couch, convinced that everyone was judging me, I felt that I could hear exactly what they were all thinking. It was like tapping into a fantastical form of empathy. If I just pushed through, I'd be able to harness the drugs' power. Same with drinking.

---

*Before you peg me as a drug addict, read Michael Pollan's *How to Change Your Mind* and see if a more respectable writer's explanation makes sense. (To be fair, Pollan discourages exactly what I'm talking about.)

I don't drink much now, but I used to have a problem. I'd drink to the point of complete numbness as a means of stress relief. I wasn't a sloppy drunk—I'd just shut down and black out. On a few mornings, I checked myself into a hospital for an IV, but I also liked the hangovers. When everything else seemed to be in constant flux, they were consistent and dependable.

I went through a decade of continuous heavy drinking, with Ambien or Klonopin every night to finish the job. It was my safeguard against growing up.

• • •

I was off medication for a year and a half. Before and after that break, Dr. Eliot and I tried a number of different drug cocktails to address my anger and curb my depression. If he had his way, I think he'd put me on lithium, but I'm too scared to go down that road. Lamictal is the latest drug we're trying, and it's interfering with my sleep. Everything comes with an adjustment period.

To this day I don't know exactly how to describe the effect that the antidepressants have on me. Lexapro took my libido away completely. I switched to Wellbutrin, which I never felt until I was off it and the manic episodes started up.

Nothing took away the thoughts of suicide. If anything, the drugs were a gasp of air between waves crashing down on my head.

Dr. Eliot prescribed me Klonopin for anxiety after I told him that I couldn't sleep at night. I was so angry. I would go to bed mad and wake up full of rage. At first, the medicine provided some relief for the acute anxiety, and I really came to appreciate the day-off Klonopin—the only way to force a pause. But over time, the medication began giving me panic attacks at moments when I would have otherwise been calm. The unease became constant.

• • •

All I ever wanted was to be normal, to think normal. I'm not a naturally loquacious person. I'm not outgoing or inclined to be a leader. I'm a wallflower. It's been like that since I was a kid. For the majority of my life I was somewhere between ashamed and afraid of my Koreanness. I wanted not to be me, which is why drugs—both illicit and prescribed—appeal to me.

The restaurants changed all of that. When I started Momofuku, I killed the version of me that didn't want to stick his neck out or take chances. Even in its larval stages, when it was more theory than restaurant, Momofuku was about carving out some form of identity for myself. It would be my way of rejecting what the tea leaves said about me. Work made me a different person. Work saved my life.

• • •

For years, at least half my sessions with Dr. Eliot were focused on how I couldn't control my anger in the kitchen. Someone would make an insignificant mistake, and I would snap. I'd lose it all the time. And I don't just mean yelling and screaming. Old-school chefs yelled. They terrorized as a management strategy, and they could turn it on or off like a spigot. But me? When I say I lost it, I mean exactly that. I lost composure. I lost control. I lost consciousness.

In many ways, it wasn't so different from being on drugs.

I've read about people who cut themselves, and I have a lot of sympathy for them. I certainly understand the need to feel anything other than what you're currently experiencing. I'd go outside and collect myself after each episode, but I'd get migraines and my head would throb long after the fact.

I am a large man, so this unhinged display is scary to witness and even more terrifying to be subjected to. It's shameful. It's not how you treat other humans. Each meltdown feels like falling off the wagon. I'm wracked with guilt afterward, putting even more pressure on myself not to lose my temper again. Dr. Eliot would tell me there were methods to prevent the outbursts. I've tried them all, including stepping away from the kitchen.

I would implore Dr. Eliot to give me an explanation. I needed to know what was wrong. I'd ask point-blank if I was bipolar, to which he would say something like, "What's going on that would cause you to ask me that, David?" Dr. Eliot would always avoid giving me specific diagnoses, because he knew that I was a hypochondriac who would immerse myself in reading everything there is to read about whatever he said I had. I wouldn't be able to stop comparing myself to other people who had the same condition. He only confirmed to me a couple of years ago that I am indeed bipolar, with something he called "affective dysregulation" of my emotions.*

What that means, practically speaking, is that some acute event will happen in the kitchen and my mind won't be able to process it. For instance, say we're preparing for a critic to come in. I'll explain the importance of the situation to the staff and what I expect from everyone. Then someone will screw up anyway. They'll lose track of a dish or make a boneheaded judgment call. They're human. But in that moment, I can only view the mistake as sabotage.

My mind interprets their actions as indifference, and I can only see that indifference as an attack on me and my values. I feel under threat. My instinctive defense mechanism is to push people away. I'll scream and yell and curse. I want to destroy them, but I know I can't, so instead, I hurt myself. I'll punch a wall, kick a cabinet, threaten suicide.

I recognize that many people will write this off as my excuse for getting angry at work. While I'm loath to make comparisons, I wonder if someone with body dysmorphic disorder might be more sympathetic.

---

* Once again, I am not an expert, but from what I've read and been told by my doctors, affective dysregulation (or emotional dysregulation) usually accompanies another condition, like PTSD or borderline personality disorder. It can manifest as an uncontrollable drive to escalate situations to the point of no return—usually through verbal aggression or self-harm or damage to property—and it's almost always associated with childhood experiences.

I look at what's happening in front of me and I just see it differently than other people. I would do anything to see what everyone else sees.

Dr. Eliot describes it as a temporary state of psychosis. I can't tell friend from foe. It's as though I'm seeing the world in different colors and I can't switch my vision back. It doesn't only happen at work, either. I will lose it at home, which is horrifying. I lose all sense of what's real and wish the worst on the people I love most. My wife, Grace, tells me that when I'm angry, I seethe with such intensity that it can't simply be emotional. It's like I'm an animal registering danger. There are times when Grace and I will be arguing and she'll plead, "Hey, I'm on your side, I'm on your side." It will take hours for me to hear her.

• • •

I hate that the anger has become my calling card. With friends, family, my co-workers, and the media, my name has come to be synonymous with rage. I've never been proud of it, and I wish I could convey to you how hard I've tried to fight it. I've been entrenched in a war with my anger for many years.

A few years ago, I was cooking at an event in Europe. The dinner had already run on for six-plus hours. Ours was the last course. I was making a simple goulash with rice, but by the time we were plating, it was past midnight. There were drunk journalists running amok in the kitchen. Most of the chefs had already left for the night. All order was gone.

René saw it coming and warned everyone. His expression seemed to say, *Get out the popcorn, friends*. It filled me with shame. I still couldn't stop myself.

A journalist lifted the lid on our pot of stew and helped himself to a spoonful. I lost it.

"If you're not a fucking cook, get the fuck out of here or I will fucking throw you out myself," I screamed, before making a huge scene.

Silence fell. The rest of the night was different. I was crushed.

• • •

"What the hell is going on?"

I call my friends and ask this all the time. They've heard me complain over and over that I have a problem accepting reality, because there's no way I deserve the kind of good fortune I've had. I used to call it impostor syndrome, but now I understand it better as survivor's guilt. All these people around me have died—literally and figuratively—and I'm still here. It truly feels like surviving a plane crash.

The odds are astronomically low for anyone to make it big as a chef. You can argue otherwise, but I think my chances were even worse than others'. I didn't know anything about running a restaurant when I decided to open Momofuku. Had I taken a job anywhere else instead, gotten better as a cook, eased into my own kitchen, things never would have panned out. I'm 100 percent sure of it. I bloomed incredibly late as a chef, and yet the timing worked perfectly in my favor. Too perfectly. It's more plausible to me that Greek gods exist and are watching my life as some form of entertainment. I'm not trying to be solipsistic.

In moments of such extreme doubt, I center myself by summoning a memory that's inextricably tied to a familiar emotion. Fly-fishing for my first permit. The first time I had freshly squeezed orange juice. The birth of my son. Having my heart broken or feeling let down. Anything that is unmistakably real.

• • •

I'd convinced both myself and Dr. Eliot that I was ready to go off meds, and I didn't start taking antidepressants again until we were getting ready to open Majordomo, our first restaurant in Los Angeles. I was scared of how I would perform in a new restaurant, and I wanted to make sure that I was doing everything I could to prevent the inevitable.

In the meantime, I got to know my unmedicated self again.

19

FAST FOOD AND ASIAN VILLAINS

Noodle Bar's tenth anniversary took me by surprise. It didn't feel like my restaurant anymore. For the occasion, we went into the vault and brought back dishes from the very beginning, offering them at 2004 prices.

I had trouble enjoying the moment. Retrospectives are about looking back from the end of the road. Looking back is not something Momofuku ever did. We had always moved swiftly forward with the intention of keeping everyone else on their toes. Now the James Beard Foundation was inducting me into the Who's Who of Food & Beverage in America—their equivalent of a lifetime achievement award. It's a high honor that I took to mean my best days were behind me.

A more charitable view of our situation was that I could trust the crews of the various restaurants to keep the operations running smoothly. We'd established our voice and aesthetic, which is more than you can say for a lot of people. In any creative pursuit, you expend most of your younger years chasing a distinctive look or sound or approach. Think about the great visual artists. They all have a recognizable style, even if it only represents a small fraction of their artistic output. Warhol and his prints. Bacon and his triptychs. O'Keeffe and her flowers. Koons and his balloon animals. Kahlo and her portraits.

We had many signature looks, and we were still creating work I liked. Paul Carmichael had taken over our midtown restaurant, Má Pêche, which was originally a showcase for Tien Ho's Vietnamese cooking. Paul started serving a $95 tasting menu informed by Japanese kappo cuisine and his own Barbadian roots.* Ko, meanwhile, was moving to a larger, more elegant space.

The real issue for me was that I could sense a palpable Momofuku fatigue in the air. It had become easy to write off our influence. Food across the country had become porkier, spicier, brighter, better. This was by no means all our doing, but the result of helping to open the floodgates meant that we no longer represented the cutting edge. There were Momofuku facsimiles all over the world. I wish I could say I was flattered, but having copycats meant that we had something that could be copied.

I knew that changes had to be made, and not just for the sake of pride or ambition. I needed to subvert people's culinary expectations within the context of making prudent business decisions. Where was the intersection between making money and making trouble?

I was struggling to figure out what my job was. I didn't know

---

*It was both novel and delicious, but the work didn't get nearly as much acknowledgment as it should have. Paul would eventually move to Sydney to take over Seiōbo, where he could see out his vision with even more clarity, yet he still doesn't get the recognition he deserves as one of the world's great chefs.

everyone's name at the restaurants anymore. I spent a lot of time in my head, thinking about whether I had anything left to say as a chef. And even if I were to return to the kitchen to make some sweeping overhaul of our cooking, who's to say that I still had the touch, or that what came next would be better? More important, for almost a decade, my creative fuel had essentially been rage. One of Marshall Goldsmith's most emphatic lessons had been that what worked for me in the past would no longer work for me. I feared what I would be without my biggest crutch. I questioned whether I even deserved another chance.

I wrestled endlessly with this shit until finally—and I can't believe I'm saying this—a football game ignited a spark.

• • •

Lucky Peach was about three years into its run and I wasn't really keeping close tabs on the team. I'd stopped even sporadically dropping ideas on the editors. They definitely didn't need me.

Then someone in the office suggested an idea for an article. Kat Crosby was an Auburn alum and a huge fan. She asked if I'd ever been to the Iron Bowl, and when I said I hadn't, she made it happen. The *Lucky Peach* team was working on the "All You Can Eat" issue, so the absurdity of a college football tailgating extravaganza would fit right in.

The Iron Bowl is the biggest sporting event in Alabama, the annual culmination of one of the classic rivalries in all of college sports. Auburn versus Alabama. Alumni fly in from all over the world to attend the game. Kat was friends with a family who owned a house in Auburn that they'd bought specifically for game days. Needless to say, they had good tickets, too. That's how we found ourselves over Thanksgiving in an Alabama college town.

In the span of one weekend, we crashed a kegger, annoyed a bunch of undergrads, and took in as many tailgates as possible. We ate Oreo pops, pecan French toast, shrimp and grits, and eight or nine different preparations of sausage. We also stormed the field after witnessing one of the top two or three college football games of all time.*

The food at the tailgates was delightful in its twisted excess but not especially delicious. We stopped at Chick-fil-A whenever we didn't have somewhere else to be. This is in the article Ying wrote about our trip:

If you haven't had one, the namesake fillet is salty and a little bit sweet, the breading not aggressively crunchy, the spices passive and savory in a nonspecific way. It is eminently satisfying. The biscuit is the best vehicle for the chicken, but you can also try it on a bun, squishy and soft as it is. The truth is that everything in a Chick-fil-A sandwich, whether bun, biscuit, or bird, is essentially the same texture—a fact that comports well with the company's well-documented homophobic politics. It's a guilty pleasure.

I loathe Chick-fil-A as a company, yet I couldn't resist giving them my business. On one visit to the chicken bigots, I was disappointed to hear we were the last customers of the night. I could see our sandwiches languishing under the heat lamp. They must have been there for hours. I pleaded with the staff.

"Come on, you're telling me you can't go back there and drop a few cutlets in the oil for us? We don't have this back home. Just this once, pretty please?"

Chick-fil-A being a godly establishment, the clerk was courteous but could not break the rules to grant my wish. She promised that the sandwiches would stay good for hours and that I wouldn't be able to tell the difference. I took what I could get.

Trapped in their bags in the heat, the sandwiches had definitely

---

*The Kick Six game. You know, the one where, with no time on the clock, Auburn returned a missed field goal 109 yards for a touchdown and the win. If you know what I'm talking about, you're almost certainly pissed that I got to see it in person.

changed. Half a day in the salty-greasy sauna had removed any sign of crunchiness. They were squishy-soft, savory, nonthreatening. They were better.

Holy shit, I thought to myself. *They sandbagged this.*

If Hogwarts were a cooking school, sandbaggery is something they would teach in Culinary Dark Arts class. It is the practice of making the job easier without sacrificing quality. Boiling chicken falls under sandbaggery. So does microwaving potatoes and corn on the cob. One-pot cooking. Coming up with a dish you can plate ahead of time for a charity event. I love sandbagging.

My conflicted appreciation for Chick-fil-A's sandwiches was only made worse by the fact that I had failed when I had tried to launch a fast-food empire with Korean burritos. These evil bastards had mastered what I couldn't. As much as I despised the company, it was the most inspiring restaurant I had visited in a long time.

• • •

Noodle Bar opened the same year as Per Se, Masa, Shake Shack, Franny's, and Blue Hill at Stone Barns—restaurants that set the tone in New York for the following decade. The new stuff coming out didn't move me. It certainly didn't intimidate me. I came to believe that we had entered an in-between phase. We'd reached the end of the culinary arms race that had seen every chef in New York trying to outdo one another with the most technically difficult dish.

The dick-swinging was over. The future wasn't going to be about capturing a specific place and time, either. Enough people had eaten at Noma to realize that all the lackluster impersonators were never going to rival the original.

I returned to New York from Auburn and told everybody I wanted to make a fried chicken sandwich. We would finally get in the fast-food game, and while we were at it, we'd crack the code on food delivery, too, another area I had failed to succeed in.

My thoughts got more complicated and extravagant as I built a head of steam. With each passing day, I grew more certain that we were onto something huge. There's more than a small chance that I was exaggerating the clarity I was experiencing because I wanted the unmedicated version of myself to be the best one.

In any case, I was confident I had discovered what was around the corner for the restaurant business. We went to work arranging for the space at 163—formerly Noodle Bar, then Ko—to return to its pre-Momofuku roots as a fried chicken shop. What I didn't tell my team was that I was simultaneously making a second play. The fried chicken business was a canvas to fuck with people.

I was far from the first person to look the other way when it came to patronizing Chick-fil-A. A lot of ostensibly decent people were willing to ignore the truth for a taste of deep-fried bird. I wanted to flip that phenomenon around to make our own point about culture.

I don't think I ever described our fried chicken restaurant as an art project, but years later I figured out that's essentially what it was. The realization came when I met the Thai artist Rirkrit Tiravanija, whose best-known pieces are interactive experiences. He'd cook curry or pad Thai in a gallery, sometimes getting mistaken for the caterer. Rirkrit told me he'd chosen pad Thai because it was the only noodle dish in Thailand that had not descended from China. He chose to cook in electric woks, because they were chintzy approximations of the real deal, and he wanted to comment on the commodification of Asian culture. Every move was intentional. All of it was designed to breathe life into what people too easily wrote off as quotidian or worthless.

Our plan was to open a fast-food restaurant that sold delicious chicken sandwiches, but if you looked a little closer, you'd see a dis-section of the Asian American experience. Like Rirkrit, we were deliberate in all of our choices, even if they didn't all emerge as fully formed as one of his exhibits. The name came easily: Fuku. A riff on Momofuku and a phonetic fuck-you to everybody who took us for granted, mocked us, or made us feel lesser for how we ate. We'd always been sparing about decoration at Momofuku. The few touches are there for a reason, and at Fuku it would be especially so. We started to line the walls with framed posters: Oddjob from *Goldfinger*, Gogo Yubari from *Kill Bill*, Uli from *Die Hard*, Lo-Pan from *Big Trouble in Little China*, Chong Ki from *Bloodsport*, and Mickey Rooney's bucktoothed Mr. Yunioshi from *Breakfast at Tiffany's*. All the ugly stereotypical Asian sidekicks and villains from cinematic history—the painful, humiliating images that somehow continued to go unchecked in American culture.

Later, we also cribbed an idea from In-N-Out Burger, the fast-food conservatives of the West Coast. At In-N-Out, the cups and wrappers all contain hidden Bible citations. Last time I ate there, I found a tiny NAHUM 1:7 printed on my trash. The verse reads, "The Lord is good, a strong hold in the day of trouble; and he knoweth them that trust in him."

I decided Ezekiel 25:17 was the ideal choice for Fuku. You've likely heard this passage even if you're not a Bible scholar. Close your eyes and imagine Samuel L. Jackson's character Jules in *Pulp Fiction* declaring to a group of slack-jawed frat boys eating fast-food burgers: "And I will strike down upon thee with great vengeance and furious anger those who attempt to poison and destroy my brothers. And you will know my name is the Lord when I lay my vengeance upon thee."

The only person I confided in about my ulterior plans was Marguerite Mariscal. Marge came on as an intern in 2011 and would eventually rise to become our CEO. I could trust her with my unredacted crazy.

We needed to open on Sundays, unlike our God-fearing opponents at Chick-fil-A, I told her.

And we needed to drop some Ls.

"Here's what we do: we print the word *Dericious!* all over the sandwich wrappers. I want white people to see it and feel completely uncomfortable saying it out loud. We are gonna reclaim all this shit."

I'm sure Marge hoped that I'd drop the whole idea before we opened. I only became more serious.

I announced Fuku at SXSW as if we were a Silicon Valley startup. I told the crowd that I was launching a beta version of a chain poised to outwit Chick-fil-A. I talked about building a mobile app, looking forward to working with tech people, and honoring the chicken spot that occupied 163 before Noodle Bar. I made no mention of racism.

When Fuku opened in June 2015, lines formed around the block. For months, the food media wrote about the crowds, how well our delivery launch had gone, new additions to the menu, expanded hours, and our forthcoming stand at Madison Square Garden.

I'd thought that if nobody picked up on the traps I had set, I'd get a smirking sense of satisfaction. Well, they didn't, and I was fucking pissed. I should have known better, but in my defense, this was before the hot-chicken craze had hit.

You see, Chick-fil-A was only one in a long line of fried chicken–related miscarriages of cultural justice. For starters, the mere act of selling fried chicken in the United States is something originally popularized by the newly freed black slaves—mostly women—of the American South. They rarely get the appropriate credit. I feel strongly that the history warrants mentioning, even if our recipe took most of its inspiration from Asian traditions. The main culinary reference was Hot-Star Large Fried Chicken in Taiwan.

How was I to know that five years later, people from coast to coast would be eating Nashville hot chicken—another African American invention—without a care in the world for where it came from? Why did I think they would care about our statement on Asian American representation?

Exactly *one* journalist ever pushed me on the branding at the original Fuku. Well after the buzz died down, Serena Dai, a very smart Chinese American reporter, sent me an email out of the blue inquiring about *Dericious!* I explained what I was trying to do, and I think she was sympathetic.

A full year after we opened, Marge and I were manning a Fuku stand at a major sporting event. I finally got what I had been waiting for. Two well-known dignitaries helped themselves to our sandwiches. One of them noticed the misspelled word on the wrapper and showed it to his colleague.

"Dericious!" they kept saying to each other, laughing like little kids. They kept at it, their pitch lowering to martial arts master sotto voce: "SO. DE-RI-SHUS."

I freaked out. I'd hoped to weaponize the racism I'd experienced as an Asian American person. I'd hoped non-Asian people would be too scared to utter the words on our wrappers or laugh at the pictures on the wall. But they weren't scared at all.

"Marge, I made a mistake. This is a disaster. We need to pull the plug."

It's been almost five years and Fuku continues to chug along, expanding into sports stadiums and different cities. I've mostly handed the reins over to smart people with business degrees. We've shelved the *Dericious* bags, the Bible citations, and the Asian bad guys. I don't regret any of it. I only wish more people had noticed.

Grace

I HATE NIGHTCLUBS.

The problem was that I couldn't come up with an excuse. I was sitting alone on the couch when my phone buzzed with an invitation to come out. The place was within walking distance from my apartment and I had nothing else to do. I had basically lived like a monk for months—off the meds and off the booze. My friend said that a bunch of his female friends would be there. I threw on a shirt.

Regret washed over me as soon as I saw the mass of people waiting outside and felt the thumping bass from within. Nevertheless, I entered. I drank water. I interacted with the pal who'd invited me to join. I stood there, looked around, and left within the hour.

My friend texted again in the morning. One of the women at the club, the one I'd asked him about but hadn't brought myself to speak to, was hosting a barbecue with her friends.

Long story short: I arrived at the East Village rooftop and found Grace and her fellow hosts going down in flames. Too many people had come. The grill was too small. They were struggling to keep up. It was a custom-made opportunity for me to impress. I felt like I was on a crowded plane when the flight attendants call out, "Is there a doctor onboard?"

Dr. Chang reporting for duty.

I saved the day and helped with cleanup, too. The weary hosts were grateful but disappointed that they hadn't had time to eat. They were starving.

"I have a restaurant down the block . . ."

• • •

After the barbecue, I headed to Wyoming for a few weeks to unwind. I resisted the urge to contact her, but upon my return Grace called to ask me out.

I had come to terms with the fact that I would never get married. All my relationships had fallen apart, usually because of me. I felt incapable of marriage and I said as much to Grace. I gave her my usual line: "I'm not looking for anything serious, blah blah blah." Over time, I'd share every messed-up detail of my romantic life with her. She never flinched or judged me.

We began dating, and one night, David Choe came over to my apartment after grabbing dinner with our friend Asa Akira. Asa is one of the world's most famous porn stars. Choe is a filthy rich artist with a love for pushing buttons. Grace didn't bat an eye the entire night. She laughed and joked along with them, and my crazy friends took a liking to her immediately. We all sat around and watched *Bojack Horseman* together. It was a good time.

As we got to know each other better, I felt a calmness. My brain told me not to commit, that it would eventually end, but my gut said otherwise. She exuded confidence and composure. (That rooftop barbecue was the first and only time I've ever seen her in the weeds.) She hated clubs, too. She'd been convinced to go that night by her friends. And like me, she straddled two cultures.

I've dated women of other races and ethnicities, but all of my meaningful relationships have been with Asian women. Try as I might, I could never shed the cultural pressure to marry someone who was Korean. With any other relationship, there would always be the nagging thought in the back of my head that it would ultimately have to end because my family would never approve of a non-Korean woman.

Grace was Korean, but it didn't feel like we were together because we were Korean. The attraction had everything to do with her heart, her generous spirit, how chill she was. These other factors actually allowed me to appreciate our cultural connection on a much deeper level. Grace and I don't have to explain ourselves to one another because we share the same idiosyncratic Korean American upbringing. She grew up as the daughter of Korean immigrants finding their way in a predominantly white suburb of Seattle.

I don't believe in soul mates or the idea that there's one person on earth for each of us, but when I try to envision someone who might stick with me for the rest of her life, I can only imagine Grace. When I think of someone I can love for decades to come, it's Grace. She's strong-willed and self-possessed. She's worked hard in the fashion world, but her true ambitions are even harder to attain. Grace wants to live generously, fruitfully, healthily, fully, and she wants to help others do the same. She surrounds herself with good people and treats them well.

I count myself lucky to be among the primary beneficiaries of her worldview. She was immensely supportive when I eventually told her I wanted to go back on medication. She guided and worked with me through manic episodes, restaurant openings, good days, bad reviews, and many highs and lows in between.

We share an instinct to nurture and protect one another. But the absolute truth is, the balance of our relationship remains shamefully lopsided. I'm striving to give as good as I get, and to stop treating loved ones like employees. I have yet to learn how to accept the love of someone else and to believe that it won't fail me. This must be among the most frustrating and upsetting obstacles a person can encounter in a relationship. Imagine having to convince your wife or husband of your love on a daily basis. I don't just mean saying "I love you," but sometimes having to plead with them in order to drag them back from the brink. I have to be better. She knows I'm trying. I love her for giving me the chance.

We got married and Grace gave birth to a baby boy whom we named Hugo. For many years I thought I'd never be ready to be a father. Now I know I just hadn't met Grace yet.

20

WHAT YOU SEE AND
WHAT YOU GET

THE EXPERIENCE OF OPENING FUKU ONLY INCREASED MY APPETITE TO undermine people's ideas of American identity. Mania gave me the freedom to follow through.

In 2015, just after opening a Momofuku in Washington, D.C., I gave an interview to Todd Kliman at *Washingtonian*. The headline— *A Long, Strange Conversation with David Chang*—says it all, but an even better headline might have been *Ever Wonder What Mania Looks Like? Read This*. They published a transcript of our conversation, which ran forty-five minutes longer than expected. It's a doozy. Such was my manic high that I didn't get self-conscious when friends called to ask if I was okay after reading the article.

I was now close to defining my life's work. My brain was on a quest to uncover the underlying systems in the cosmos and then bring that knowledge back to the dining room. I really thought this. The ideas came quickly and were all over the place, I could see that even then. But let's not confuse being manic with being wrong. It was around this time that I wrote a piece for *Wired* magazine with the obnoxious headline *David Chang's Unified Theory of Deliciousness.*

I'd had a series of overlapping epiphanies, not all of which were original ideas, but as far as I knew, they had never been expressed in a culinary context before. The first was that the best forms of creativity are born from paradox. Think of M. C. Escher's paintings of staircases leading nowhere and hands drawing one another. Or René Magritte's *The Treachery of Images,* in which a painting of a pipe is accompanied with a subtitle: *Ceci n'est pas une pipe.* This is not a pipe.

In kitchens, we are told that a dish is seasoned properly when it's neither undersalted nor too salty. *That's not right,* I thought. The best dishes exhibit both extremes simultaneously. You want a dish that tastes too salty one moment, perfect the next, and then maybe even underseasoned after that. True balance is not an average. It is two forces in equal measure. A bowl of rice is bland. A chili relish is too salty and spicy to eat alone. Eaten together, they're perfect—a constant pull between intensity and mildness. It's an idea that is baked into our understanding of the universe. Picture the yin-yang symbol. It's a balance of black and white, but it's not just a gray circle—it's two hemispheres perpetually swirling into each other.

Returning to the salt analogy, imagine a row of glasses filled with salt water that proceed in order from least salty to saltiest. If you taste them one by one, you'll be able to sense the progression. But if you stop in the middle and go backward, the previous glass will no longer taste salty at all. Try it sometime. What we consider to be the objectivity of our senses is actually tied deeply into our frame of reference, which is always moving.

This idea of shifting perspectives brought to mind a memory from childhood.

One day, my parents bought me a Transformers toy and briefly made me the most popular kid on the block. A few neighborhood kids came over to play. When my mom served dinner, one of them took a sniff of the kimchi. While she was away from the table, he said, "No wonder you people eat dog." They all started barking.

I don't know where that kid is now, but it wouldn't surprise me to hear that he loves kimchi. It's everywhere. I can go to the bodega down the block and spend ten minutes debating which boutique brand to overpay for.

Humans have innate biological predilections, but the most important factors in determining our tastes are societal. Cultural conditioning can convince a person to recoil from a dish that's exactly like one of their own staple foods. Scientifically speaking, sauerkraut and kimchi are basically identical. That conditioning can also force us to cling to notions that prevent the evolution of deliciousness (and society).

I specifically say *us* because I'm also guilty. It used to drive me crazy to see a white chef making kimchi, but really, it shouldn't have. What's the alternative? We all stick to our lanes rather than make an effort to see something new? I'd far prefer to see a white chef trying to make kimchi instead of barking at it.

Cuisine has always evolved through collision, even if we don't always notice. To wit: over the course of my life, I've eaten hundreds of tacos al pastor. I've always considered them the emblem of Mexico City. Only recently have I learned that the vertical spit used to cook al pastor, the trompo, originated in Lebanon. It's the same exact device that gave us the shawarma, the döner kebab, and the gyro. Lebanese immigrants brought the vertical spit with them to the Americas, where the technology met new ingredients and people, yielding fantastic results. It shouldn't have come as a shock to me. Deliciousness is a meme. Its appeal is universal, and it will spread without consideration of borders or prejudice.

I began to question the validity of various cultural truths. Who gets to assign value to certain foods? What makes something acceptable or not? Why was MSG villainized in Chinese restaurants but fine when it occurred naturally in Parmesan?

Let me frame this yet another way. There's a famous clip from a 2010 Lakers game. Matt Barnes and Kobe Bryant have been jawing at each other for most of the night. In the third quarter, Barnes pump-fakes a pass at Kobe's face at point-blank range. Any mere mortal would flinch, but Kobe does not so much as blink. You could end any argument about who held the title of most cold-blooded basketball player of all time by summoning the clip.

A few years later, the Internet dug up a different angle of the same play. From the overhead camera, you could see that the ball hadn't come as close to Kobe's face as millions of people had thought. Our limited perspective had fed the narrative we wanted. The new angle didn't make it untrue, but it shows how fragile our convictions are. Yes, Kobe was one of the most fearless, unflappable athletes of all time. No, this was not an example of that.

I wanted the food at Momofuku to serve the same purpose as that second clip: to reveal that our beliefs may only be a matter of perspective, and that multiple things can be true at once.

All these ideas were nascent at the time, born from mania. I must have sounded like an idiot to anyone who was listening, but I was growing in certainty. It would all come to bear when we opened our first sit-down restaurant in New York in five years.

• • •

We were forced to expand because we'd taken on outside money. I can't concisely explain why I'd finally agreed to bring in outside money, or justify why I personally guaranteed the loan—remember the physical I took to prove that I wasn't going to die before the bank could get its money back?—except to say that we needed it. I was still so far from understanding how a business should work.

But even though we'd taken the money, there was none to speak of. We used a good chunk to build out a new larger home for Ko near the Bowery. Our D.C. restaurant was massively expensive, too. The rest of our money was going to supporting passion projects like *Lucky Peach,* which was still alive at the time.

For the sake of cash flow, I agreed to open a second Noodle Bar in New York, in Chelsea. It would be the first step in a harebrained scheme to scale up. We would open a commissary kitchen in Sunset Park, Brooklyn, that would handle most of the cooking. A bus would make the rounds between the boroughs, dropping off items for small teams at various Noodle Bars whose kitchens were outfitted with only the essentials. They'd be paint-by-numbers kinds of deals; training would be standardized so anyone could hop aboard any Noodle Bar and learn to do the job with ease, ad infinitum.

I tapped Josh Pinsky, a hardworking cook from Ko, to run it. Pinsky understands that the organizational side of a kitchen is just as important as the creative. He is also a direct communicator.

A few months before the opening, I asked if he was excited.

He wasn't.

Anyone at Momofuku will tell you that I'm constantly preaching honesty and transparency. I insist that I want people to push back against me. Now ask the team if that's true, and they'll say . . . "No comment." To be honest, I'm trying to get better at hearing answers I don't like, but what Pinsky was telling me had the benefit of being both true and something I wanted to hear.

Scaling Noodle Bar carried all kinds of baggage related to the idea of selling out or selling ourselves short. Deep in my gut, I was hoping for an out. I knew that Pinsky wanted to be a chef with a capital C, and it was a relief to hear that he didn't want to be the chef of a fleet of Noodle Bars.

Pinsky told me he prided himself on being the pasta specialist at Ko. That's the sort of stuff he really loved to cook. An idea instantly crystallized. *An Italian Momofuku? Are you kidding me?* I couldn't think of a better place to put all this philosophical deliberation to the test.

Most people have already forgotten that not long ago, Italian food was written off as an inferior foreign cuisine. These days, the average New York diner can share their opinions about favorite olive oils and identify the various culinary regions of Italy. I love Italian food as much as the next guy, but I also longed for the chance to fuck with it mercilessly.

I put the matter to a vote in the office. Should we open another Noodle Bar, or do something completely different? The team was clear. They wanted to push for something new.

I went to Home Depot and bought a wooden dowel so I could roll noodles. The resulting dish came out looking like chicken and dumplings to most people, but to me it was Korean su jae bi. Cut slightly differently, the noodles might have also passed as mafaldine. When I tasted it, I couldn't decide which reference was most prominent. It's all about how you look at it.

Case in point, when an Italian restaurant charges $25 for pasta pomodoro, very few foodies will balk. We picture the pastificio kneading the pasta dough the way his nonna taught him. We assign a high value to tomatoes grown and canned in Italy. We picture the skilled cook stirring al dente spaghetti and sauce together with a splash of pasta-cooking water at the perfect moment so that it becomes a unified dish. Every dollar is justified.

Now let's say a Chinese chef uses four times as many ingredients and spends three times longer making a bowl of noodles. Even the cultured foodie still expects to pay no more than eight or ten bucks. False cultural constructs tell us that pasta can be expensive, while noodles have to be cheap. The same dichotomy exists between almost any Asian (or African or Latin American) dish and its Western analogue. To me, there is literally no other explanation than racism. Don't even try to talk to me about how the price differential is a result of service and decor. That shit is paid for by people who are willing to spend money on safe, "non-ethnic" food.

At Nishi, we would erase the invisible divide between pasta and noodles.* Our customers would order an Italian dish, something they'd eaten hundreds of times. If all went according to plan, they would love our version more than any other, only to learn that it was made from ingredients that sounded more like a recipe for lo mein than amatriciana. It would be a Trojan horse that upset people's biases not only in terms of what they liked, but *why* they liked it. In fact, we wouldn't even advertise ourselves as an Italian restaurant.

We didn't want to force dishes together. That's fusion. We wanted to encourage natural convergences that would predict what food will look like down the road. I thought about the pasteis they sell in the markets of São Paulo, empanada-dumpling hybrids that developed through interactions between Europe, Asia, and South America. I thought about the culinary blending of Asian and Latin influences in Los Angeles. It was too logical not to be inevitable.

It's not so different from what Quino and I had done years ago at Noodle Bar. This time, instead of imagining that my Korean family had traded places with Quino's Mexican forebears, I pictured a family from Turin swapping places with another family in Seoul. What would happen when the Koreans ran out of soy sauce? In a pinch, would they incorporate Parmesan into their recipes?

In northern Italy, they eat bollito misto, a classic dish that can succinctly be defined as tough meats simmered slowly in stock and then sliced and arranged onto a platter. In Korea, they eat suyuk, a classic dish that can succinctly be defined as tough meats boiled in stock and then sliced and arranged onto a platter. At what point between the two does the bollito misto cease to be bollito misto and the suyuk cease to be suyuk? At what point does something come out that's a natural hybrid with the same universal appeal?

More and more, I noticed how the most impactful Momofuku

---

*The word *nishi* means "west" in Japanese. It made sense as a name, both geographically (the Chelsea location relative to our other restaurants) and conceptually (the first Momofuku menu ostensibly specializing in Western cuisine).

dishes were ones that lived in this in-between dimension. For the past ten years, Ssäm Bar has served a dish of spicy pork sausage and rice cakes. Here's the origin story: Joshua McFadden, one of our first chefs, asked if he could make a Bolognese ragù. I said yes, on the condition that he limit himself to Korean ingredients. He and the other Ssäm chefs ended up making an absurdly tasty dish: I could understand the Bolognese reference when I tasted it, but thanks to the starchy gumminess of rice cakes and the liberal use of chili oil, I also thought of mapo tofu. The dish was more than the sum of its cultural parts. It derived its magnetism from the tension between the familiar and the foreign—the diner could decide which was which—and was firmly committed to both.

The breakthrough Nishi dish, the one that best encapsulated our vision, was the cacio e pepe: nominally Italian but made with almost no Italian ingredients. For years, we'd been fermenting chickpeas in our test lab to make a kind of miso we called hozon.* The flavor had always reminded me of cheese. I tried making a cacio e pepe with the hozon standing in for pecorino, and it was extraordinary. The fact that chickpeas are called *ceci* in Italian set us up for a cool name, too: ceci e pepe.

I wrote the final menu myself. At first glance, it read a lot like a typical Momofuku effort: DISH NAME—X COMPONENT, Y COMPONENT, Z COMPONENT. But there were subtle differences. Each section of the menu had a Korean translation. And at the bottom of the page, there were ten footnotes, little clues that read like an artist statement:**

---

*The lab was built to conduct fermentation experiments but also to scratch the exact same itch as Nishi. We wanted to make products that upend people's ideas of not only what is valuable but also what's possible with food. One of our earliest outputs was a pork version of katsuobushi—the dried, smoked, fermented fish flakes that are one of the foundational ingredients of Japanese cooking.

**When I reread the menu now, it makes me hungry, but it also makes me want to punch myself in the face. The biggest lesson I took away from this period was to do more and talk about it less.

1. Dry Aged Happy Valley Eye Round: Crudo × Carpaccio
2. Mul Neng Myun (-) Noodle and Beef (+) Momofuku Pickles
3. Bagna Cauda × Caesar × Ho Chi Minh
4. We encourage eating the head and the shell
5. Notes from Parmesan come from chickpea hozon. No cheese
6. Su Jae Bi × Malfatti × Cracker Barrel
7. Golden Century's Pippies and XO × Fideos × Vongole
8. Ma Po Tofu × Chili Pan Mee × Lamb & Mint
9. Jampong × Ladner's Jalapeño Crab Spaghetti × Grandpa Woo
10. Kathy Pinsky's Bundt Cake 2.0

• • •

When Nishi opened in the first week of 2016, we only took walk-ins. Inside, it was cramped and lively. There were a few Escher prints hanging on the walls. Pinsky and I spent our days and nights cranking it out together, fine-tuning. For the first time in my career, I went into the dining room to "touch" tables, gathering feedback and apologizing if certain items ran out. Mania made me decidedly more gregarious.

I sent out a company-wide email surveying people about our potential weaknesses. I wanted everyone to be a step ahead of the critics, specifically Pete Wells at *The New York Times*.

> **From: david chang**
> Date: Sun, Jan 31, 2016 at 10:43 AM
> Subject: Pete wells Paranoia.
>
> Just a heads up.
>
> With Nishi opened he will be not only eating at Nishi
> for review but certainly noodle bar and Ssam
>
> I predict a double review Nishi + Ssam or noodle or ma
> Peche but you never know

I don't know if we will be able to catch him every time.
Best way to maximize time and energy is to not focus on
just one person but to improve and examine our entire
operation. If we do miss him than so be it. He should
get the same meal as everyone else.

So we need to reemphasize humility in how we cook
and service guests. Tighten certain procedures that
are loose. Improve existing dishes that we just don't
have time.

Let's get Pete wells px fires going on very night where
we have portioned off soigné pieces for him. To hammer
into the cooks that the precious few seconds in a
service can add up when you need to come through for a
critics table. Let's artificially increase the pressure
load on everyone. Let's get so regimented in how his
table gets touched by the room that no gets nervous
when he finally shows up.

This week can all the restaurants mentioned above share
their plan of attack for Pete wells:

- a list of potential criticisms or weak spots at each
restaurant (menu, facility, music, service, a specific
dish . . . anything)

- how we will remedy those ailments

- a check list that that is unique to each restaurant
(so if we do catch and spot him we ensure certain things
are in play). For example. We have soigné food and best
server already reserved. The reserved soigné food is
important to set aside daily whether it's a sauce or a
portion of noodles.

We make sure that the tables around him are being
handled and they are happy. The facilities are all in
a good place. Etc etc. I mean a literal check list that
needs to be reviewed rapidly when he is here. So we
don't miss anything.

Let's not let Pete wells dictate our future. We should
be the ones who write that. We may very well not exceed

his subjective expectations, but if we are truly our
hardest critics, we should be ready for anything Pete
Wells related. Let's kill him with the most delicious
food and service.

Thanks guys. If you have questions please email me. Dave

Marge raised a red flag about the lessness of the Nishi space—
no backs on the seats, no cushions, no bread service—but I reasoned
that that had always been our style. People also noted that prices were
high, or they looked high. We were testing out a no-tipping policy
to compensate everyone on staff more fairly. But even without the
tipping-inclusive model, Nishi's prices were steep in comparison to
Noodle Bar. *That's the point,* I told myself. *This is an Italian restaurant.
We have to charge Italian prices.*

Before Wells could chime in, Ryan Sutton of *Eater* and Adam
Platt of *New York* magazine panned us in the same week in March.
Panned. They each gave Nishi one star. A week later, Tejal Rao, then
the critic for Bloomberg, sang the same tune: one star there as well.
The restaurant was not just uncomfortable; it was aggressively unin-
viting. The food was uneven, they said.

From: david chang
To: Roundtable
Date: Tue, Mar 15, 2016 at 5:56 PM
Subject: Nishi review: eater

I'm gonna keep this short . . . but I first want to
apologize to the entire company for letting everyone
down. I made the decisions that made Nishi what it is
today, which was a rushed project with inherent physical
short comings.

Regardless, Nishi is a restaurant with great food
and service but misses the mark on everything else
including ambience, pricing and comfort. It unfortunate
that I haven't been able to best showcase everyone's
hard work.

We will not panic and we will reevaluate our prices in
the coming weeks. There are many things to take into
consideration and Ryan Sutton brings up many good points
but these are not quick fixes. Making quick decisions
put us into this current situation,so we will take our
time to make the right decisions moving forward.

- We will address the dining room both in comfort and
acoustics

- We will explore the no tipping policy and our price
point to make it work

it should be noted how great Josh, Carey and Sara
have executed. Especially considering that it was to
be a Fuku/noodle bar a mere three months ago. So I
really want to congratulate them on their great work.
No one says the food or service is bad, in fact I
think they are terrific. Critics just think the nishi's
idiosyncrasies are insanely stupid and that's on me.

Anyway I could ramble forever but wanted to make sure I
addressed the eater sutton review.

Everyday we will get a little bit better. Any all
suggestions welcome. Thanks for understanding. Dave

In fairness, some of the bad decisions at Nishi weren't mine. But at the end of the day, our failings were on me. It had been a while since I'd opened a restaurant in New York, and I'd lost my confidence to communicate my ideas.

"We can take their criticisms constructively," I told everyone in person. "But we have to remember that the big one hasn't written his review yet. Eyes on the prize."

Wells would be the final word. We still had a shot.

The fact is that I have benefited as much as any chef from positive reviews in *The New York Times,* but it's also absurd to think of the amount of time that I have dedicated to following the lives and understanding the minds of their food critics. At times, it can feel existentially frustrating, especially when you realize that diners generally don't question the authority of their local critic. Critics are assumed to be infallible or, at the very least, deserving of the benefit of the doubt. For whatever reason, it is incumbent upon the chef to meet the critic on his or her terms. While we waited on Wells, I tried to imagine all the angles: the best reviewers don't merely inform readers if the food is good or bad. They offer important cultural criticism. So, what was the peg going to be? He could write about our resurgence and tacitly imply that his peers got it wrong. He could also say we'd sold out. Wells had written one of the first major magazine pieces about Momofuku, in which he placed me as the fiercely independent foil to the clubby, high-volume, corporate Asian-y restaurants that were showing up on the scene when Noodle Bar opened—places like Megu and Tao, where you ate under a thirty-foot statue of the Buddha. Or he could be informed by the zeitgeist. He was fresh off destroying Thomas Keller in an unprecedented takedown of Per Se. He was either making room for someone to take Keller's place in the firmament or he was in the mood to drop the hammer on more big names. Or maybe it meant nothing. I started to get especially nervous when *The New Yorker* called; they were writing a big profile on Wells and they wanted a reporter to be there with me while I read the review. I declined.

I was in the HBO offices when my phone started to flicker. We were pitching *Lucky Peach* as a TV show to try to inject some cash into the magazine. I had done the fact check for the review with Wells the night before, so I knew it was coming out. Under the table, I snuck a peek at the headline—*At Momofuku Nishi, David Chang's Magic Shows a Little Wear*. What does *a little wear* mean? I scrolled through, focusing in on random lines. I excused myself when I got to the rating: one star.

Like everyone else, Wells said the food wasn't good enough to justify the lack of creature comforts. He characterized the menu as annoyingly self-referential, which stung. Big picture, he suggested that maybe it was time for everyone to realize that Momofuku had had its moment and served its purpose.

In my mind, he was saying one thing loud and clear: *Thank God that the Momofuku era is finally over.*

• • •

Nishi was our first across-the-board failure. Grace didn't sleep the night the review came out because she was worried that I was going to hurt myself. I had worked so hard, I thought, to get out of the hole. "The gradual unfucking" is what Marshall Goldsmith used to call it. I was nicer at Nishi, with fewer outbursts. I was trying but I was unsure about how to be this other kind of leader. I assumed that people would give us a chance to make mistakes while we found our footing. I thought I was being transparent when I told Sutton and Wells we were working on the sound levels and other issues, but really I was trying to preempt their criticisms. Scrambling, I even considered speaking more publicly about the financial realities of the company, how we didn't have the budget to make improvements as quickly as possible—how I was personally leveraged against the business, how we were still living day-to-day.

But who was going to believe that? And why would that be their problem? The Yankees don't get an extra out because somebody left a mitt at home.

We had missed the mark. I was pissed at myself for not being above reproach. And I was pissed at the reviewers. Showing some wear? What do you want from us? We're trying to do something remarkable. There was nothing worn about it.

For years, I had treated the restaurant business with the same mentality that Coppola took into *Apocalypse Now*. He approached making a movie about the Vietnam War with the intensity of someone going to actual war. I knew how unhealthy it was. For once I hadn't pushed hard enough, hadn't lived like I was ready to die. And the moment

I'd started trying to see the bigger picture, I'd put the business at risk.

I was on the verge of getting back on my feet after a very bad year, but the reviews of Nishi knocked me flat on my back again. I'm hesitant to admit this, but having to live through it a second time when *The New Yorker* published its profile of Wells put me in a bleak state of mind. I'm embarrassed that I let criticism affect me so intensely, but I felt closer to suicide in that period than I had in years.

I wanted credit for trying to be multiple things at once, but they all said we weren't being enough of a restaurant. Whether or not we deserved it, no one gave us a pass for trying. And we had been trying so hard for so long. This meant everything to us. Couldn't they see that?

21

BLIND SPOTS

If I'm going to call out critics for what they've failed to see about Momofuku, I also have to take a moment to explore my own blind spots. The obvious one—the big, glaring, ugly thing I didn't grasp—was about the women in our industry.

I'm not going to sit here and tell you that #MeToo awakened me to some hidden injustice. Nor will I pander to the moment and tell you that we'd all seen this coming for a long time. The truth, for me at least, is somewhere in between.

Within days of Brett Anderson publishing his earth-shattering article in *The Times-Picayune* about the New Orleans chef John Besh and the atmosphere of pervasive sexual harassment and aggression at his restaurants, a different chef was fired from a restaurant group I really admire.

As the company's executive chef, he oversaw multiple restaurants. An employee at one of them had been showing around an
inappropriate photo of a female co-worker. The chef saw but didn't
report it. When the woman in the photo went to HR herself, they
conducted a full investigation and ultimately fired both the chef and
the general manager of the restaurant where the incident took place.
The guy who shared the photo had already been let go for unrelated
reasons.

My gut reaction was to think that the punishment was harsh.
A suspension, I could understand. But firing a chef over a nude
photo that someone else took? I knew that the chef was extraordinarily busy. I imagined him working on the line when this employee
showed him the photo on his phone. He was probably creeped out.
Maybe he even said something like, "Dude, put that shit away." He
could have made a mental note to deal with this cook later. Then one
small emergency or another pulled his attention away. The day kept
piling on and eventually he forgot about it. I could see the same thing
happening to someone in my company.

Did he really need to be fired? I continued to turn it over and
over in my mind. What was I not getting?

Ultimately, I asked myself what kind of photo would have caused
me to drop everything I was doing, send the chef packing immediately, and alert everyone in management to the situation. As self-
centered as that approach may sound, it helped me understand what
I was missing. What if a cook had been spreading around some racist
meme he'd made of an Asian co-worker? What if my chef ignored it
and I found out about it later? I imagined the years of insecurity and
humiliation flooding over me, and the sense of betrayal I'd feel after
my staff had let it slide. How would I have reacted? I would have
lost it.

It had been so easy for me to imagine the male chef's perspective, but it took more effort to empathize with the woman. I dedicate an inordinate amount of time to thinking about professional

kitchens, and I pride myself in my empathic abilities, especially when it comes to other cooks and chefs. I count myself as an expert in the restaurant business. And yet, with all of the evidence in front of me, telling me that this was wrong, that the restaurant group had acted appropriately and responsibly, I hadn't immediately seen it. Some expert.

• • •

I'm literally one of the poster children for the kitchen patriarchy. In 2013, *Time* magazine put a photo of me, René Redzepi, and Alex Atala wearing chef whites and satisfied smirks on the cover of their magazine and called us "The Gods of Food." I didn't question whether any women would be included in the issue's roundup of the most important chefs in the world because frankly it never occurred to me to ask.* Even years before #MeToo started in earnest, the backlash to the all-male lineup was swift and deserved.

At the time, I thought the point was about representation: there should be more women chefs covered by the food media, just as there should be more people of color. But no, we're talking about something much more vicious. It's not just about the glass ceiling or equal opportunity. It's about people being threatened, undermined, abused, and ashamed in the workplace. It's embarrassing to admit how long it took me to grasp that.

I counted Mario Batali and Ken Friedman as friends. If you're looking for stories, there's nothing that you can't read about in *Heat*. It's right there in black and white in the pages of Bill Buford's acclaimed book about studying at Batali's feet. Throughout, you'll find Mario looking up servers' skirts and comparing every ingredient

---

*I also can't believe I didn't stop dead in my tracks when I heard the phrase *Gods of Food*. I must have been so happy not to be called a *celebrity chef* that I didn't even stop to think about how much more obnoxious this new moniker was.

he comes across to a sexual organ. There were countless eyes on Mario, which made many of us think that what we were seeing was all right.

But something terrible *was* there under the surface and I simply didn't look hard enough. Mario offered the clues freely, but I, for one, was too ignorant to ask questions.

• • •

I considered writing this book without talking about #MeToo. In fact, I received plenty of forceful suggestions from colleagues to that effect. *There's no way for you to get it right,* they told me. *Better to keep your head down.*

This might be a little ungenerous to say, but I imagine that as #MeToo gained momentum, most chefs in America immediately started scouring their own backyards for past mistakes. I get it. Fear, even when you know you're "clean," is a powerful motivator.

I'm no exception. I asked my staff to investigate our company's history, compare our HR policies to others', and ensure that we were above reproach. I felt some degree of comfort. I was satisfied with who we were as a company and certain that we could defend our record. But I wanted to make sure we could address any possible grievances with a truthful and satisfactory answer, so we kept digging.

Then one day, I called everyone in Momofuku's management team and told them I was wrong. To feel comfortable while others continue to suffer is the ugliest form of contentment. I'd been so concerned with being right that I hadn't considered whether we were doing right. In our restaurants, we'd never settled for "good enough so that we won't get in trouble." What kind of standard is that? Why would we think that way about how we treated our own people?

The team pivoted its focus from the past to the present and the kind of company we wanted to become. The company-wide directive was to shoot for the moon with our ambitions, even if it seemed impossible that we'd ever achieve them. We needed to look outside ourselves and our industry for ideas, and I was happy to see the team coming up with solutions that I wouldn't necessarily have seen on my own. Leslie Ferrier, our vice president of human resources, sent out a company-wide email with the number for a hotline run by a third party that would hear and investigate any reports of discrimination or harassment. That was a start.

But there's a long way to go—I know that. I also know that, contrary to what I once thought, the way I see the restaurant industry is not the full picture. Every day I speak to a cook or chef or journalist who changes my understanding of what it means to cook and serve food professionally. I'm writing this at a moment when I'm reassessing everything I thought I knew.

I'm striving to be honest about my past shortcomings, but hindsight is not enough. I'm nowhere near as empathetic or aware as I want to be. I can't promise that I'll ever get there, or that Momofuku will become the company we're working toward. There will always be mistakes and miscommunications. The only fatal error would be to stop trying.

• • •

You remember those Magic Eye books that were popular in the nineties? At first you'd flip through and see nothing but meaningless patterns, like pieces of ugly wallpaper. Then someone would tell you to "unfocus your eyes" or something like that. You looked again and suddenly a three-dimensional image emerged. You'd flip back through all those same banal pages and see dinosaurs, pirate ships, wolves howling at the moon.

Once you learned how to see it, you could always do it. You couldn't look at one of those patterns again without seeing something else.

I know it's painfully simplistic, but that's the best metaphor I have. Once it clicked, flaws appeared to me where they hadn't before.

Even this book, written with the benefit of greater knowledge and better perspective, is still riddled with problems. I've talked a great deal about the importance of failure as a learning tool, but it's really a privilege to expect people to let us fail over and over again. There are too many dudes in my story in general, and you can still sense my bro-ish excitement when I tell old war stories. Almost all the artists and writers I mention are men, and most of the movies I reference can be found in the DVD library of any frat house in America. It's my truth, which is why I'm leaving them in here, but I wish that some of it were different.

Recognizing my flaws doesn't mean I'm "cured," nor does wishing that I'd done things differently. I still regress from time to time, but I'm trying to be the person I want to be. I'm trying to build a company that is better than I am and an environment where the next generation will have better answers to the questions we're facing.

The mental and physical toll of working in restaurants is corrosive. I don't know how long it will take to undo the harm and build an industry that is equitable for people of all genders, races, ethnicities, sexualities, and beliefs. I think it begins with being accountable to one another. Respecting one another and ourselves. I know that better education and communication will be key.

I'd really like to tie a more satisfying bow on this, but I'm now realizing that that may be a brutish impulse, too. *How can I hammer out a resolution to this right now? Whose fault is it, and how do I make them pay?* The need for quick resolution points to a desire to get it over with, when, in fact, the only solution is to sit and marinate in how uncomfortable this all is. I have to commit the years it will take to learn about the people around me and reject my baked-in biases. I'm somewhat soothed by one thought: we are supposed to grow as people. We're meant to ask questions, see things differently, build empathy. That's the hope, anyway.

I'll give you an example. In *Kitchen Confidential,* Tony wrote about the salacious appeal of working in a restaurant.

In the kitchen, they were like gods. They dressed like pirates . . . They drank everything in sight, stole whatever wasn't nailed down, and screwed their way through floor staff, bar customers, and casual visitors like nothing I'd ever seen or imagined . . . I saw a lot of bad behavior that first year in Provincetown. These guys were master criminals, sexual athletes . . . the life of the cook was a life of adventure, looting, pillaging and rock-and-rolling through life with a carefree disregard for all conventional morality. It looked pretty damn good to me on the other side of the line.

It's awkward to think about how much I enjoyed reading his stories and the many others—mostly told by men—that glamorized the crude brutality of the kitchen. But I did.

Cooking brings out the best and worst in me, and I think the same went for Tony. I've tried to do some growing up and whittle away my uglier tendencies. Tony grew up, too. I watched him mature on television and in person. I know it pained him to think of his role in glamorizing this part of chef culture, but we forgave him because we could see that he was evolving. My hope is that the people in this business can undergo the same kind of growth without leaving the kitchen.

Restaurants saved my life, but they've also hurt and betrayed many of my peers. I believe our industry can still be a place of healing—a refuge where people nurture one another physically and spiritually—but only if we make it so.

22

CONSIDER THE LOBSTER

CHANGE IS GUARANTEED, BUT GROWTH ISN'T. IN MY EXPERIENCE, IF YOU want to grow, you've got to want it. In fact, you've got to want it so bad that you'll toss out everything that got you where you are.

No one used to complain about the music being too loud in restaurants. Most of the time, there was no music at all. If there was, it was all classical, jazz, or some innocuous Italian or French soundtrack played at a barely audible volume.

You didn't really hear music in kitchens, either. When we opened Noodle Bar, Quino and I were in our twenties and music meant so much to us. It was our place, so why couldn't we listen to music while we worked? We brought in an iPod and a CD player, bought the jankiest speakers available at Circuit City, and set them up on the top shelf. We had never worked in an open kitchen before, so it didn't dawn on us until the first night of service that if you play music in the kitchen, everyone in the dining room is going to hear it, too.

We listened to the same stuff we listened to when we were by ourselves. Pavement. Silver Jews. Velvet Underground. Yo La Tengo. GZA. Fugazi. Pixies. Metallica. Galaxie 500. Wilco. There was a stretch where we played a ton of country—a lot of Waylon Jennings. Lambchop's "Your Fucking Sunny Day" was a really important track to me. It's a great, chill, happy song, but when we put it on the playlist, I thought someone might complain about the profanity. We kept asking ourselves, *Are we allowed to play this?*

Whoever ran the pass was the DJ for the night. One of the nice perks of working with all the cool, young kids in the East Village was that they would expose us to so much good shit. As a rule, we avoided playing music that people knew too well. My greatest fear was re-creating that moment from *Almost Famous* when the whole bus starts singing along to "Tiny Dancer." We played songs and albums that didn't get a lot of radio play, and we saw that these bands were meaningful to a lot of our guests, too. One day a guy walked up to me in the kitchen and said, "Are you playing The Who B-sides? This might be my favorite restaurant." Music became a natural filter for the audience we were hoping to serve. It was a nice spiritual complement to the kind of food we were cooking.

We learned to calibrate the volume levels to suit our needs. When you've got an empty space at the start of the day, you can't blast the music. But as the room fills up with sound-absorbing bodies, you have to crank it up or you can't hear it at all. If anyone complained that it was too loud, our response was always to turn it up.

Playing loud music discouraged people from lingering in the restaurant. I took my cue from the way McDonald's designed their seats so that you lose circulation in your legs if you sit for too long. When your business depends on maximizing the number of people coming in and promptly getting the hell out, you need to help them along.

You could interpret a lot of our decisions back then as hostile, but I swear we were acting out of necessity. We developed a reputation for being unfriendly to vegetarians, and God knows I talked a lot of shit, but honestly, even if we wanted to accommodate vegetarians, we didn't have the time or space to prep any extra mise en place. Our opening beverage program consisted of canned beer and $1 bottles of Poland Spring water. We didn't concern ourselves with serving you dessert or a cup of coffee. We needed to turn tables, and we didn't want you regaling your friends with one more cool twenty-minute story.

• • •

It was clear from Nishi's poor reviews that we needed to revamp the restaurant, but in the subtext, I saw an indictment of all our restaurants. It wouldn't be enough to fix Nishi. We needed to show that we were capable of evolving everything about ourselves.

In many ways, Ssäm Bar is the beating heart of Momofuku. It has always won the most praise from both the public and critics. It changed the restaurant game, and no one wants to be the person who screws that up. But whenever there's been a period at Ssäm Bar where it wasn't very good, it was because we were afraid to change. This was one of those periods.

Working against our own legacy was a new test for us. I've always loved underdogs and I never imagined I'd be anything but one of them. Now, it was as though Momofuku had been traded to the defending Super Bowl champions. There were many long-standing aspects of Ssäm Bar's operation that we had never questioned because the numbers didn't support the idea of change. But just because it's profitable doesn't mean that it's right.

Marge spearheaded the transformation, along with Momofuku's president, Alex Muñoz-Suarez. It had to be them. If I'd learned anything in the past few years, it was that I couldn't be the person to lead the charge. And while it may not have looked like it to the untrained eye, Marge and Alex completely changed the restaurant.

The songs stayed the same, but we lowered the volume on the music. We added soundproofing, bought new plates and silverware, and installed chairs with backs on them. We put in banquettes, wallpaper, and a wine cave. The menu was now bound in leather.

Max Ng would be the new chef. Max had come to America from Singapore seven years earlier to work with us. He'd spent time at both Ko and Ssäm Bar, but he wasn't really ready to be a chef. That's exactly why I wanted him. He knew our ways, but he didn't know enough to let himself get stuck in the same old tired routine.

Max wanted a Michelin star. He wanted to be number one on the World's 50 Best list. He wanted accolades and awards, and he wasn't going to let the limitations of our space prevent him from reaching his goals. I loved that Max wanted to chase all that stuff. Just because the restaurant didn't look the part of a world-class establishment didn't mean we couldn't aspire to be the very best of the best.

I told the team to kill our existing menu and do whatever they wanted. They didn't disappoint. The first efforts were unbelievable. Belacan-rubbed skate cooked in a banana leaf. A caviar bun with bacon-ranch dressing. A taiyaki, the fish-shaped Japanese waffle cake, stuffed with foie gras instead of the traditional red bean. I was thrilled with where we were headed. With time, I thought, it could be something truly great.

Wells had only visited the restaurant a handful of times since he'd taken over as the *Times* critic. Then one night, I was putting in a shift as expediter—something I rarely do. In walks Wells. He sat right by me at the pass. I felt less confident about the meal we served him than anything we've ever done.

We had changed the very identity of the restaurant, killed the old Momofuku. I didn't know which way was up or down anymore, and there wasn't any time to figure it out. I was convinced that

Wells would demote us from three stars to two. That may not sound like much to you, but coupled with his spurning of Nishi, it would cement the perception that Momofuku was old news.

Wells returned a couple months later, and then his review came out.

Three stars.

I've never been so happy about maintaining the status quo. This review from a critic who had only recently questioned our relevance was a validation of our efforts. I set aside my misgivings about criticism in general and enjoyed the first victory of the new era, and the first piece of evidence that we were on the right path.

• • •

I want to say a little bit more about Marge. When Nishi first opened, Marguerite was among the very few people on staff to speak up with her concerns. Since she joined us as an intern in 2011, she's always been incisive and vocal. *Is there a reason the service is subpar? Why do we still have no backs on the stools? Why can't we have an overarching vision while treating each restaurant differently in terms of food, service, and mission?*

Marge not only helped revamp Ssäm Bar, she led the Nishi rescue mission as well. We closed for a renovation and relaunched in October 2017, just before the re-review of Ssäm. At Nishi, Marge pulled off the same magic act. What's more, she did it with almost zero resources. She remodeled the dining room and rethought how we communicated with diners. We started telling people it was an Italian restaurant, for one thing. Thanks to Marge, people could read our menu and feel like they were visiting a restaurant and not solving a math problem. Without ever asking Pinsky to overhaul the menu, Nishi got better and busier.

It all confirmed what I already knew: I am the wrong person to operate Momofuku. The irony of us growing up as a company is that we needed to get younger to do so. By the time we made it official,

I'd already been delegating much of my responsibility to Marge. She took over as CEO right before her thirtieth birthday, in 2019.

We set her up with an executive coach to help her ease into the role. After one meeting, the coach told me that giving the keys to a twenty-nine-year-old was a huge leap of faith. She said that Marge was not very communicative, and that when she trained fifty- and sixty-year-olds, they had much more to say. I nearly exploded.

Who was this stodgy suit to tell me Marge wasn't ready? I chose Marge specifically because she wasn't a jaded stereotype. I was tempted to pull her out of training right then and there. I decided against it. It would be better for her to go through the process and see for herself what she was up against. Marge's moral compass is stronger than that of anyone I've ever met. I had no reason to fear that she would be deterred or discouraged by this poor judge of character.

I'm not betting on Marge being perfect tomorrow. I want her to make mistakes. I don't want a CEO who thinks they've already seen and done everything. I want someone who's just as eager to be right as they are to be proven wrong.

• • •

There's an old myth that lobsters are immortal.

What leads people to believe this is the fact that lobsters show no signs of getting old. As they age, lobsters don't stop growing or reproducing. They can grow back limbs. There's no limit to how big a lobster can get. They don't slow down until the day they're cooked and eaten.

Lobsters grow by molting. They shed their old shell to reveal a new, soft shell that will eventually grow and harden around them. By the time they're done, there's no sign of the lobster they were. It's an exhausting, dangerous process. It takes a tremendous amount of energy and leaves them exposed and vulnerable while they're in the middle of it.

Want to know the only sign that a lobster is dying?

It stops molting.

I had happily killed a lot of lobsters before I learned this fact. Suddenly the lobster became Momofuku's unofficial mascot. Never again would we fear the grueling work of breaking ourselves down and gluing ourselves back together again. That cycle of building and destroying and rebuilding is not something to overcome. The human equivalent of not wanting to molt is trying to make life easy, refusing to grow or be self-reflective.

I can't say if it's healthy or normal to be so concerned with growth, but I know for sure that it makes Momofuku a hard place to work, especially because our definition of growth isn't restricted to a straight arrow on some financial projection. Sometimes our obsession with learning and improving can actually be to the detriment of the bottom line. Marge is with me. She gets it, but not everybody does right away.

I was in a Fuku board meeting recently when someone told me that I was the worst businessperson they'd ever met.

Fuku is supposed to be our scalable fast-food concept, but I was suggesting we make more items to order and diversify the menu; I was saying we should slow down a fast-food business. I know how dumb it sounded, but I had seen pretty clearly that the key to a successful QSR (quick-service restaurant) business was hospitality. People want to see their food being made. I'm not just talking about scooping it out of a steam table into a bowl. Let's not treat people so cynically.

No one liked my ideas. I'd surrounded myself at Fuku with smart people with business degrees and proven track records, so I deferred to them.

On the other hand, when we had the chance to open a small, standing-room-only restaurant on the third floor of the Time Warner Center down the hall from Thomas Keller's Bouchon Bakery, I vowed to do the exact opposite of what a Harvard business study would tell you to do. We were opening a full-size Noodle Bar next door, which would be our main source of revenue. In the adjoining postage-stamp-sized space, we would be free to take a chance on something we'd never done before.

At the time, we were also busy working on pre-production for the second season of *Ugly Delicious*. Among the subjects we were exploring was one I've mentioned before: the vertical spit and its various uses around the world, from shawarma and gyros to al pastor. Wherever this ingenious meat-cooking device lands on earth, a culinary tradition seems to develop. It all feeds into this universal human compulsion to wrap meat in some kind of bread.

We'd been working on our own flatbread recipe based loosely on both Chinese and Korean traditions—a yeasted dough that we would roll out to order, griddle on a flattop, and call *bing* after the Chinese term for flatbread. The idea of making cooked-to-order flatbreads in a mall flies in the face of traditional reason, which is why I immediately loved it. At Bāng Bar (*bang* means "bread" in Korean), we would serve a hybrid creation: made-to-order bings wrapped around spit-cooked Korean barbecue.

The pushback from the kitchen came hard and fast.

We won't be able to make enough bread!

"Well," I said, "we'll just make as much as we can."

Next, I told them to try putting mortadella on the spit.

It looks so stupid. And the fat all renders out!

First of all, I couldn't care less about it looking stupid. Secondly, there was no shortage of pork fat at the restaurants. Why not cure some of it into lardo and layer it between thick slices of mortadella? We did, and it was awesome.

I want Bāng Bar to be completely antithetical to common sense. I want it to be a safe haven for working stiffs in an upper-crust shopping center. The food is cheap—much cheaper than anyone at the company thinks is smart. But if we can do it, why not? Most of all, I want everyone to eat there. It's the restaurant where we've

emphasized hospitality more than anywhere else. While you're waiting in line at Bāng Bar, we do our best to keep you fed with snacks.
Potatoes roasted under the spit. Congee. Just a little something to tide
you over, served on proper plates with silverware. I tell the team that
I'll be happy when we get complaints about how many blue-collar
people we've brought into a fancy shopping complex.

• • •

We recently held our first company-wide leadership conference. After
a period of rapid expansion, we needed to pause for a moment to help
the company feel more like one entity and less like a bunch of splinter
groups. So we called all the managers and leaders of the restaurants
and flew them to Asbury Park, New Jersey, for two days of discussions and team building. The team at headquarters came up with the
idea and made it happen. I was just there to do my best impersonation
of a motivational speaker.

In my welcome speech, I talked about prizing vulnerability over
perfection. It's better, I insisted, to admit that you don't always know
the answer. It's okay to ask for help. I also pointed out the problem of
prior success: You may, for instance, find yourself dreading another
busy night of service at the restaurants, but can you snap out of it and
see how privileged we are to have customers? Can you remember to
treat every guest as though their business will make or break us?

Marge spoke about fearing apathy and embracing empathy,
which has become our central tenet. She cited Neil Young and *Rust
Never Sleeps,* his album of live recordings made during a tour in which
he forced his band to do something different every night, lest the act
get stale. She addressed life balance and "saving something for the
swim back."* In speaking about the importance of team culture, she

---

*It's a reference to the movie *Gattaca,* which we talk about all the time. See rule 33
in the appendix.

borrowed the line "The score takes care of itself" from the great NFL coach Bill Walsh. If we invest in one another, she said, success will follow. She handed out little booklets codifying Momofuku's philosophy, as well as printouts of David Foster Wallace's "This Is Water," the late author's commencement speech about identifying and challenging one's inherent biases.

Over the course of the two-day retreat, there was bowling, karaoke, a beach bonfire, a crockpot-cooking competition, and a screening of the mountain-climbing documentary *The Dawn Wall*.

There's no way to know how each Momofuku leader will take what they heard at the retreat. I hope they've internalized what was said and can see a way to translate it into tangible, sustained action. I hope they know it's not all supposed to change overnight. The company we want to be is still theoretical, but we have to start somewhere.

OUT WEST

WHEN I TURNED FORTY, GRACE AND I STARTED TALKING ABOUT MOVING to the West Coast. The plan was to rent a place for a couple of months, acclimate, and search for a permanent home. We figured Los Angeles would be a better place to start a family. For me, the move was as much symbolic as anything else. It would be my effort to embrace new challenges and a new city as part of a healthy regimen, rather than as a distraction from the hurt. I would pick up the pieces of the recent disasters and try to make something new.

I would try to help others grow, too. The true measure of a great chef is how many of their alumni have surpassed them in stature and success. I've never done a good enough job of preparing others to take me down. Like many chefs, I've been guilty of complaining about how it's impossible to find good cooks these days, and that young people aren't motivated to succeed. In private, I referred to it as the Millennial Epidemic.

More recently, I've started to see it another way. I suspect that a good portion of the people who work with me *do* want to get somewhere, but they don't know how. If they don't get where they want, it isn't their failure, it's mine. This improved attitude won't fix the affliction that makes me snap when I see something I dislike in the kitchen, but maybe it can make me a better teacher in the times when I'm not impaired by my brain.

And so, even though I had half a mind to quit the business, focus on making TV shows, sell Momofuku, do anything but open another restaurant, I went ahead and did it anyway. I went back on the meds for fear of all the potential triggers that would come with putting on my chef whites. At Nishi, I'd worked on menu development, but I hadn't played a day-to-day role in the kitchen for years. It was what the situation required.

Maybe it was the lingering effects of Nishi's poor start, but when we first announced that we were coming to L.A., the food media didn't seem to take any special notice. In my mind, Majordomo felt like our last stand. About six months before we opened, the staff and I locked ourselves in the LINE Hotel in Koreatown. Roy Choi had recently closed his restaurant there and loaned the space to us to conduct what you might call R&D. What transpired was more like boot camp.

I was terrified to be opening in a place that none of us knew very well with a crew who were effectively strangers to one another. I hadn't worked directly with our chef, Jude Parra-Sickels, since 2006. I was friends with our chef de cuisine, Marc Johnson, but we had never cooked together. Our GM, Christine Larroucau, was new to Momofuku. I'd worked with our wine director, Richard Hargreave, before, at a few of our restaurants. That was it.

We did almost no cooking in the first month. We spent the majority of our days talking. *Where would the restaurant be in five years?*

If it's a success, why do people love it? If it's a failure, why did it fail? What would the criticisms be? We ran through these conversations over and over and over. There were history lessons and homework, discussions about culinary theory and values. *What do you believe in and what makes you believe in it?*

This time was invaluable. It was a moment when I was able to share how I thought and how I hoped the staff would think. I knew that building a culture was paramount, and that we would have to continue to feed it, protect it from negative influences, and adapt with time. It's like a sourdough starter. You have to keep it healthy or it'll die.

• • •

A week or two before opening, I noticed a new sous chef doing a sloppy job of labeling his mise en place. I told him he didn't need to use so much tape, and that even if it was just for his station, he should try to write more clearly.

"Okay, chef. I just didn't think we were being so serious yet."

I threw a fit for the ages. *It doesn't matter that we're not open yet, we're always fucking serious. If you don't fucking respect your station it means you don't respect yourself and you don't fucking respect your co-workers.*

I was shaking. When I finally calmed down to the point where I could speak at a normal volume, I told everyone to stop what they were doing. I delivered a half-hour screed on care and the common good. Had my only goal been to stop people from using too much tape, I accomplished it. But I paid the price in morale and trust. On one end of the spectrum there's constructive criticism. On the other, there's this. Destructive criticism.

I'd been afraid of this exact moment. Whatever progress I'd made with Marshall Goldsmith and Dr. Eliot had happened in a vacuum. If I truly wanted to become a better leader, I'd have to deal with my anger in full view of everyone, under the extreme duress of opening a restaurant.

Triggers were everywhere. The first year of a restaurant's life is unending turmoil, especially when it comes to staffing. People come and go as you try to build a lasting team. Every chef is deeply familiar with the torture of investing time and money into training a new cook, only to have them bail as soon as they're ready to step up.

One day after we opened, a cook explained that he and his wife had been talking. He couldn't support his family on a cook's salary, and it didn't seem like that was going to change anytime soon. His plan was to pivot, attend community college, find a normal job.

This cook was in his early thirties. I can't count the number of times I've told young people who are interested in this profession to get a college degree instead. But this guy had worked for close to a decade at some of the best restaurants in the country. He was valuable to us and to the industry as a whole. More important, he'd told me that he loved cooking.

In the past, he would have been dead to me before he could finish saying, "I appreciate the opportunity." But I was trying to see things differently. He was telling me he needed something that I hadn't been quick enough to offer.

I suggested that I could be his personal mentor, if he wanted. We sat down in the dining room and plotted out his goals on a piece of paper. I told him that he was young and this was the time in his life to be taking chances, not playing it safe. I offered to speak to his wife and explain my position. I also told him that there are no guarantees in this business.

He returned the following day. He and his wife had decided that he'd work at the restaurant in the mornings and attend school at night.

That's a best-case scenario, which is more or less useless as a barometer. A better test would be Ricky and Max.

Ricky and Max were friends before they started working at Majordomo, and they had been working with us for less than six months when they told me they were going to leave to pursue a long-time dream.

"We're going to open a late-night food truck that caters to cooks after service."

Upon hearing their plan, the last thing I wanted was to help them, which is why I offered to do so. I talked them through the challenging economics of what they had in mind. They remained unfazed.

"Listen, if you stick around here for a full year, I'll support you," I said. "You can work part-time while you get the truck ready. You can use our purveyors, store and prep product here. You can open the truck next to the restaurant, and we'll send customers there. I don't need to have any skin in the game."

While they deliberated, I grew more impatient. I had never made a concession like this in my life. I was investing even more in these two, knowing full well that they would ultimately be leaving. I was pissed that they didn't recognize the value of what I was offering them.

After a few weeks, they announced that they were going to leave. They were rejecting my help.

I delivered a parting message: "Looks like I'm getting into the food cart business."

I was bluffing, but I wasn't kidding. If they wanted to succeed, they needed to imagine a hundred people like me breathing down their necks. I told them that they were now my competition, and that their only hope was to outwork me. "Every time you take one of my dollars, I'm going to work harder to put you out of business." In the old days, I might have actually followed through, opened a food truck, undercut them in price, and outhustled them. So I guess you can count that as progress.

• • •

As for the menu at Majordomo, I told everyone it would be like a Korean American Cheesecake Factory. There would be a big menu and large portions. It would be fun, and you'd eat dishes without knowing exactly what they were or where they came from. We would resist the urge to overdescribe our thought process, as we'd done at Nishi. It would require a tremendous amount of thought and planning to create a new food philosophy that fit Los Angeles, but if we did our jobs right, you wouldn't see that work at all.

Going into it, there were only a few items I knew we'd have on the menu. Both were big, spectacular beef rib dishes. First was a take on the kalbijjim at Sun Nong Dan, an L.A. institution that specializes in a bubbling pot of spicy braised short ribs with a heap of melted cheese on top. The other was a whole smoked plate beef rib, inspired by the meat master Adam Perry Lang. The first time I tasted APL's smoked ribs, he was simply slicing and serving pieces by hand over a picnic table. No sides, no sauces. Just meat and a little salt. My immediate reaction was that I would have paid any amount of money to eat those ribs. It was event cooking—something I would travel for to eat.* At Majordomo, our twist would be to season APL's ribs with my mom's kalbi marinade.

I was preoccupied with the notion of celebratory dining. The only reason why Angelenos would fight traffic to get to our restaurant would be if they felt that eating at Majordomo was a special occasion. For our opening night, I suggested we roast a whole animal on the patio.

The team would be cooking for two hundred paying customers for the first time. There was plenty on their plates already. "We've got so much outdoor space" and "How sick of a surprise would that be" were the reasons I gave for this dumb, punishing idea. We didn't even know what permits we would need to cook an animal al fresco. The team groaned.

---

*There's a very short list of dishes like this, and in my mind, Peking duck is at the top.

I'd noticed that as we crept closer to opening night, everybody was beginning to feel comfortable, and that comfort was driving us toward efficiency. It's understandable. They saw their priorities as dialing in the menu and polishing up service, so that the operation would run as smoothly as possible when the time came. I threw out a second idea for opening night. I told everyone that instead of seating guests at the kitchen counter as we'd planned, we'd use the bar as a literal ssam bar. Guests would line up and help themselves to pork butt and all the fixings. A logistical nightmare.

What I truly wanted wasn't a roast goat or pork buffet, but for everyone to embrace the paradox of feeling completely prepared and completely unprepared at the same time. By tossing outlandish propositions at them, I hoped the team wouldn't flinch at an unexpected crisis. They'd be simultaneously loose and on high alert.

I know I sound like the Joker ranting about chaos being for the greater good, but I swear it's true. When diners walk into a room that's about to burst with excited energy, they can't help but feel it, too. Sometimes you've got to inject a restaurant with that vitality however you can.

I scrapped both plans before our first service, but the spirit remains central. For example, one of my favorite Majordomo dishes is a whole boiled chicken. We present the bird to the table in a big pot, bring it back to the kitchen to carve it, and then return with a beautiful platter of rice topped with the sliced breasts and two different sauces spooned over the top. Once guests are finished with that, we bring out a soup made from the carcass. It's so good.

After we opened the restaurant, I had to return to New York for a few weeks. Every night, I read the daily reports from L.A. Here's what the Domo team wrote in one dispatch:

We've been cooking a "presentation chicken" lately to
help get the chickens out earlier. That is, when the
first bird is fired, we usually cook two & have one
just for presenting so we can butcher the chicken that's

```
rested, while we slow the other chicken, which speeds up
the time it takes between seeing the chicken & receiving
the rice. The extra chicken at the end of the night is
also butchered into our stock the next day, since we
always like to use those bones from carcasses for the
soup that follows.
```

They had cooked enough services to realize they could improve flow and make things easier on the staff with a little bit of bait-and-switch. A smart decision and common practice. The guest would have no idea that the chicken they'd seen wasn't the same one they were eating.

I wrote to Jude and the rest of the Domo team saying we would discuss it upon my return, which they accurately interpreted to mean we were going back to the hard way.

It had nothing to do with integrity. I didn't care about fooling the diners. What concerned me was the precedent we were setting. I worried about the mindset of the server whose job it would be to parade a stunt chicken around the dining room. I was terrified of our culture stagnating. The dish was meant to be a difficult pickup that required constant coordination between the front and back of house. That was what made it great. If they wanted to sandbag it, they needed to figure out how they would make up for the lost energy elsewhere.

• • •

Hugo was supposed to be born in L.A., but he ended up a New York baby. After a complication with the pregnancy, Grace felt more comfortable being close to her doctor in New York. It wasn't what we intended, but we made our way back to the East Coast, where we had an apartment and a community of friends. For once I couldn't just force a plan to happen simply because I thought it would be good for work. I had a family to consider.

Hugo is my totem. I look at him, and I am grounded. My son.

The purest love I know, and my greatest responsibility. I'm worried about how I'll provide him with the friction he needs to grow into a strong, self-possessed person. My instinct is to spare him every ounce of potential pain, but I know that what he needs is to feel the hurt of heartbreak and rejection. He needs to fall down, so he can learn to get back up. He'll have it easier than I did, and I'm nervous about it.

I think about Hugo all the time at work. I wonder if being a good father and a good leader are the same thing. Every day at Momofuku, I'm confronted with the temptation to tell people how to spare them-selves some frustration or pain, but I know that's not going to make them better.

A year after Majordomo opened, some of the staff began to burn out. That place is a beast. It's one of our busiest restaurants and Momofuku's first foray into the West Coast. The creative and opera-tional demand is extraordinarily high. Not that anything terrible was happening. The team there is too talented and conscientious to allow much to fall through the cracks. But in some ways, that was the problem.

For instance, the chefs were looking to spend more time with their families. I did some quick math and told them that they could probably save more than fifty hours a week if they trained some-one else to expedite. In case you aren't familiar, expediters are the air traffic controllers of the kitchen. They keep track of all the order tickets coming in and keep the various stations coordinated. Usu-ally, the person expediting is the executive chef or one of the sous chefs, but I've begun to see that as a total misuse of time. Sure, in a small tasting-menu restaurant, the chef can stand in the center of the kitchen and have their eyes on everything. But at a place as large as Majordomo, I'd much rather see my chefs wandering the kitchen teaching young cooks, ensuring quality across the board, than hun-kering down at the expediter station.

Expediting is exhausting, unrewarding work that chefs only embrace because it's something they know they can control. It's a classic behavior. You get put in a position of leadership and suddenly you gravitate toward what you hate most—paperwork, expediting, inventory—because you know how to do them and it gives you some sense of security.

I proposed that if they could give it up and focus on the bigger picture, they could be home every night. I suggested that they try giving some young cooks a shot at expediting for a couple of hours each night. Or train some front-of-house people to do it. Or just hire expediters.

A few weeks later, I asked how it was going.

"We tried, but it didn't work."

I asked how many times they'd tried. Once.

At first, it made me crazy. I'd given them what seemed like a direct path to more time, but in my opinion, they'd given up way too early. I want them to have life balance, and I thought I'd provided them with a direct path to finding it on their own. But the fact is that their only sin was wanting to soldier through and do things correctly. If it was anyone's failure, it was mine as a leader. I'm asking them to walk a near-impossible line.

As another example, after we opened Majordomo, I tapped Eunjo Park to head the kitchen at our next restaurant, Kāwi. We were opening in Hudson Yards—a megadevelopment in New York that everyone in the city was apprehensive about. It was a huge mall and—you may be sensing a theme here—the last place anybody would be looking for an interesting dining experience.

Jo is one of the most talented, tough, honorable, and caring young cooks to ever come through our doors. She also has a ridiculous résumé that reads like a foodie's bucket list. Everyone at Momofuku respects her. But she had never been the chef of her own restaurant before. She'd never even been a sous chef. By all traditional metrics, she was too green for the job. Nevertheless, I was certain she would go on to be an important chef who could, under the right conditions, single-handedly change what it means to cook Korean food in America.

The glaring inconsistency about Momofuku has always been that I'm Korean, but the restaurants have Japanese names and serve more nominally Japanese food than Korean. (I got away with it because many Americans don't care to distinguish between Asian cultures.) My preference for Japan can be at least partially explained by my grandfather, who, as I've mentioned, basically grew up thinking of himself as Japanese. There's also the fact that Korean culture tends to be extremely wary of outside interpretation, whereas the Japanese will freely incorporate whatever influences come their way. Even as a Korean American who is more or less an outsider to my mother culture, I'm constantly fighting off the impulse to protect Korean traditions.

Years ago a friend invited me for a meal put on by a Korean chef at a private supper club in Tokyo. I can't remember the chef's name, but I remember her celery kimchi.* I hated it. It was so delicious and so offensive to my traditionalist sensibilities. For days I thought about that meal and the liberties the chef had taken with Korean cuisine. There's no way she would have been able to do what she did in Korea, but in Japan, she was free to explore her own cuisine. I began to understand that what holds us back from culinary progress is often some cultural roadblock that we honor in the name of preservation—the kind of arbitrary roadblock that says, *You're not supposed to do that with kimchi.***

I spent a good portion of my career avoiding the perception that

---

*For many years, dating back to my pre-Momofuku days, I kept handwritten journals with detailed notes about almost every restaurant meal I ate, and stored them in the basement of Ssäm Bar. During Hurricane Sandy, the basement flooded, and I lost all of it, as well as my entire collection of rare cookbooks.

**I think the reason why minority chefs in America find cultural appropriation so upsetting is that we feel obliged to uphold these arbitrary proscriptions, while white chefs do whatever they want. We're following the rules and they're not. Most of the time, they didn't even bother to learn the rules. I decided that I should just start playing the same game.

I was messing with Korean food. For many years at Momofuku, we buried any sign of Koreanness under other influences and disguises. While cooking has enabled me to fight battles and explore subjects that I'm too scared to approach in real life, I couldn't overcome the shame and anxiety I'd felt about Korean food since I was a kid.

I've slowly become more comfortable exploring my heritage. After all, if you could buy gochujang-flavored potato chips on American grocery store shelves, maybe it was safe for this gyopo to cook Korean food, too. Over the last few years, I've begun to feel an urgency to see what Momofuku can do with Korean cuisine.

While we didn't serve banchan or bibimbap or tofu stew or any other obvious Korean signifiers, Majordomo had actually been our most Korean restaurant to date. There were more Korean names on the menu than ever before, more Korean spirit to the service, more Korean design touches. The goal was to keep asking hard questions about cultural truths, specifically what makes a Korean restaurant Korean. I looked at what we were doing as a form of appropriation, with the appropriator being me, an Asian American man.

At Kāwi, I wanted Jo to take the idea even further. With the opening more than a year away, I flew her to Los Angeles to spend a few weeks living with me and Grace. Every day she was in town, I gave her the same assignment: cook her version of a traditional Korean dish.

Everything she brought to the table was too polished. Too European and overly technical. Jo knew how to cook this food in her bones, but it was being filtered through years of training and learned habits. When I asked her what she wanted to say with her food, she said she wanted to change people's perceptions. She wanted to capture the joy of the food she ate growing up. But it wasn't showing up on the plate. I know it sounds maniacal. If I knew what she was doing wrong, why didn't I just tell her what to do?

Finding a point of view and expressing it through one's cooking is a near-impossible task. I could see the hurt that was in store for her and all the other young chefs at Momofuku. I could see them all grappling with the same issues I had wrestled with, and I desperately wanted to step in and do it for them.

For the next twelve months, Jo struggled. There were tears and sleepless nights, disastrous test dinners, whole menus scrapped. She inched her way forward, day by day. When she opened Kāwi, I was ecstatic for her and the team, but the fight is far from over. She's still finding herself. I'm so fucking proud of her.

A NEW DEAL

I WAS DEATHLY ALLERGIC TO THE WORD *MEMOIR* WHEN I STARTED WRITING this book, adamant that the details of my life don't explain me or Momofuku. I convinced myself that I'd hunker down for a year and then turn in a collection of third-person essays, a focused meditation on mental health, and a comprehensive guide to the culinary arts. Sure, at first the publisher would balk, but they'd come around.

Much of my reluctance was due to the fact that I felt like it was too early. I don't have the answers. And yet here we are: my editor has expressed concern over the fact that I have yet to address the question you probably started asking fifteen chapters ago.

"What happened to Dave killing himself?"

In one sense, I did kill myself. I killed the version of me that was meek and afraid of dying. I considered my mortality and reached the

conclusion that if the worst possible outcome is death and we're all
going to die anyway, then nothing else should scare me, whether it's
pain, hard work, embarrassment, failure, or financial ruin. So long as
I'm not hurting anyone else, there's nothing to stop me from doing
anything I want to do. Very early in this book, I mentioned that I
consider the myth of Sisyphus to be an inspirational tale. It's an idea
I obviously adapted from Camus. In the eyes of the gods, Sisyphus's
endless task of pushing a boulder up a hill is a punishment. But by
accepting his fate as unchangeable and continuing to do the task,
Sisyphus can reject the gods' view of him and thus be happy. Not
happy in other people's eyes—only his own. In other words, we may
not be able to reject our fortune or fate, but we can reject how we
approach it. Every day, we have the chance to kill the way the world
sees us and push the boulder up the hill with a big, fat smile on our
faces. To live life without amends.

But that's not what you're asking. You want to know if I still
think about suicide. Well, there are periods when I don't, and when I
do, it's usually more academic than emotional.

I think about how nothing I've achieved would have been possible if I hadn't been ready to die from the outset—how my success is
completely tied to my depression. I fear losing more of my heroes to
suicide. I think about whether I'll eventually grow tired of pushing
the boulder myself. I wonder out loud to my friends if we've been
sold a false idea of happiness, and I worry I'm just telling myself that
as an excuse to be unhappy.

"Come on, Dave," you're saying. "What the hell do you have to
be depressed about?"

Nothing. There's nothing to be depressed *about*. For those
who know me well, it can be a struggle to reconcile my depression
with the look of joy on my face when we're eating and goofing off
together. You know how much I love my family and my job and the
people I work with. But if you've fought depression or know somebody who has, you know that no amount of money can fix it. No

amount of fame. No logic. The continuing stigma around suicide and mental illness tells me that not enough people truly understand it. I don't really blame them—it's impossible unless you've lived it. But there's this puritanical notion of suicide as evil, depression as some kind of failure of character. Too many of us assume that antidepressants and suicide hotlines and generalized compassion are antidotes—that painting the train station a calm color is going to stop people from jumping. You wouldn't suggest to a cancer patient that calling a hotline would cure them, would you?

To fight this, you need help. Medicine, yes, but people are key. You can't do it alone. I'm lucky to have Dr. Eliot. The mere routine of talking to him has kept me alive. I speak to him even when it doesn't seem necessary or feels like a chore. He brings out my most thoughtful and considerate self. When we're talking, I'm the version of me that's happy to wake up and face whatever challenges lie ahead. It's frustrating that I can't be like that all the time.

I'm unbelievably lucky to have met Grace. I'm trying really hard not to let work be an excuse or a buffer between us. But for years, my best coping strategy has been work. I have assumed so many responsibilities and said yes to so many things. Working hard creates my own gravity. The more I work, the more I am on terra firma. Even on vacation. When I'm out of the office, it usually means that I'm cooking dinner for twenty friends. I've developed a pretty serious fly-fishing habit, and it's not the relaxing kind. It's work. When I read or watch a movie, I get overly invested in the characters and overthink the plots, no matter how atrocious they are.

This all raises the question of whether depression is something you can control by simply sucking it up. My answer is no, I don't think you can overcome it with willpower, but I do believe that dealing with depression is a choice that needs to be made. You have to choose to stand up every day and keep going. To reject your default settings. To offer another silly analogy, I always liken it to being a Jedi. It's easier—and probably cooler—to give in to the dark side.

The only way to be a Jedi is to do the hard thing and reject your base instincts.

On good days, the fight will push you into experiences you would never have known otherwise. You will have purpose, even if the purpose is only to stick around.

• • •

The last time I saw Tony Bourdain was in the spring of 2017. We hadn't talked in a while, and when we did, we kept it mostly superficial. He liked to give me a hard time for not taking Brazilian jiu-jitsu more seriously. As with anything he was interested in, he'd gone all in on the sport.* Whenever I knew he was in the city, I resisted the urge to bug him. I never liked taking away from the time he had with his daughter. That spring, I broke my rule. I couldn't think of anyone else who could understand the dark place I found myself in after Nishi's poor showing and the collapse of *Lucky Peach*.

I suggested we meet up at the Coliseum, a pub near his apartment on Columbus Circle that I used to visit with the crews of Per Se and Jean-Georges. I arrived early to snag a spot, angling to get a table in the back. The place was packed with rec-league softball players drinking cheap beer.

I got the attention of the older lady behind the bar. She seemed to be in charge.

"I hate to be this guy, but I'd pay money if you could help me get a table with a little privacy," I said sheepishly.

"There's two seats over by the window," she replied.

"I don't know how to say this, but my friend gets interrupted by a lot of strangers," I tried.

---

*I ended my short BJJ career shortly after Alex Atala, who is as good at grappling as he is at cooking, choked me out with my own arm.

She cocked her head and looked at me quizzically. "Are you talking about Tony? He comes in all the time. Usually likes to sit right here at the bar."

Tony and I drank for four hours. As things got tipsy, we called in an air strike of jalapeño poppers, chicken tenders, curry fries, and mozzarella sticks. There may have been fried calamari, too.

"Jesus Christ, this is disgusting," I said, surveying the catastrophic scene of sauce-stained napkins and half-eaten appetizers.

"What you need is a cigarette, my friend."

He had started smoking again. I had quit years earlier, but always partook with him. Out on the sidewalk, he recommended a change of venue.

"Why don't we go have dessert somewhere quieter?"

We soon found ourselves in a banquette at Porter House in the Time Warner Center. His local. Tony ordered a ribeye for two and an exceedingly nice bottle of red burgundy. The amuse bouche was a slab of bacon that could pass for a steak. There were French fries to go with the pommes purée.

Full and a little drunk, we went our separate ways after dinner—him to pack for yet another excursion, me to my apartment downtown. In the cab, I played back the night in my head. I'd wanted to ask so many questions. I'd blabbed a lot, but had I explained everything I needed to explain? What was it he said I should do, again? He had so much wisdom. I worried that I'd wasted my precious Tony time.

On the car ride home, I got an email:

From: Anthony Bourdain
Date: Thu, Apr 20, 2017 at 8:02 PM
Subject:

Be a fool.

For love.

```
For yourself.

What you think MIGHT possibly make you happy. Even for a
little while.

Whatever the cost or good sense might dictate.

Good to see you.

Tony
```

• • •

We found out that Grace was pregnant the day after Tony died. I was a wreck. I tried to find pleasure in the moment, but I was afraid that I'd missed the chance to feel the elation of becoming an expectant parent for the first time.

Then we FaceTimed our parents. I knew they would be happy to learn that their biological needs were being met, but between the tears and sobbing wails, I realized I was witnessing a form of joy I'd never seen before. I wept, too. This was the pure, uncut version of the feeling I got from cooking for people. And yet it had nothing to do with restaurants. If anything, Momofuku had made it harder for me to encounter it.

It was only a brief détente in a complicated lifetime with my family, but that moment will always be my mental image of happiness.

The thing about seeing a therapist for close to two decades is that you realize it's always going to come back to your parents. For years, I would talk endlessly about anything with Dr. Eliot to avoid discussing the tea leaves, my father, the go-kart accident. But since going back on my medication and starting this book, I've been forced to reflect.

In the lead-up to my son's birth, I told myself it was time to start letting go of some old burdens, to stop being so angry at my past and the people I hated. I didn't know how to let go of rage, resentment, insecurity, or my general pettiness. I'd relied on those attributes for so long that they'd come to define me. As ludicrous as it sounds, I was scared that if I learned to forgive, I'd disappear.

For the sake of my son, I began making amends with people, one by one. Some were big, emotional reconciliations with former friends. Others were quick conversations that reopened lines of communications with old colleagues. Throughout the process, I couldn't feel any of the anger or resentment draining away.

Then, when Hugo was born, I suddenly realized that in nine months, I had unknowingly accomplished my goal. I felt at peace. It's like physical therapy. You don't think these silly exercises are helping until one day you stand up and don't feel the pain anymore.

When Hugo got sick for the first time, I instantly felt the parental instinct to do whatever I could for my child's health. We took him to the hospital, where we were surrounded by much worse-off kids and their parents. I was overcome with a single thought: *I wish none of these people had to be here.*

Hugo was fine. A few weeks later, we had his 백일 (baek-il)— the traditional Korean celebration of a baby's first one hundred days and a chance to wish for their continued well-being. Other Asian cultures celebrate their children's first hundred days as well, but I think it's especially important for Koreans, given our country's history of famine and struggle. For Hugo's baek-il, Grace and I had dinner with my parents. I looked at my dad across the table and realized that I was around the same age that he was when I broke my leg as a kid. I replayed the episode in my mind again. A wooden cart. Steep hill. My left leg. Yellow couch. Yellow-red ointment.

We didn't go to the hospital for five days.

I'd always rationalized this as Dad's way of parenting. He was trying to make me tougher, or at least I prayed that was what it was. Over dinner, I told him that I was writing this book. I explained that I didn't want to dwell on my childhood too much, but that I did want to ask him about the femur incident.

"I don't understand why you didn't take me to the hospital right away. What were you thinking?"

My dad is eighty years old and usually takes a minute to answer questions. His response that night was immediate: "I don't know what I was thinking." He told me that he had consulted with several members of the church and that they recommended a particular specialist. I pointed out that half the people in our congregation were doctors and that he had taken me to an acupuncturist for a fractured leg.

Grace held my hand under the table.

"I don't know what happened," he said. "I'm just dumb. I'm just dumb."

My mom cut my dad off to defend him, explaining that he had raised me the only way he knew how—the way he had been raised.

I really do believe that my dad has tried to become a better, more thoughtful, loving person in his later years. I'm trying to give him credit, not just for the man he's trying to be but for the way he raised me. If he'd been the father I wanted him to be, I wouldn't be the man I am.

But even now, as a dad myself, I still see a vast gulf between us.

Dr. Jim Kim once told me that I would never understand what it's like to live through war. He's right. I can never understand the experiences that shaped my parents, how it felt to come to America without speaking a lick of English, the racism they must have endured, the violence they'd fled, or the sense of longing they felt for their homeland. It's why Asian parents want their kids to study unambiguous subjects like math and science, be good at golf and violin, and avoid liberal arts like English or philosophy or political science or cooking—anything subjective can be taken away from you. If I could stop being so angry, maybe I could understand my dad.

My siblings tell me that he and I are exactly the same.

EPILOGUE

I was calling Ying every other day to discuss Cubism and how I thought it applied to what I was trying to do at the restaurants. Eventually he got tired of humoring me, so he invited the art critic Jerry Saltz to come on my podcast. Saltz had just won a Pulitzer for his writing at *New York* magazine, and he agreed to an interview on the show to indulge my amateur art commentary, yet another sign that my life has become ridiculous.

I'm a newcomer to art. I'm one of those guys who used to look at one of Rothko's big blocks of color and roll my eyes. When I first saw Marcel Duchamp's "Fountain"—a porcelain urinal on a pedestal—I had no idea what I was looking at.

My interest in Cubism was a relatively new development. I was trying to understand what made these screwy portraits so valuable. A lot, it turns out. The Cubists broke all the rules of perspective and composition because they could. You couldn't do it in real life, but you could do it with art. In a painting you could depict multiple angles of the subject at the same time. You could paint what you felt rather than what you saw. The power of paradox at work again. Shit—no wonder people liked this stuff.

Jerry sharpened my understanding. The paintings were valuable because nobody had ever done it this way before. The newness was lost on people like me, but at the time it must have been like discovering a new continent. Same with Rothko and the abstract expressionists. And Duchamp. His Readymades series, of which "Fountain" is a part, was a monumental statement: "This thing you piss in is art because I am an artist and I said so."

I found myself thinking back to that night onstage with Tony and how I'd criticized Bay Area cooking. Even if it was blown out of proportion, people had rightly taken my "figs on a plate" comment as an indictment of the movement that Alice Waters started. In truth, I *did* consider California cuisine as more of a lifestyle than a cooking philosophy. Like I said, I loved Alice, but I didn't count her among the true visionaries of modern gastronomy: the Adriàs, Blumenthal, Aduriz, Juan Mari Arzak, Passard, Gagnaire. She wasn't one of those guys with their ultra-cool, ultra-technical cooking. The thing she did seemed too obvious to be innovative. Of course the ingredients in California are good. Of course you should treat them simply. Of course a cozy restaurant with a strong philosophy and excellent food like Chez Panisse is a nice place to eat. So what?

But then, all at once, something occurred to me: these facts were only obvious *because* of Alice. She was the most radical, confident American chef of the past one hundred years. She put figs on a plate at a fine-dining restaurant and said, "This is cooking, because I am a chef and I said so."

Was it really that long ago that I'd been unable to see it?

Every Sunday that we were in Los Angeles, Grace and I would drive over to the farmers market off Hollywood Boulevard to eat some pupusas and pick up fruit. I had never worked with better produce than what I saw every day in California. It's everything they say it is—flavorful, abundant, huge, endlessly diverse. During one of our trips, I bought a hundred bucks' worth of peaches and nectarines from one stall. As I struggled to hold it all in my hands, Grace looked on, amused and slightly embarrassed.

"What are you gonna do with all that fruit?"

33 RULES FOR BECOMING A CHEF

For those who became chefs because they *had* to, it's crazy that anybody with other options would *want* to work in restaurants. But any chef who has found some degree of success—no matter how illusory that success may be—will end up fielding the same question: *How do I become a chef?*

For my answer, I've cribbed a format from the great Jerry Saltz, who wrote an incredible essay for *New York* magazine titled "How to Be an Artist." In the spirit of Jerry's thirty-three guiding principles for aspiring artists, what follows are my thirty-three rules for becoming a chef. Or, I should say, thirty-three rules for becoming a *good* chef. Nobody needs rules to become a shitty chef.

I've covered some of this material already, but it's all worth revisiting. Or, if you skimmed over the past 250 or so pages, you're in luck. All my salient observations about the restaurant industry and usable advice are contained herein.

I briefly considered getting a bunch of well-known chefs to sign off on this list but ultimately decided not to force my perspective on my friends. In that spirit, keep in mind that these rules are all highly subjective and that I've broken nearly every one of them at some point. That's part of the process.

PART ONE

Do You Love Washing Dishes?
Important questions to get you started.

Rule 1: Being a chef is only partly about cooking.

Before you drop out of school or put in notice at a comfortable job to chase the dream of being a chef, you should make sure you know what you're getting into. Let's see how you respond to the following questions:

Do you love washing dishes? How about mopping floors, taking out the garbage, unloading boxes, and organizing the refrigerator? These constitute 90 percent of the job of being a chef. It helps if you enjoy them.

Are you hungry? Sorry—I'm not asking if you want to eat. I'm asking if you're ready to outwork everyone else around you. Hard work is the great equalizer in the kitchen. If you can grit it out, you can overcome a significant lack of talent, experience, and privilege.

Were you a theater understudy and/or second-string benchwarmer in high school? Good, because you will need to love being on a team and not always getting the spotlight.

Are you inherently jealous of your friends? Be honest, because you will experience FOMO like never before in your life, as you get into the habit of missing Friday and Saturday evenings, birthdays, weddings, and anything that involves not being at work at night.

Do you intend to support a cushy lifestyle on your cook's salary? Hopefully not. (Note that the same applies to the people you work for. Look for someone who has bet it all on cooking.)

Is there anything else you could be doing for a living?

Is cooking your only hope?

Are you still with me?

Then let's proceed.

Rule 2: Don't go to cooking school.

Theoretically, cooking schools are a great idea. They provide a curriculum, experienced instructors, and job placement opportunities.

A degree from the Culinary Institute of America will open doors to a perfectly comfortable career track in a hotel restaurant or corporate kitchen that pays a decent salary with benefits.

But you wanted to be a *chef,* right?

On a practical level, the scenarios presented to you in culinary school bear no resemblance to a restaurant kitchen. In the real world, you don't have five people working one station during an easy lunch rush with a forgiving audience. Make no mistake: cooking schools are businesses that are selling you on the illusion that you will emerge from their programs as a bona fide chef. They prey on your not realizing that you can learn all this stuff for free (see rule 9). Of my graduating class of thirty-five at the French Culinary Institute, I can think of only one or two other people who are still cooking professionally. If medical schools had that kind of failure rate, there'd be congressional hearings.

Rule 3. Study Shakespeare instead.
Even if you're 100 percent sure that you want to be a chef, I would still urge you to go to college over culinary school. Culinary technique makes cooks. If you want to be a chef, you need a far broader set of skills.

Go to college and major in engineering, chemistry, microbiology, history, philosophy, or literature. Any of these will come in handy, whether or not you become a chef. Learn about Asian, European, African, and Latin American history and pay attention to how culture evolves around the world. Study the Medicis, the Ottomans, Genghis Khan, the Aztecs, Jared Diamond, Darwinism. I was a religion major, and studying the *Bhagavad Gita* changed my life. So did studying logic and Gödel's incompleteness theorems. Join the debate club. Practice piano. Write for the college newspaper. Take an interest in your fellow classmates and their stories.

Pick a state school with low tuition in a vibrant food city like Austin, Houston, Los Angeles, Chicago, San Francisco, or New York, and get a job in a restaurant or a bar. Give them twenty hours of your time a week, and don't just work in the kitchen. Work as a busser or server, too. You will get a sense of the atmosphere and the rhythms of a hospitality operation. Most important, in getting a college degree while working at a restaurant, you'll test your ability to follow through on your commitments. Plus, a bachelor's is a way better safety net than a culinary degree.

Rule 4. See as much of the world as humanly possible.

Go on vacation with your parents. Stuff your belongings into a duffel bag and hit the road yourself. If you're a college student, study abroad. If you're already a cook, here's the good news: you can cook anywhere. Do *not* let the language barrier be an excuse. You don't need an interpreter to understand what the chef means when they gesture over to the pile of plates sitting by the sink. You might have to stay in domiciles with questionable plumbing. That's what being young is for. I stayed in a homeless shelter while I was working in Japan. It was all I could afford.

You need to be surrounded by people and understand why cuisine happens the way it does. Eat everything you can. Take it all in—not just the food, but all the beauty, heartache, wealth, poverty, struggle, racism, history, and art you can find. It's going to help you empathize with people, which is the most powerful tool at a chef's disposal.

Rule 5. Fight for the job you want.

When it comes to picking a place to work, aim for a restaurant with a kitchen that will push you beyond your skills and comfort zone. If you're lucky enough to land a job interview, show up early. Shower and look presentable. Bring all your equipment in case they want you to stage right away.

If the restaurant tells you they're not hiring, but you're sure this is the place for you, don't give up. For a young Magnus Nilsson, the place was Pascal Barbot's tiny kitchen at l'Astrance, in Paris: three Michelin stars at the time (now ridiculously downgraded to two), a highly influential style, and no shortage of capable cooks. Magnus showed up one morning to ask for a job. Like hundreds before him, he was denied. How did Magnus take it? He showed up every single morning for months until they finally granted him a chance. Sometimes getting your foot in the door means wedging it in.

<u>PART TWO</u>

All My Favorite Singers Couldn't Sing
Don't worry if you lack talent or skills.
Tenacity is all you really need.

Rule 6. Come prepared.

There's a good chance that the restaurant will furnish you with many of the items necessary to do the job, but you'd be an idiot not to have your own gear. It shows that you're serious and will make you feel invested in your work. Start with these:

- Sharpies, pencils, and pens
- A notebook
- Blue tape, for labeling
- A chef's knife, serrated knife, paring knife, vegetable knife, cleaver, and knife guards for each of them
- A whetstone and a sharpening steel. Sharpen your knives before and after every service.
- Offset spatula, cake tester, bench scraper
- A Kunz spoon, a quenelle spoon, a perforated spoon. And you should know how to hold them properly (like a pencil or paintbrush, not like a toddler demanding dinner).
- Calculator and gem scale
- A pepper mill. (The best I've found is actually a Turkish coffee grinder.)
- Advil, bandages, burn ointment (get a prescription for Silvadene), medical tape, and gauze
- When they replenish the medical kit at work, grab a couple of packets of Pain-Aid, which is basically Tylenol with caffeine.
- Footwear. I've never been a clog guy. Wylie got me hooked on steel-toed boots, which are comfortable and nonslip, protect against dropped items, and raise you off the floor a little bit.
- A hat
- Grease from working the line makes having contacts or glasses a nightmare. Consider Lasik.

- Sweatbands for your wrists, as ridiculous as it sounds
- Chopsticks or tweezers. I'm all for chopsticks.
- You don't necessarily need to bring your own towels, but start stashing clean ones wherever you can in the restaurant and remember your hiding spots.

Rule 7. Everything is mise en place, including you.

In the most literal sense, mise en place refers to the prepped ingredients you need to work your station during service—the raw proteins, vegetables, sauce bases, seasonings, fats, and everything else that will go into your assigned dishes, plus backups for each of them. And backups for your backups. But the idea of mise en place extends more broadly to a sense of readiness (and can apply to life as a whole).

To that end: get some sleep at night. Exercise, if you do that kind of thing. (Take special care of your back. Can't emphasize this enough if you intend to be in this business for the long run.) And use the bathroom before service. You can forget about leaving the line once there are guests in the dining room. Spare yourself the discomfort of needing to poop during the dinner rush. Get your body on a schedule. It's not that difficult.

What *is* difficult is avoiding more dangerous habits. You will be surrounded at all times by self-destructive ways of alleviating stress, and you will almost certainly turn to them from time to time. Don't come to work drunk or high. Set boundaries and try to think of your body's long-term well-being. Smoking cigarettes is ubiquitous and okay for a while—I find that it dulls your sensitivity to salt and acid, which is actually beneficial in a professional kitchen—but given that it will eventually kill you, you should really let it go at some point.

Rule 8. Develop a new relationship with time.

Be the first one to work, not only because it shows your commitment to the job, but because you're going to need all the time you can get, especially in the beginning. Keep your phone in your locker. Once service starts, don't look at the clock. Ignore all measurements of time other than minutes and seconds. From the start of service to the last table, you should only think in terms of how long you need to complete the dish in front of you and whether you're synced up with the team.

Ignoring the clock will also prevent you from being the asshole who starts to mail it in at ten p.m. Treat every table like it's your own family, even if it's a slow night and you've started cleaning up your station when a two-top walks in five minutes before the restaurant closes. Your brain may immediately assume that they are wealthy and privileged and don't care that they're keeping the hardworking kitchen staff from enjoying a well-deserved beer. But remember that you don't actually know who these people are or where they're coming from or why they've come in search of nourishment at such a late hour. You don't know anything about them, and you need to assume the best. Imagine that every guest has chosen to eat their last meal with you.

Rule 9. Learn by doing.

Volunteer for every available task, regardless of whether you know what the hell you're doing. One day, while I was working at Craft, Marco Canora called to me from the pass and said he needed gremolata. Without hesitation, I began nodding furiously and said "Yes, chef." As I hurried back to my station, it dawned on me that I had very little idea of what went into gremolata and no clue how to make it. I swallowed my embarrassment and returned to the kitchen to ask chef for a recipe. He wasn't upset. He liked my hustle and can-do attitude (even though I literally couldn't do the thing he was asking for). I appreciate the same approach in all my cooks.

To that end, work the morning shift, where most of the prep gets done, not just dinner service. Learn how to make everything on the menu from start to finish. Know every aspect of a restaurant.

Rule 10. Make great family meal.

One afternoon, I walked into the kitchen at Craft to find our sous chef Akhtar Nawab making samosas. It was a strange sight. We had never served anything even vaguely Indian before. "Samosas on the menu today, chef?" I asked. He told me that they weren't for guests; they were for us.

Akhtar had come in early to make family meal. Every successful chef I know approaches family meal with deadly seriousness. After all, if you don't care for the people you work with, how will you ever care about the strangers coming into your restaurant? But it's not simply about showing respect and love for your peers. Family meal is an amazing creative outlet. It's the one chance for cooks on the bottom rung to express themselves, and an opportunity to practice making something delicious from scraps and leftovers.

Rule 11. Choose the harder path.

You're in the basement doing prep, and you realize that there are multiple ways to approach the task, including one that will be much quicker than the method your chef has called for. Chances are, no one will be the wiser if you take the easy route. But you still choose the more arduous path. Why? Because you realize that you're not cheating the customer or your chef. You're cheating yourself. You are cheating yourself out of practice and cheating yourself out of building the kind of fuck-you mentality that is vital to your survival.

In 1986, when he was at the height of his powers, Larry Bird decided to play a whole game as a lefty. He recorded forty-seven points and a triple-double using his off hand. Why? Because he wanted the challenge. If you've got your station down pat, it's up to you to make things more difficult. Don't be jealous of your friend who's already a sous chef while you're stuck on garde manger. Garde manger is the coolest job and teaches you the most skills. You're in this to be the best, not just climb the ladder.

Rule 12. Become a master sandbagger.

Another Craft story: there was a critic in the house. It was the peak of spring, and they ordered an asparagus dish. Except we didn't have it. The asparagus from the greenmarket had come in late and there wasn't time to trim all of it for service. Tom Colicchio calmly entered the kitchen, hoisted the massive crate onto the counter, and with one swift, deliberate movement passed the entire box through a bandsaw, yielding perfectly prepped asparagus stalks.

My favorite chef stories are all about sandbagging—the dark art of saving time through tricks that are as ingenious as they are frowned upon. I call it a "dark art" because you don't want to make a habit out of sandbaggery. Do it once when you need it and you've hacked the system. Do it too often and you're a hack.

I realize that this sounds like a direct contradiction to the previous rule, which brings me to . . .

Rule 13. Embrace paradox.

As discussed earlier in this book, I firmly believe that the greatest forms of creativity are born of paradox. In your role as a cook or a chef, sometimes you need to make things harder on purpose. Other times, you want to save time and effort. The challenge is to figure out how to commit to both ideas simultaneously and fully. It's a moving target. As you find success, buy new equipment, pay yourself and the staff better, make life easier where you can. But know that the struggle is what gives you and your restaurant life. For everything you make easier, make something else more difficult. Buy yourself some time so you can spend that time pushing yourself in new directions.

The same idea applies to cooking, by the way. In my mind, a perfect dish is not one where the flavors are uniformly in balance, but rather one that is both too salty and not salty enough at the same time. Taken together, it is in balance. Leaning into this paradox is how you make food that is both delicious and unpredictable.

Rule 14. When you're in the weeds, stop.

I'm not a beach person, but from what I understand, if you're ever swimming in the ocean and you find yourself being pulled out to sea by a riptide, you're supposed to swim parallel to the shore. Fighting the tide will only tire you out and expedite your death by drowning. The same applies when you're in the kitchen, and the orders are piling up, and you're running out of mise en place, and you can feel control slipping out of your hands—a situation commonly known as being "in the weeds."

Your survival instinct tells you to work faster, harder, messier. It may take you years to come to this realization on your own, but when you're in the weeds, the only thing you can do to save yourself is to stop. Take a step back. Breathe. Assess. Organize your thoughts and your station. Then calmly get back into it. It will go against all your default settings, but it is the only way to survive.

Rule 15. It's okay to quit every day.

The kitchen will not provide you with the positive reinforcement you desire, and when you fuck up, you're going to hear about it. The job will never seem like it's getting any easier until the day you realize it's too easy. You may be tempted to quit after every poor service. It's perfectly fine to feel that way.

The trick is to pick yourself up the next morning.

I've found that the cooks with the brightest prospects are the ones who are hardest on themselves. The trick is to direct that dissatisfaction to your advantage. Every day as a cook can be a fresh start. There are no lingering effects from the previous bad service. Yesterday's mistakes are gone. Resolve to be better today. Just know that in three or four months' time when you move to a new section, it's all going to feel freshly impossible again.

Speaking of which, here's a basic road map of your path as a cook at a restaurant: you will begin as a completely useless burden on your colleagues. Eventually you will learn and grow and become an irreplaceable part of the team. As the next crop of young cooks comes through, you'll train them well enough to make yourself obsolete. This is when it's time to move on. You and the restaurant have both given as much as you can to each other.

You need to be careful how much you learn when you work for someone else. Just as there are cooks (like me) who fail by not seeing out a full year at a restaurant, there are cooks who stay put for way too long. At some point, you need to leave the nest.

PART THREE

Say Anything

You've managed to become a chef with your own kitchen to run. Now it's time to find your voice.

Rule 16. Be the glitch in the Matrix.

For the most part, actors fall into one of several different camps. There are comedic actors and dramatic actors, improv specialists, method actors, and theater diehards. The same applies to cooking. Those with extreme patience may choose the path of the shokunin—the single-minded dedication to perfecting an existing style or technique. Plenty of people have found success in the restaurant business by imitating others or mastering an existing style. I don't want to diminish that, but

I believe the more effective path these days is to give people something they haven't had before.

Twenty years ago it was ramen for me. That was the subject I loved that most other Americans didn't care about yet. But if I were starting out today, I'd move to Hunan province or study Keralan cuisine or consider the possibilities presented by tired dining sectors like shopping malls. You're looking for anything that's been written off as cheap or ignored because it's not cool. Cool is your enemy.

Whatever you decide, make sure to do the homework. If improv is the equivalent of creative cooking, then the best chefs are improv actors who have also studied serious technique. Immerse yourself in whatever interests you. Don't be one of those chefs who travel to San Sebastian for a long weekend and return thinking they can open the city's best pintxo bar. That's a bad look and a surefire path to mediocrity.

Rule 17. Don't edit in your head.

A man of genius makes no mistakes. His errors are volitional and are the portals of discovery.
—James Joyce, *Ulysses*

Let me build on something I've said multiple times in this book: there *are* bad ideas, but all ideas are worth chasing. Sometimes when you're sure a certain idea will be a failure, you end up surprising yourself and it turns out better than you thought. But I promise that if you take the idea as far as you can and try as many ways of getting there as possible, at some point you will learn something that makes it worthwhile. I see so many young chefs who dismiss a thought without first seeing how it turns out. Every dish and service is an opportunity to collect data. It's only a mistake if you don't learn from it.

Rule 18. Apply guardrails.
It's much more challenging to be creative with all the freedom in the world than it is when you have limitations. For instance, if I say, "Make me something delicious," your brain will start racing in five hundred directions at the same time. On the other hand, if I say, "Make me something delicious with carrots," your task is much clearer.

Define the principles you believe in and use them to guide you in the kitchen. When Noma first opened, René Redzepi gave himself specific limitations about the kind of restaurant it would be: ingredients had to be hyperlocal and the overarching mission was to unpack and expand on Nordic tradition. Since then, Noma has moved its guideposts, but those initial boundaries were crucial to its success.

You may also find it useful to define the broader parameters of your professional life. Come up with best- and worst-case scenarios that represent complete success and irredeemable failure. Aim for the former, don't let yourself slip past the latter, and avoid spending time thinking about what happens in the middle.

Rule 19. Copy, don't steal.

There's a lot you can learn about technique, history, ingredients, and creativity by trying to replicate someone else's cooking. You should do it. You should try to understand what makes the food you love special. And then you should be very careful about your next step.

Throughout Momofuku's history, we've served dishes that were directly inspired by other chefs. Whenever we've done so, we've been careful to note the connection right there on the menu. I feel confident in saying that we've always tried to do right by the cuisines and people to whom we paid homage. If you're 100 percent sure that including someone else's idea is vital to the story you're trying to tell at your restaurant, then acknowledge where it came from. And under no circumstances should you serve something worse than the original. Do not cut corners. Do not do a watered-down version. If it makes the dish better, inject some of your own perspective, but adding cheese to something doesn't make it yours.

Rule 20. Start a cult.

Whether you're trying to get more business in the door or raise money for your own restaurant, you need dedicated followers. I'm not talking about fans; I'm talking about believers.

You need to move diners with your cooking to the point that they will support you when the rest of the dining room is empty. You need investors who will put money into your restaurant with no expectation of return. You need to kill the critics with the strength of your convictions. Do not cook out of fear or shy away from your vision.

After spending some time with me, a journalist once said of my approach to Momofuku, "I've never met anyone who takes something so seriously." That is the impression you need to convey at all times. People, whether critics or diners, will respond to someone who approaches their work as a life-or-death proposition. They are not accustomed to it, and they will be drawn to it.

Therefore, most important of all, you need to believe more deeply than anyone else. You build a cult by showing everyone that you are willing to go further than all of them to see out your vision. You can't ask everyone else to swallow the Kool-Aid if you're not going to take the first gulp.

PART FOUR

Nuts and Bolts
We exist to nourish people. Try not to
feed the sharks while you're at it.

Rule 21. Immerse yourself in all the awful, boring shit.
A good chef can speak a second language with moderate fluency. A great chef speaks at least twenty. More specifically, they have learned the jargon and bureaucratese needed to deal with the state liquor authority, community boards, landlords, labor laws, human resources, the power company, restaurant-supply stores, the Department of Buildings, the Department of Health, the fire department, laundry services, trash disposal, accounting, heating and air-conditioning, banking and loans, office equipment, payroll, and the POS system.

I'm forgetting many, many other dialects, but the point is, you need to know all of this horrible nonsense if you're going to survive. Otherwise, you're almost certainly going to be taken for a ride by someone. There's no substitute for burying your head in the minutiae.

Rule 22. Pay for what you can get.
Hire whatever lawyers, accountants, and construction firms you can. Try not to buy used equipment if you can avoid it. Buy the nicest

new products you can afford, and accumulate more and better as you grow. Customers will feel the effort you put into keeping up with better-financed operations. (There's a metaphor in here about self-reliance, but I'll let you spell it out for yourself.)

There's another reason to keep your operation as slim as possible. I opened Momofuku with minimal decor, backless chairs, no coffee, and no desserts, because I couldn't afford any of that shit, but it was also because I wanted people to feel the energy of a fast-paced eatery. I wanted to turn tables quickly, without seeming like we were rushing diners out the door. It's all about channeling the energy in the direction you want it to go. No amount of fancy decor can match the atmosphere of happy people eating.

Rule 23. You are your best publicist.

Don't waste your money on hiring a PR agency, especially at the start. There's so much food media these days, you don't need to pay someone to get stories written about you. You just need to have something to say. Use the money you would otherwise use on a PR agency to hire an extra cook, pay people better, or buy the equipment you need. The return on your investment will be much greater.

But, Dave, I don't know how to talk to media. I need help.

I grant that not everyone has a knack for this—I was absolutely horrible at talking to journalists at the beginning—so here are a few basic principles I've learned:

- *Be transparent.* Most journalists are smart enough to detect when you're bullshitting them, and even when they're not, there's no use in bullshitting yourself. Here's a better strategy: stick to your moral compass, give everything you have to doing good work, and speak honestly.
- *Know the power of "off the record."* Even when you're being completely honest, you don't always want everything you say to make it to print. It changed my life to discover that I could qualify something as off the record and journalists would abide. Suddenly I could have an honest, open conversation with a writer about my plans and goals and opinions, without them spilling the beans to their readers. It's a devastatingly effective way of communicating what you're about without giving away the whole

store. Just be explicit when you request that something be off the record.

- *Let the work speak.* Journalists receive hundreds of emails every week announcing menu changes, special events, and other promises of novelty. Don't waste time cluttering their inboxes. Put the time and resources into making what you're doing impossible to ignore. If you nail it, then every customer who comes to your restaurant will do the PR for you. Of course, easier said than done.

- *Read what's being written.* It amazes me how little some chefs know about the people covering their restaurants. They view critics as the enemy and yet they don't arm themselves for battle. They don't know what the critics look like, how they think, what their tastes are, who they hang out with, or where else they're eating. You would be surprised by how many critics say they don't like eggs! It's all right there for the taking if you simply read what's being written (and not just the articles you're mentioned in). Study. Bone up. Prepare yourself.

- *You never know who's going to hold the keys to the castle.* It's tempting to think you're too important to speak to the young intern who's been sent to interview you or the blogger who only has fifty followers. But if they approach you respectfully and earnestly, you should never be so stupid and arrogant as to dismiss them. If you brush off one too many smart kids, you're bound to make a lifelong enemy out of a future media mogul.

Rule 24. Always plan for worst-case scenarios.

In the restaurant business, "friends-and-family" dinners are an opportunity for you to practice with an obliging audience before you open the doors to the paying public. In exchange for a free meal, your guests know that the food and service might not be perfect.

Of course, in practice, friends-and-family is usually a shitshow. Because they don't have to pay, all your friends and family will try to bleed you dry in one night. You let it happen because that's what you're supposed to do.

The smart restaurateur will look at friends-and-family as an opportunity to explore the worst-case scenarios with a group of people who aren't going to run and blast you on Yelp as soon as they get home.

At a typical Momofuku friends-and-family, the lights may go off in the middle of service. Or the gas. Or the POS system. An unexpected six-top of VIPs will show up at the busiest possible time.

A guest in the dining room may suddenly inform his server that he is going to be dairy-free after the fourth course. It makes no sense, but they have to comply.

Another table may send a dish back, complaining that it is over-seasoned, though it looks an awful lot like they added a mountain of salt to it themselves. There's nothing the kitchen can do. The customer is always right.

The managers and chefs will scurry around, wondering why the fuck this is all happening.

Ninety-nine times out of a hundred, it's because I orchestrated it. I want to see how people react under duress. I want to see who remains calm and collected.

We have this one chance to push ourselves with a safety net. Why not use it?

Rule 25. Know your weaknesses.

You will not be the best at everything you do. Accept that as quickly as you can, so you can adapt. Most chefs are control freaks who feel compelled to have a hand in every decision. But if you want to build something sustainable, you need to learn how to step aside and empower others. In sports, the best players often make the worst coaches. Same with cooks and chefs. The smart thing to do is to admit your weaknesses, even if you keep them to yourself. Trust the people you hire. Don't be intimidated if they're better than you in certain areas. You want employees who feel empowered. They may not always make the same choices as you would, but that's really the best result you can hope for. You're trying to build the best team, and no team needs ten quarterbacks. You need players with different strengths.

Rule 26. If a fast-food manager can control their temper, you can, too.

I had an epiphany at the airport recently. I was standing in a long line for breakfast at McDonald's. I was watching the staff as they tried to keep up with the onslaught of orders from stressed-out travelers. Things were getting a little hairy. The cooks were losing control. Even though it was a McDonald's, any chef on earth would immediately recognize this situation as a crew in the weeds.

I turned my attention to the manager, expecting to see him lose his shit. But he didn't. He remained calm. He slowed down and organized his troops. He'd seen this before and he knew how to get out of it.

Anger has traditionally been woven into the fabric of the kitchen. Cooks like me came up in a world where yelling and shouting was an acceptable form of communication. Working in kitchens tapped into something ugly within me, and I've been working for the better part of twenty years to correct it. Watching that McDonald's manager calmly control his kitchen was yet another reminder that I can still be much better. The outside world might see fine-dining kitchens as superior to fast-food ones, but I honestly think that may be a fallacy.

PART FIVE

Welcome to the Ride That Never Ends
You've defied tremendous odds to find success as a chef. You have no idea what comes next.

Rule 27. Reject prior success.
Let's say you've managed to carve out a little recognition for your work as a chef. Maybe you've won a Michelin star or two. Maybe a James Beard Award. Cooks are banging down your door to work for you. Diners are lined up around the block. You're on easy street now, right?

Wrong. You are entering the most dangerous phase of a chef's trajectory. If you or your staff come to work feeling like you deserve all that recognition and praise, you're fucked. Entitlement and complacency are your enemy. It's equivalent to the struggles of inherited wealth. Customers can smell it on you, and believe me, they will disappear the second they get a whiff. When you feel the job getting easier, your task is to find a new challenge. Not for some puritanical reason, but because it's the only way to make it in the long run. The day you stop making mistakes is the day you stop growing. The only mistake is not to learn from your errors.

I don't feel any more secure or steady now than I did when I first started Momofuku, which is the only reason I feel at all confident that we're doing things right.

Rule 28. What worked in the past won't work in the future.

The more successful you become as a chef, the further you will be taken away from what you're good at. It begins with your first promotion to sous chef or chef de cuisine. You were the fastest, most adept cook in the kitchen, but suddenly your days consist of all these new responsibilities that have nothing to do with cooking. Now you're doing inventory, training people, designing menus, doing interviews. I've seen this realization crush countless young chefs, who thought they'd reached a peak only to find that the skills they'd built up won't help them anymore. They've got to develop a completely different set of muscles. Customers can't eat awards, reviews, or the past.

If it helps, think of it as a video game. As you progress, you have to learn new moves, fight more difficult bosses, navigate more challenging levels. It's supposed to get more difficult or else it wouldn't be interesting or rewarding to play. How boring would it be to play the same level over and over again?

Rule 29. Every dish is a crime scene.

Chief among the new skills you will need to learn as a burgeoning chef is communication. You can no longer afford to play the lone hero. People are counting on you to relay your vision and methodology to them, especially as you are drawn further and further away from the kitchen.

Once you've learned to be a good communicator, other people failing to communicate will become the bane of your existence, which means that you'll need to develop a complementary skill set: forensic science. On a recent night at Kāwi, our Korean restaurant in Hudson Yards, I tasted a dish of thinly sliced, pickled brisket and found it inedibly salty. I went to the kitchen to investigate. Nobody could tell me what had happened. We tasted the dressing, which was fine. I asked the cook who plated the dish whether she'd added additional salt. She hadn't. As I dug deeper, it became clear that the briskets themselves were overseasoned. The sous chef who prepared them the night before had decided on his own to add salt to the recipe. He found it odd that the brisket braise was underseasoned and took it upon himself to add salt to the whole batch without informing anyone.

The problem is that we'd purposely left the briskets unsalted, knowing that the dressing would be plenty salty. It's possible that his idea would have resulted in a better end product, but only if he'd informed other people about what he was doing. Working backward like a police detective was the only way to identify the problem, which, to no one's surprise, was a lapse in communication.

Rule 30. If life is a nature documentary, we are the wildebeests.

Chefs literally exist to nourish others. Metaphorically, we're also easy prey for predatory landlords, business partners, investors, and brands. Generally speaking, restaurant people are underinformed in all manners pertaining to business. Like a wildebeest at the watering hole, you've got to be on high alert at all times for lions in the tall grass. Study all the jargon and legalese that's designed to confuse you—waterfalls, pro rata, super voting rights—and learn about investor strategy. Do your due diligence on potential partners. See if they have a winning track record. If the deal seems too good to be true, it is. Don't trust anyone who reaches out to you once you're successful. And I'm sorry to say, but almost zero partnerships between chefs work in the long run.

In business, they tell you to negotiate from a position of strength, but we're almost never in that position. Your only choice is to assume that everyone is trying to screw you over. When you take money from sophisticated people, they will baffle you with byzantine contracts. Two general rules: (1) The only surefire way to win is to own your own real estate. (2) You will never make money selling your restaurant unless you have something scalable.

This all poses an existential problem for chefs that's best demonstrated with this question: Can you think of any chef who has retired as a chef?

Plenty of chefs have profitably transitioned into restaurateurs, or branched into media, consumer goods, fast food, and other food-related business ventures. But I can't point to a single chef who has finished their career by walking out of the kitchen and into retirement. It's just not something our industry allows for. I hope that will change with time, but you should know the score before you get in too deep.

Rule 31. Keep your eyes on the prize.
Being a chef is one of the dumbest professions you can possibly enter.
It's also the best job in the world.

Don't take all my warnings and negativity to mean that I don't love
what I do, and please don't lose sight of what makes this job great.
Feeding people is a beautiful act. With your cooking, you can transport people through time and space. You are a conduit for celebra-
tions, and a comfort in hard times. You champion the work of farmers
and ranchers and artisans. You tell stories. You connect people and
break down barriers. You are an artist. Don't forget it.

Rule 32. Employ the buddy system.
There have been a few documentaries about rock climbing recently.
Free Solo won an Academy Award for documenting Alex Honnold's
solo, untethered climb of the three-thousand-foot rock formation
known as El Capitan in Yosemite National Park. Honnold and his
remarkable accomplishment get a lot of attention, but I'm on Team
Tommy Caldwell.

Before Honnold performed his solo feat, fellow climbers Tommy
Caldwell and Kevin Jorgeson made history by free-climbing a different
route up El Capitan together. You can watch their journey in *The Dawn
Wall,* but I'll recap the most relevant bit for you. At one point during
their three-week journey up the rock, Jorgeson gets stuck, unable to
complete the most difficult part of the climb. He urges Caldwell to proceed without him. But as he approaches the homestretch, Caldwell
stops and decides that he won't finish without his friend. He goes
back down and spends days helping Jorgeson, so they can finish the
ascent together.

Why? In the words of the documentary, "I can't imagine a worse
outcome than doing this alone."

Most people will view what Caldwell did as an act of selflessness.
I would argue that helping his friend was actually the only possible
choice for Caldwell. He had harnessed years of tragedy and heartache into this impossible undertaking. Climbing El Capitan would both
define and redeem him. But with his goal in sight, he realized that it
would be meaningless to stand on top of the mountain by himself.

The more I learn about this world, the more I am humbled. So much of success comes down to factors beyond our control—where we were born, our race, our parents, the help we got along the way, and where we were at any given moment. We have less agency in our lives than our egos would like us to believe. No victory is achieved alone.

As you become successful, you will see that the only path of any value is to stop short of the peak and make sure you're not alone at the summit.

Rule 33. Save something for the swim back.

I'll end with one final movie reference. I used to watch the science-fiction movie *Gattaca* for motivation. I saw myself in Ethan Hawke's character, Vincent, who grew up being told he was inferior to his genetically engineered brother, Anton. When they were children, the one time Vincent ever beat his brother was in a contest to see who could swim farther in the open ocean. In the movie's climactic scene, Vincent repeats his victory and defeats his brother a second time. A disbelieving Anton asks Vincent how he had the stamina to continue as kids and again as adults.

"This is how I did it, Anton," says Vincent. "I never saved anything for the swim back."

That line always gave me goose bumps. As someone whose tea leaves never pointed toward greatness, I gravitated to the notion that if you worked like you had nothing else to live for, you could overcome whatever obstacles came your way. For many years, that was how I approached Momofuku. I was on a one-way ride going as far as my arms and legs would take me. Eventually I might drown, but not before I outlasted everyone else.

I have no doubt that this philosophy is why I'm successful. I know that if I'd given anything less than everything I had, Momofuku would not have made it. But recently, I've come to understand the ramifications of living this way. It's not just my life anymore. I have a wife, a kid, friends, and colleagues whom I want to see happy. I don't want them to sacrifice everything for me or Momofuku, and the only way to ensure that is to change my own perspective.

I am so lucky that this business didn't kill me. I feel blessed to have realized my shortsightedness while there's still time to change. My advice to you is to save something for the swim back, but also to be ready and willing to change your perspective. Right now, at age forty-two, I feel certain that I know all the answers to this business. But if I'm living the way I should, then hopefully I'll think back on this time and be embarrassed by how shortsighted and foolish I was. I'm expecting to open this book in ten years and cringe like I'm staring at a picture of myself with a bad haircut. I'm looking forward to it.

AFTERWORD

This book was scheduled to be published on May 19, 2020, but that date came and went.

Two months earlier, on March 14, all of our restaurants went dark. We weren't the only ones. The Covid-19 pandemic thrust nearly every independent restaurant on earth into a fight for survival. A staggering number of restaurant workers are currently unemployed; chefs have seen their life's work erased in an instant. And that's to say nothing of the millions of other jobs lost or the hundreds of thousands of lives taken by the virus so far.

Then, on May 25, George Floyd was killed by police officers in Minneapolis, setting off a worldwide movement against systemic racism and police brutality.

The events of the past few months have posed monumental questions about our country's prevailing wisdom and priorities. Let me be clear, though: The need for change was urgent even before any of this happened. And if you ask me, much of it was already coming—at least as far as the restaurant industry goes; it's just that the world has condensed that change from a timeline that would have probably been ten to fifteen years down to a matter of months.

That doesn't mean we're there yet. Not even close. This is just the beginning. And while what's happened in the past few months has generated incredibly painful realizations about our society, we must hold on to hope. As impossible as it may seem, I believe that we can build a better version of our world, a world where no one is left vulnerable to the diseases—both natural and man-made—that plague us today.

But we have to learn from our mistakes. We can't keep up with a world that changes this quickly if we don't have a firm grip on the past. In that spirit, I've left this book unchanged from what I submitted to the publisher months ago. I really believe you can read this book as you would a history text about the excesses of the Roman Empire. Over the past twenty years, as the food world was growing and expanding—and my career along with it—we were all guilty of buying into our own hype. I hope this book will help us see the stupid areas that we gave too much attention to and the vital issues to which we didn't give enough.

So what now? The next version of America is still unformed, which is exciting and daunting at the same time. My approach, as always, is to start by defining the extremes, the parameters of success and failure. So, at the risk of looking like a complete idiot, allow me to pick an arbitrary point in the future—let's say 2035—and present two possible visions of tomorrow's world.

2035: WORST-CASE SCENARIO

- America remains divided along its fault lines. Politics continue to prevent progress on what should be apolitical issues: the environment, public health, and especially institutional racism. Social media deepens these divides and makes reconciliation all but impossible.
- Climate change has continued to accelerate. There's been no widespread behavioral or structural changes, and billions of people around the world are at grave risk due to rising temperatures, droughts, wildfires, and extreme weather patterns.
- We thought Donald Trump was the worst possible president, but

he only lifted the curtain on something much more entrenched. He may as well still be in office.

- In the wake of Covid-19 (and other subsequent pandemics), the vast majority of independent restaurants have been allowed to die. Fast food won. People who tell stories about the restaurant-dining era are dismissed like music fans who never got over Elvis.

- The remaining hourly-wage restaurant employees—especially undocumented workers—have seen no improvement to their salaries, benefits, or job stability. Tipping is still the dominant model for hospitality workers, and the minimum wage is still too low to sustain a life.

- We've lost a great many family-run restaurants, as well as the knowledge they held. More important, new opportunities for people with nonwhite perspectives remain woefully limited. As a result, there has been a distinct narrowing of voices in food and food media.

- Robots and ghost kitchens dominate the culinary landscape. We've seen the death of the chef as a celebrity figure and cooks have fallen to the very bottom rung of the social order.

- Mental health deteriorates around the world, yet nobody recognizes it as a public health issue.

2035: BEST-CASE SCENARIO

- Aliens have invaded. Or some other momentous global event has finally awakened us to our common humanity. We've begun to build things together again, including a national identity that derives its strength from its diversity.

- We've seen small actions compound into radical, sweeping changes in policing, the prison system, voter rights, immigration, health care, education, the environment, and foreign aid, to name but a few key issues.

- Innovative farming and advances in food production, in combination with widespread changes to people's eating habits, have helped curb climate change. Meat has once again become some-thing to be celebrated, cherished, and stretched.

- In the wake of Covid-19, the government recognized the essen-tial work of the food industry and helped independent restaurants recover from the financial toll of the pandemic. Restaurants, in turn, adapted and diversified their revenue streams, leading to better pay and better protection for employees.
- With greater financial certainty and freedom from a reliance on best-of lists, awards, and critics, restaurants are now hubs for craft and creative expression.
- New establishments mean new voices. There are no hierarchies anymore. The restaurant world is a meritocracy, meaning there is equal opportuniy for those who have traditionally had less access to capital and opportunities. As a result, a broad range of cultural knowledge has been preserved.
- More people are cooking and growing food at home.
- Cooks and chefs helped lead the way out of the Covid-19 pan-demic, both by feeding those in need and by leveraging their expertise to help the world safely adapt to a new landscape. We've seen the death of the chef as a celebrity figure as the cooking pro-fession has been elevated as a whole. Getting a job as a cook is now on par with becoming a doctor or a software engineer.
- Mental health is much better understood by the public and treat-ment has been completely and utterly destigmatized. Seeing a doctor for help with mental-health issues is as commonplace as getting a flu shot.

These are only my scenarios and I recognize that not everyone will agree with my priorities, which is why you should spend the time considering the future *you* want to see. Beyond that, my only advice to you is to aim for the best and fight like hell to avoid the worst.

—DC, JUNE 2020

ACKNOWLEDGMENTS

Frankly, it would be impossible to list every person to whom we're indebted, so we'd simply like to thank our families and friends for their innumerable contributions to this book (and our lives in general), particularly the entire Chang family; the teams at Clarkson Potter, Majordomo Media, and InkWell Management; and everyone at Momofuku, past and present.

That said, we need to make one exception: If you enjoyed reading this book, and if it feels like there's been a consistent footprint throughout, it's undoubtedly because Chris Ying was carrying us.